FROM SCRATCH

FROM SCRATCH

10 Meals, 175 Recipes,
and Dozens of Techniques
You Will Use Over and Over

MICHAEL RUHLMAN

PHOTOGRAPHS BY QUENTIN BACON

ABRAMS, NEW YORK

FOR

Emma Kate Smith

AND HER FATHER,

Walter Smith

Contents

Mayonnaise from scratch

Introduction

A bacon, lettuce, and tomato sandwich began this book, early in June 2009. I'd posted a short essay on my website with a recipe illustrating how easy it is to make salted and dried pork belly. Ten years ago, curing your own pork at home was still a fairly novel idea, even among avid home cooks. After explaining how to make pancetta, I suggested any number of uses, one of which would be to put that pancetta on a BLT.

My blog had a legion of readers who shared my love of opinionated food writing and cooking great food and were quick to respond. The very first comment on this post was by a culinary enthusiast (former line cook and pastry chef by his own blog's account), Gareth Mark, who wrote: "Okay, fine. I'm already growing tomatoes and lettuce and baking bread. Mayo isn't hard to make. I guess it's only right to make my own bacon. Bet it'll be a really fine BLT."

I thought, yeah, I'll bet it will be, too.

About twenty-five comments down, I came across someone identified only as "Carrie," who wrote this: "Oh lord, now I'm obsessed with making a BLT from scratch."

That's when I thought, *You know, they're right.* It would be really easy to make a BLT from scratch, but also enormously satisfying. And so I wrote a post on that day asking people to do it, make a BLT from scratch, meaning: (1) Bake your own bread, (2) Grow your own tomatoes and lettuce (it was June, thus a reasonable and easy suggestion), (3) Cure your own bacon, and (4) Make your own mayonnaise. And I said that I would do it, too.

After more than a hundred enthusiastic comments, I made it official. I turned it into a challenge, with categories (traditional, deconstructed, and best photograph). And the entries poured in. The winner, an American sous chef working in Sydney, Australia, went so far as to make his own salt with which to cure the bacon and add to the bread dough (he reported that 25 liters of sea water yielded 1 kilo of salt).

But it was another story that cut me to the quick. A man named Walt Smith, in West Virginia, read my post and told his youngest child, ten-year-old Emma Kate, about it. *Let's do it!* she said.

When I posted the winners, I concluded with a new category: "Most Inspirational BLT (because this post merits a Hollywood ending)."

Walt Smith wrote to me by email:

Dear Michael,
. . . Instead [of entering the challenge myself], we used the contest as
a learning opportunity for Emma Kate and a bonding opportunity
for us both.

She took this entire process very seriously and was, I thought,
very creative in her approach. She added ginger to some of the cured
bacon (though she didn't want to use it for the sandwich) and it was
also her idea to add the lemon thyme to the mayo.

With the exception of the knife work and heating the smoker,
Emma Kate created the entire sandwich without help or input from
me. It really is so easy a kid could do it!

Emma Kate typed the message below and chose the pictures that are
attached.

Thanks Michael,

Walt Smith

Mr. Ruhlman,

I had fun making my BLT. First, my dad and me planted a garden in the summer. Then the tomatoes and lettuce sprouted. In September I cured the pork belly with some pink salt and put it in the refrigerator for one week. When it was done curing I put it on the smoker. When it was done my dad cut it on the slicer.

I can't eat gluten (wheat, barley, rye), so I had to make Gluten-Free bread. First, I mixed some egg yolks into some rice flour with milk and yeast. Then we let it rise and put it in the oven.

I picked the tomatoes and some lettuce that looked like an oak leaf. My dad and I cooked the bacon then he cut some vegetables while I made mayonnaise in a little red mixer. I put lemon thyme in it, it's my favorite herb. I didn't like the mayonnaise but everyone else did.

I made the sandwiches and we had friends over for a dinner party. Everyone said it was the best BLT they ever had.

Thank you for having the contest.

Emma Kate Smith

When I scrolled down to see the photo of that ten-year-old girl smiling in front of her BLT-from-scratch, I felt tears running down my cheeks. And I knew I wasn't alone. In the first comment on this post, Claudia Young wrote, "So wonderful . . . made me cry the good cry."

Yes, I had a cry. Why? See for yourself: just google "ruhlman blt winners." And I knew very well why: Several powerful emotions coalesced in her smiling face as she presented her sandwich, summing up so many benefits of cooking our own food. (I tried to reach her when I was writing this book but was unable to. I hope she continues to make people happy with her cooking.)

The girl was happy and proud—she felt good, and cooking does this to the cook. It makes you feel strong. It was a chance to connect with her father, and he with her—they did this together. Father and daughter had come together over food and then, of course, the whole family and friends got in on it. "Everyone said it was the best BLT they ever had." A simple sandwich had brought everyone together, and that ultimately is what I love about the power of food.

I write this during a hard time in our nation, a time when so many of us feel divided. Food, more than anything—more than *anything*—brings us together. Everywhere around the globe, it does this. It's part of our humanity.

As I've written before and will never tire of arguing, preparing food and sharing it with our families and those we love was the mechanism for advancing *Homo sapiens* past other early upright species to make us the most successful species the planet has ever known.* Cooking made us human, and I believe that cooking can keep us human. And *that*, ultimately, is what that ten-year-old girl brought home to me so simply and touchingly. And it's also, ultimately, why I'm writing this book.

I want people to cook their own food for the people they love. I want people to feel comfortable in the kitchen and know that they can accomplish anything they wish, because, as that girl's father said, it's so easy a kid could do it. Whether you are the kind of cook who loves to take an entire day to make a meal, or you simply want to get a little better so that weeknight meals are simpler, less stressful, and still delicious, I want this book to be accessible to you.

> The concept is simple:
> By exploring several familiar, staple meals,
> we can learn just about everything
> we need to know in order to cook, well, anything.

The BLT is a lesson in making bread, curing bacon, and making an emulsified sauce (here, mayonnaise). The lessons of lasagna, or steak frites, or paella, or cassoulet, or a simple omelet are abundant—a whole range of sauces, custards, rice and bean dishes, easy sausage making, making your own pasta or working with dried, braises, roasts, sautés…and the bistro staple profiterole leads to a fleet of dessert techniques.

Contained in their preparation is all you need to know, whether you have twenty minutes to get a nourishing meal on the table or an entire weekend to

---

* I learned this from Richard Wrangham, *Catching Fire: How Cooking Made Us Human*, which was published in May 2009—interestingly, a month before my BLT-from-scratch blog post.

mess about in the kitchen. If we pause even to think about a roast chicken, we see all kinds of sauces and techniques and offshoots: how to make stock, how to make a simple pan jus at the last minute or an ethereal tarragon sauce brought to nappe consistency with beurre manié, how to make great soup, how to turn leftover chicken into amazing meals, and how to cook all the things around a roast chicken—roasted vegetables and all manner of potato cookery. Roast chicken is one gateway into the realm of great cooking. The omelet is another. The slow-roasted pork shoulder yet another. The abundant and versatile curry—from any number of regions in Asia, from India to Thailand—yet another.

Some people presume that because I wrote *The French Laundry Cookbook* with Thomas Keller and other such books that I must be a food snob. On the contrary. If I have only twenty minutes to get dinner on the table, I think a rotisserie chicken is a great option (and then I make overnight stock with the bones while I sleep—see page 38). This morning I had toast made from a loaf of Wonder Bread because it was what we had. I put a poached egg on it, so simple and satisfying. (I actually prefer Wonder Bread for sandwiches with soft ingredients—egg salad, for instance.)

But I do want us to be honest with ourselves. Is this the best I can do with the ingredients on hand, the time I have, and the energy I feel like expending? What if I want to make the *best* roast chicken ever—how would I do it? What if I put that poached egg on some bitter greens and make a bacon vinaigrette? Do I even know how to make a bacon vinaigrette? Well, because I know how to make a standard vinaigrette, I can figure out how to make a warm bacon vinaigrette. And then you are cooking—and once you are cooking, it's hard to stop. Because cooking our own food is so good for us and so satisfying.

Eating food that we or someone near us cooked makes us happy, as our body absorbs its deep nutrition. Savory food we cook for ourselves is almost invariably nutritious, because it's a balance of all the things we need—protein, carbohydrates, and fats. And you sense deep in your primitive brain, in the limbic system that registers taste and aroma, *I want more of this. This is good.* Just as our ancestors did when they shared both the work of preparing food and the pleasure and nutrition of sharing cooked food, developing the nuanced language required to tell each other stories, stories that described where more food was and where adversaries might be.

I know people are busy. I'm busy. I don't always have the time or energy to cook. Or sometimes I just feel like Chinese takeout. But I recognize the importance of cooking, and sharing food, and so I do always want it to be a part of my weekly routine. Happily, I have a wife who loves to cook, so it's easy to share the time it takes to shop, cook, and clean up.

Also, I just *love* to eat. And I love to make people happy. And I love life most when we come together over food.

Time, Tools, and the Food Itself

Cooking takes time. So does going out to eat. So does watching TV while you wait for food to be delivered. *Everything* takes time.

This is why I have always resisted the call of thirty-minute meals and those recipes claiming to be "quick and easy"—not that there's anything wrong with either, per se. But the emphasis on "quick and easy" obscures the fact that nothing in all of cooking is particularly difficult. Sometimes there are simply more steps to a dish, so a recipe can be more involved. But "quick" and "easy" both mean the same thing: fewer steps. And sometimes that's just what I need. I also believe that "I'd love to cook, if only I had the time" is just an excuse. You don't need an excuse not to cook. There is nothing wrong with choosing to do other things instead of cooking, so just acknowledge it. Our culture, happily, has recognized that cooking is important, but that also comes with a judgment—that you're somehow a bad person if you don't cook for your family. This is a horrible judgment to put on anyone. Our lives are complicated and busy; no one should be judged for not cooking. Just be honest with yourself about your capabilities, your time, and your obligations. One of the most stressful things we can do is try to prepare a meal when we don't have enough time.

The time factor is important in cooking. This is why I've created a kind of timetable list of recipes so that you can see which ones can be done in under an hour, as opposed to those that involve a lot of steps for special-occasion meals, like cassoulet (page 193) or a BLT from scratch (page 279).

Obviously, sometimes you need to get dinner on the table lickety-split. And other times, even if you have more than an hour, you're so tired you just want something that doesn't take a lot of effort, something with only a few steps (like pasta with tomatoes and basil, page 116) or a simmering pot of hearty beans (page 189).

I like to cook. If you're reading this book, you probably do, too. Or at the very least, you believe that cooking food for the peopbele you live with, for friends and family, is important. Indeed, I believe that the benefits of cooking food are vast and worth the time and effort that gathering food, cooking food, and cleaning up after it requires.

The Importance of a Plan

When I talk about time, I must also talk about planning. This is one of the biggest obstacles that makes cooking difficult, and it is an obstacle of our own creation. We don't plan ahead. It's five P.M., you'll be leaving work shortly, and it's your turn to cook dinner that night. "What am I going to make for dinner?" This can be a roadblock. Even though you *knew* you were going to be needing to make dinner on this night. You simply failed to plan.

I fail to plan all the time. I try not to, but life can get busy and suddenly it's seven o'clock. My friend Russ Parsons, journalist, author, and former food editor of the *Los Angeles Times*, once criticized my suggestion that roast chicken was a great weekday meal (when my kids were young, I roasted a chicken every Monday night, which would then give me some form of chicken soup later in the week or chicken salad for lunches). He maintained that by the time you got back from the store, it was too late to preheat the oven and roast a chicken.

"Russ!" I wanted to shout back. "What does going to the store have to do with it? You should have already bought the chicken."

Giving yourself enough time simply means planning ahead. You know what days of the week you'll be cooking dinner. Plan it out on Saturday or Sunday and shop for three weeknight meals at a time. When you shop on Sunday, get the stuff you need for the chicken dinner on Monday (page 30) and an easy pasta dish for Tuesday (your favorite pasta topped with Summer or Winter Tomato Sauce, page 101), then on Wednesday make Chicken Noodle Soup (page 39) from the overnight stock you made from the chicken carcass—three meals right there, two of which come together in twenty minutes. Every time you go to the grocery store, plan an extra day ahead and buy food for that meal as well.

If you plan, you will have all the time you need because you have controlled the time. Try not to let time control you.

The Food You Buy: Think Nourishing, Not "Healthy"

Of course, the quality of the food you buy determines the quality of the food once it's cooked. As Thomas Keller said to me, "If you have better ingredients than me, you can be a better chef than me." So buy vegetables at their peak. Organic is best if you don't mind spending a little more—there's evidence that the pesticide residue on conventionally grown produce can affect our gut biome, and perhaps other parts of our bodies. And whatever kind of vegetables you choose, buy plenty of them. I know the chapters in this book are heavily meat-centric, but we all need to make vegetables a main part of what we eat. It's a good thing to keep great and satisfying vegetarian dishes in your repertoire (some vegetable curries, a few pasta dishes) and when you do eat meat, reduce the quantity. Nobody needs 12 ounces/340 grams of steak every night. Buy quality meats and eat them in moderation—4 to 6 ounces/110 to 170 grams is usually an appropriate serving. And buy quality meats, those that were well raised and aren't loaded with hormones and antibiotics. This is intuitive and should go without saying.

A lot of people ask me how to cook "healthy." I tell them that's the wrong word, and it's made for a lot of confusion at the grocery store. As a doctor friend of mine says, "Our food isn't healthy, *we* are healthy. Our food is *nutritious*." Or should be.

When you're shopping, ask yourself, "Is this food nutritious? Does it have a lot of nutrients?" Almost all foods that must be cooked are dense with nutrients and fiber—all vegetables and fruits are rich in nutrients and fiber, legumes especially. Even starchy vegetables such as potatoes are nutritious and also have a lot of fiber. The orange sweet potato is an especially nutritious tuber. Another good saying: Eat all the colors you can—a variety of different colors on your plate indicates a variety of nutrients.

All dairy contains nutrients and fats essential to good health. Meat, chicken, and fish are rich sources of protein. Seeds and nuts are loaded with fiber and essential fatty acids. And don't even get me started on the wonders of the egg—they could fill a book (they have, in fact, filled many of them, including one by me).

Cook with these items and you are by default cooking "healthy."

Asked to name a good diet, the food marketing researcher Harry Balzer said, "You want a good diet? Cook your own food. Eat anything you want—*just cook it yourself.*"

Wise words.

The Importance of Small-Batch Stock

I cannot overstate how much better meals can be when you use homemade stock. If there's one thing you can do in your kitchen to elevate your cooking, it's making your own. Build it into your cooking routine by making it in small batches.

I think the stockpot killed stock-making in the home kitchen. A stockpot connotes *big*. And *big* connotes lots of meat and bones and vegetables, simmered on the stove for hours and hours, then strained and strained again and stored. In other words: A Project. Well, it can be, and if you love to cook, there are few more valuable essences in the kitchen than a well-made brown veal stock (page 146).

But a few sweet vegetables simmered in a pot of water for forty-five minutes gives you a delicious stock as well. You don't even need to strain it. Just ladle it into whatever you're cooking. Try the vegetable stock on page 114—it's fabulous for cooking and is even excellent drunk straight from a mug.

But the most versatile stock for most kitchens is chicken stock. If you're going to roast a chicken, it would be a shame to throw out the carcass. It's so easy to cover it with water and add an onion and a carrot and put it in a low oven overnight. The next morning you have a beautiful homemade chicken stock without really having done anything (see page 38). Or you can buy a package of chicken wings and do the same.

If you have a pressure cooker, you can make rich, full-bodied stock in less than two hours. Set the cooker to its lowest pressure setting, and after an hour and a half remove it from the heat. Then—and this is important—let it cool on its own rather than releasing the pressure all at once, which will bring the stock to an immediate vigorous boil and muddy the stock.

I sometimes leave my overnight chicken stock out on the stovetop or in the oven if I'm not using the oven, covered, using it as needed all week long. Having stock at the ready is an easy luxury. If you do this, it's important to bring the stock to a simmer each day, in effect pasteurizing it lest any spoilage bacteria take over. I've left stock on the stovetop and used it over the course of as many as five days. But not in summer, when it's too hot—an excessively hot kitchen will spoil the stock fairly quickly, so strain and refrigerate it.

Beef stock is another useful elixir to have in your refrigerator. Ordinarily it takes a long time to coax the gelatin from those big old bones—six to eight hours. I offer on page 142 a quick version, using meat (where all the beef flavor is) and powdered gelatin (which is often made from beef bones). It makes a delicious cooking liquid for a stew or can be reduced and used in a sauce. And it makes a terrific pho (page 144).

If you simply will never make your own stock because the boxed stuff is so convenient, try this: When you're using a lot of it for a soup or a braise or a risotto, dump it all out of the box into a pot. Add a chopped onion and carrot (and fresh herbs if you have any) and simmer it for thirty minutes. You'll be amazed at the freshness and flavor that one little trick can do to store-bought broths.

Learn What Foods Can Be Made Ahead

When you know what foods can be made hours or even days before serving them, you have more control over your time. For instance, say you're planning a very nutritious and delicious steak, potato, and green bean dinner for tomorrow night for guests. But you want to spend all your time with the friends and family you're cooking it for—not dutifully move through your prep list. If you know that you can cook and shock your green beans a day ahead and keep them in the fridge wrapped in paper towels, and that the baked potatoes can be made early in the day while you're doing other things or as soon as you get home from work and then simply reheated, then the actual cooking of dinner requires only ten minutes of active

time—sautéing the steak and, as you do, reheating the beans (either in the micro-wave with a little butter or in a pan with butter or olive oil, maybe adding some cumin and red pepper flakes).

How do you think four cooks working the line of a busy restaurant can put out two or three hundred complex meals? They're not boiling green beans to order. On super-busy Saturday nights at the only restaurant I ever worked at, the chef had me "cook off" (sear) about a dozen filet mignons at five P.M. so that I didn't get crushed. I wouldn't finish cooking some of those steaks until eight P.M.

Pretty much all green vegetables can be cooked and shocked (plunged into an ice bath) and then reheated later.

Pretty much all root vegetables can be cooked many hours before being reheated. Just don't chill them; keep them at room temperature until you need to reheat them, and their flavor will remain bright. Now that I think about it, cauliflower can be handled this way, too.

All meat can be started in advance and kept at room temperature. If you want to serve grilled meats, you can start them over a smoky charcoal fire earlier in the day, then finish them in the oven and they will taste pretty much the same as if you started and finished them on the grill minutes before serving them.

Anything cooked low and slow in the oven can be cooked up to three days before you want to serve the dish. (See just about everything in the slow-roasted pork shoulder chapter.) Often, especially with braised foods, they're even better the next day.

All soups can be made in advance.

In fact, there are very few things that can't be at least started well before finishing and serving them. You can make a salad hours ahead of time, but you shouldn't dress it until just before serving time. Gougères (page 310) are best straight out of the oven, still warm. Paella should be cooked start to finish and then brought immediately to the table. But really, that's about it. Some high-end restaurants have been known to do only *à la minute* cooking, but for the most part, the entire fine-dining industry is based on the ability to prepare most components of every meal in advance. By putting this fact to use in your own kitchen, you give yourself more control over time.

A Few Food Staples

Salt The most important thing to know about salting food is to use the *same kind* of salt for all general seasoning. I use Morton's coarse kosher salt because that was what was available at my old grocery store, and I got used to it. But it's heavier than the other main brand of kosher salt, Diamond Crystal. So, whenever I use Diamond Crystal, I'm not quite sure how much to use, and I tend to underseason food when using it. Most professional kitchens use Diamond Crystal salt because Morton's has an anti-caking agent, making the former a "cleaner" salt. I can tell the difference only by its weight, not flavor.

One advantage of using Morton's goes to people who do not have a scale to weigh their salt because it has a near equal volume-to-weight ratio: 1 cup, which is 8 ounces by volume, weighs pretty close to 8 ounces. So, if you measure only by volume, I recommend using Morton's for these recipes. Fine sea salt can be used, but that too has its own feel to it. This is why it is important to use the same salt consistently, so that you can learn to season by sight and touch.

My favorite of the finishing salts is Maldon salt, harvested in southwestern England. It adds a delicate crunch to soft foods that benefit from last-minute salting. It's great on meats, of course, but it's even a delight on a chocolate tart and caramel sauce.

Butter This again is a matter of preference and what you are used to. I've always used salted butter, and that's what I continue to use. If you prefer unsalted butter (most chefs do), that's fine. Always use the same kind. The quality of butters does vary, but when using butter for everyday cooking, I use grocery store commodity butter. If the butter will be featured or is particularly important in the dish, you may want to spend extra on a high-quality butter, now widely available in supermarkets.

Oil I use vegetable or canola oil for most cooking. Sometimes I use inexpensive olive oil for cooking if I want the oil to add its own flavor. I reserve extra-virgin olive oil for finishing foods and for salads. Peanut oil is the best oil for deep-frying because of its high smoke point, but I tend not to use it because it's more expensive than vegetable oil.

Eggs I use generic grocery store eggs for most cooking. Organic eggs can be of a little higher quality, and if organic is important to you, then this is what you should buy. If I have access to farm-fresh eggs at a local market, I usually buy them, but I reserve them for scrambling, poaching, or frying so that I can appreciate them on their own. Often their yolks are very deep yellow or orange, owing to what the chicken ate, and these can make for very vivid scrambled eggs. If you're lucky enough to have these especially flavorful and nutritious eggs available to you, they're worth more than you'll pay for them.

Tools

I've long preached a less-is-more approach to outfitting a kitchen. You need only five items to cook anything. Of course, your kitchen drawers will fill up with all manner of hardware claiming to make cooking easier and faster (I'm often appalled at my own drawers, but I'm sorry, I'll never give up my lemon juice press). But all you really need is a sharp knife, a good surface to cut on, a pan to cook in, a heat source, and food. When you have only five things to focus on, you can see that the better each of those items is, the better and easier your cooking will be.

Knives The biggest problem in American home kitchens is dull knives, usually a lot of dull knives. A dull knife is the biggest obstacle to easy food preparation because it forces you to press down too hard to cut through a vegetable so that you're smashing through it rather than slicing through it. This makes prep work unnecessarily difficult and also affects the flavor of the food. It can also result, when the knife slides off the food rather than through it, in bad cuts on your hands. A sharp knife is a safe knife.

So, either find a wet-grind knife-sharpening service in your area or buy an inexpensive Japanese stone and learn how to use it. It takes practice, but once you get the hang of it, you will never be handicapped by dull knives. I sharpen my knives with a King brand Japanese sharpening stone, with a 1000/6000 combination grit, and I finish them with a honing steel.

You need three knives: a chef's knife or some form of large knife for most of your cutting, a paring knife for cutting small things, and a serrated knife for

cutting bread. Don't spend money on a big block with a dozen knives. Invest in three good ones.

Are you looking for a gift for a loved one who likes to cook? Remember this: Nothing says "I love you" better than a really sharp knife.

The Cutting Surface You need a good, heavy, and, most important, large surface to cut on. The second biggest problem in home kitchens is a lack of work space (visit me when I'm cooking in my teensy New York City apartment and you'll see what I mean). If you can, give yourself plenty of room to cut, and space for all the stuff you're cutting to go after you cut it. If you have room, get a Boos board, at least 18 by 12 inches/20 by 30 centimeters, but preferably 20 by 15 inches/50 by 38 centimeters or larger, and 1½ inches/4 centimeters thick. Thinner polyurethane boards of those dimensions are acceptable as well. (And remember, if you're doing a lot of cutting, put a damp dish towel underneath it to keep the board in place.)

Pots and Pans If I could have only one pan in the kitchen, it would be a cast-iron skillet. There's almost nothing you can't cook in these things, on the stovetop or in the oven. It's the perfect pan to roast a chicken in, or make a sauce, or sauté a steak, or stir-fry vegetables.

It's helpful to have large and small saucepans and sauté pans. And nonstick pans are wonderful for cooking eggs and crêpes and other delicate things that can stick, but they shouldn't be your default pan. Invest in one good nonstick pan and keep it clean and protected. I either hang mine or put a kitchen towel in it in the cupboard to prevent other pots and pans from scratching it.

I'm also a huge fan of my cast-iron enamel Dutch oven. My favorite is a 7-quart/7-liter pot, but if you typically cook only for two, a 3.5-quart/3.5-liter pot may be right for you. A good one, such as Le Creuset, is extremely valuable and will last forever.

Spatulas, Spoons, and Such And last, you need something good to stir with, something that is sturdy and has a flat edge that can sweep across the bottom of a pan. A flat-edged wooden spoon or heatproof spatula is valuable for everyday cooking. Round wooden spoons are ubiquitous and may be beautiful objects, but they are a handicap, so I manufacture and sell my own flat-edged wooden "paddles."

The rest of your tools are a matter of preference and convenience. Here are a few of my preferred tools:

- *A sturdy pair of* TONGS. *Make sure they grip well; those without a scalloped edge force you to squeeze food too hard, damaging it. And tongs are not just for food: I also use them to remove hot pans from the oven.*

- *A large* PERFORATED SPOON.

- *A variety of* PYREX MEASURING CUPS (*they're great for storing food in as well*).

- *A variety of* PYREX MIXING BOWLS.

- *A sturdy* METAL SPATULA *for flipping food (I prefer a slotted one that allows fat to drain through easily).*

- *A heatproof rubber or silicone* SPATULA.

- *A good set of metal* MEASURING CUPS *and* SPOONS. *Avoid boutique-y or fancy versions, as their measurements can vary.*

- *An instant-read* THERMOMETER.

- *An* IMMERSION BLENDER. *I use this all the time for making soups and sauces (see Winter Tomato Sauce, page 101), and the whisk attachment makes mayo a snap (see page 286).*

- *A* STANDING MIXER.

- *A* FOOD PROCESSOR.

- *A* KITCHEN SCALE. *This is not strictly necessary, but if you learn how to use a scale, recipes are much easier and turn out better. And if you bake a lot, a scale is truly invaluable. I've designed a scale by My Weigh called the Maestro, which has a micro-scale built into it, but all the My Weigh scales are excellent, durable, and affordable. I can't do without a scale in the kitchen.*

And that's it. All you really need to cook everything. Actually, more than you need.

WHAT DOES "FROM SCRATCH" MEAN?

If you cure your own bacon, grow lettuce and tomatoes, and make your own bread and mayonnaise, in my opinion that's emphatically a from-scratch BLT. But is a roast chicken dinner "from scratch" if you didn't raise the chicken, grow potatoes and green beans, or make your own butter? Is a cassoulet "from scratch" if you didn't make and stuff your own sausage? My dear pal Blake Bailey told me with pride that he regularly makes from-scratch lasagna, even though he uses jarred tomato sauce for the Bolognese. Did I tsk-tsk? Not a thought of it—he puts all the components together: boils the pasta, creates a soft cheese mixture, and bakes it for his wife and daughter. And by his account everyone is delighted with the results.

In this book I will show you how to make a wide range of dishes from scratch, from relatively simple fare to elevated and complex meals, involving many steps and components. I've spent years observing how some of our most accomplished restaurant chefs do what they do, and I will share some of their thinking and techniques in ways that home cooks can easily put to good use. My wife, Ann, and I cook dinner for each other almost every evening we're home, and we both take great pleasure in the smells, flavors, and nourishment of a home-cooked meal. Nobody should be intimidated by the thought of cooking or feel that a shortcut (jarred tomato sauce or a rotisserie chicken) is a compromise; it's a choice, depending on our circumstances. Cooking delicious food is something we're all capable of. And preparing your food from scratch, however you want to define it, should likewise be an invitation to embrace rather than a mountain to climb.

Take popcorn, for example. Can popcorn be "from scratch"? Few of us grow our own corn, make our own butter, or harvest our own salt. Microwave popcorn has become dominant in today's household, and it can't be beat for convenience and no cleanup. Open a box, remove a cellophane wrapper, microwave for three minutes, and then open another bag to get at the popped corn covered in oils and chemical flavoring. This is definitely not from scratch by any reasonable measure. Stovetop popcorn is a wholly different product, to my mind—one of my very favorite things to eat, in fact.

The following—which my son, James, then age six, called "pot popcorn" to my (initial) alarm—takes 5 minutes:

For 4 people, combine a cup of popcorn with a tablespoon of vegetable oil in a pot over high heat. Shake the pan and swirl the popcorn continually to ensure all the kernels heat evenly (this is the most important stage of the cooking, to ensure all kernels pop; you can also use the time to put some butter in the microwave). When the corn begins to pop, cover it and leave it alone. Once it's really rocking, start shaking the pan up and down frequently so that unpopped kernels fall to the bottom of the pan. When the popping stops or mostly stops, empty the popcorn into a large wooden bowl, drizzle with butter, and sprinkle lightly with salt. Devour.

So, can popcorn cooked on the stovetop be considered "from scratch"? An unqualified yes. You've taken a raw, inedible product that looks as it did when it was harvested, transformed it with some heat and care into something edible and delicious, enriched it with butter, and seasoned it with salt. The bottom line for me is this: "From scratch" is an attitude, not a recipe or a rigid set of instructions. Take a whole chicken, place it in a skillet, roast it in a hot oven for an hour—dinner from scratch.

CHAPTER 1

Roast Chicken

I have written about roast chicken in at least two of my previous books. I've discussed it on my blog and on Twitter and on Instagram. I've published a recipe for roasting chicken that recommends, as a part of the recipe, sex with your partner. I've written about the roast chicken on behalf of chef Michael Symon. I channeled Thomas Keller's version of roast chicken for his father, a story that opens the cookbook *Bouchon*. And I concluded a TEDx presentation in Cleveland with an image of a roast chicken, because it is an emblem of cooking, and of my personal conviction that cooking our own food and sharing it with one another, and appreciating this fundamental act for all that it is, might be a way toward a better understanding of how to live. And yet I've never told the whole story of a roast chicken from a purely practical standpoint.

The roast chicken may be the most generous of all our common meals. It almost defies a complete telling because of this generosity, its changeability, its ubiquity throughout so many cultures. There's a reason that the most commonly cited favorite meal among chefs is a roast chicken. Not only is a meal centered around a roast chicken economical, nourishing, and delicious, it also connotes *home* in ways that few other dishes do, especially to those who cook most of their meals in a professional kitchen for people they don't know. When a chef imagines a meal that makes her or him happy, it's a roast chicken that most think of, the crispy-skinned bird still in its roasting skillet, fat sizzling, set on a trivet at the center of a table around which family and friends have come together.

Home. The greatest sense of ease and pleasure. That's what roast chicken means to me: home. And here I want to describe not just a recipe for roast chicken, but one that integrates side dishes and includes variations on that roast chicken, and then variations on those side dishes that go so well with chicken. Not only to describe a perfect roast chicken, no corners cut, but also that speedy roast chicken dinner when we can't or don't want to take our time with each step, a few hacks when you still crave the satisfaction and nutrition of a roast chicken dinner (I know of no one, professional chef or home cook, who hasn't been caught on the wrong side of the clock). And I'll discuss what to do with the chicken after the meal, using leftover chicken and, of course, making the best of all possible stocks, which you can literally do in your sleep.

Roasting a chicken scarcely needs its own recipe. Indeed, I went on a blog rant about the ways Americans are trained to think that cooking is too hard to do on our own, that we're too stupid to cook, and wrote what I called "The World's Most Difficult Roasted Chicken Recipe." Here's the recipe: a chicken, a hot oven, salt, and one hour. That's pretty much all you need for the best roast chicken ever.

So, for me, what makes the roast chicken so important to write about is what happens around that chicken: the pleasure of it at the table, the way the smell of its roasting permeates a home and relaxes us, making the side dishes while the chicken cooks, making a jus while the chicken rests, cutting it up, and thinking about the luxurious stock the carcass will make as you dream sweetly through the night into the next morning, the chicken weaving one day into another.

Herewith, then, is as complete a rendering as I can of the story of a single roast chicken dinner, told through a dozen recipes and many techniques. First, I present a recipe that integrates all components of a complete meal, all ingredients and steps, into one. I follow this with variations on each of these components, then suggest hacks for the hurried, and, finally, what to do when the initial meal is done.

It's a whole story.

Make a ROAST CHICKEN DINNER (30) a part of your weekly cooking routine and you'll see how generous this meal is. It teaches you economical side dishes such as simple GREEN BEANS (add lemon zest!), (30) QUICK SAUTEED BRUSSELS SPROUTS, (44) ROASTED BROCCOLI WITH GARLIC, (44) and any kind of potatoes— THE AMAZING BAKED POTATO, (47) MASHED POTATOES (47) (make mashed potatoes by baking them, and save the skin for cheesy POTATO SKINS (48)!

A roast chicken dinner is a dinner that keeps on giving!

It teaches you all kinds of SAUCES— A SIMPLE AU JUS, (30) proper GRAVY (33) (plus a thickening lesson: ROUX), or a refined TARRAGON sauce (32) (plus a thickening lesson: BEURRE MANIÉ) (32) or maybe

you want to BRINE (34) your chicken first. And of course you'll want to have several variations to keep the roast chicken from feeling routine — with a SALSA VERDE, (35) or with JALEPEÑOS, LEMON and GARLIC. (36) or maybe you don't have time!

Go for that rotisserie chicken in your grocery store and focus on the sides, for a LIGHTNING FAST ROAST CHICKEN with MASHERS AND GRAVY. (37)

However you find yourself with left-over chicken, you'll want a way to use it —

when you roast a chicken it teaches you all kinds

CHICKEN SALAD (50) (curried, jerked, with tarragon) or a CHICKEN POT PIE (54) (see chapter 2 for an EASY CRUST).

Or, if ever you find yourself with a chicken carcass, you'll want to make the EASY OVERNIGHT STOCK (38): 2 minutes work and the next morning a whole bath of fresh chicken stock awaits. Make a classic CHICKEN NOODLE SOUP (39) later in the week, or buy some tortellini for TORTELLINI EN BRODO (40) or make your own using the pasta recipe in CH 3!, use the stock for the CHICKEN POT PIE, (54) or learn to make THE coolest, most refined chicken soup known: CHICKEN CONSOMMÉ (41)!

ROAST CHICKEN AU JUS WITH MASHED POTATOES AND GREEN BEANS SERVES 4

This is one of my favorite meals, one I never tire of. It makes me feel good having eaten it, and it usually leaves plenty of leftovers or at least enough for a second meal of soup. I love to serve it with simple mashed potatoes because they are so easy and delicious and quick to prepare; they can be made well before the chicken is done (they'll keep for hours—just don't let them get cold). Green beans are likewise inexpensive, easy, and tasty, buttered and seasoned simply with lemon zest and salt. The only key to making this easy on yourself is to make sure you've done the shopping ahead of time.

Later on I'll show ways to cut down on the time if you don't have much but still want a roast chicken, but here I assume you control all your time. You will need to allow for 90 minutes of total cooking time (after your oven is hot), and plan to spend about 45 minutes actually in the kitchen. So plan ahead. Say you want dinner on the table at 7 P.M. but don't want to be rushed. Then you'll want the chicken to go into the oven at 5:30, which means turning on your oven at 5:10 or so. Chicken in at 5:30, out at 6:30 to rest while you complete the meal, served by 7. If you're quick with a knife and generally deft in the kitchen, you can shave 10 or 15 minutes off the 45 minutes of actual cooking, but if you don't have to rush, take your time and enjoy the process.

Of particular note here is how the jus comes together in the cooking pan. The pan will contain plenty of flavorful fat and juices from the bird that will condense on the bottom of the pan. Wine adds its own flavor as it deglazes, lifting the stuck skin and browned bits, or fond, from the pan. Thinly sliced carrot and onion add aromatic sweetness to the sauce. And the two complete reductions allow those juices, as well as the sugars extracted from the vegetables, to brown and develop even more flavor. All of this takes place in 15 minutes or so to create a delectable and nutritious jus to finish the meal.

And finally, oven temperature. The chicken cooks best at 450°F/230°C. But this is well above the smoke point for animal fats, and any residue in a dirty oven, so it helps to have good ventilation and a clean oven. If you don't have both, use a lower temperature, 425°F/218°C, to avoid smoking yourself out of the kitchen.

1 (3- to 4-pound/ 1.4- to 1.8-kilogram) chicken, *preferably at room temperature*	2 large russet potatoes (*1½ to 2 pounds/680 to 900 grams total*)	1 small onion or ½ large onion	1 cup/240 milliliters dry white wine
1 lemon	1 pound/450 grams green beans	½ cup/120 milliliters whole milk, *plus more as needed*	2 cups/480 milliliters hot water
1 tablespoon kosher salt, *plus more to taste*	1 carrot	6 tablespoons/ 90 grams unsalted butter (*or more to taste*), *cut into pieces*	

Preheat your oven to 450°F/230°C (or, if your oven isn't clean, 425°F/218°C).

Rinse your chicken and dry it inside and out (I discard the liver, and reserve the gizzard and heart for the sauce, but feel free to discard all).

Zest the lemon, reserving the zest. Put the zested lemon in the carcass of the bird. Truss the bird if you want a gorgeous presentation. The best way to learn to truss a chicken is to watch a video of it. (Go to ruhlman.com and search "how to truss a chicken" to see my colleague Brian Polcyn do an impromptu demonstration. If you do truss, you don't need to put the lemon in the carcass. Both trussing and inserting a lemon will prevent hot air from circulating inside the cavity, which can overcook the breast.

Sprinkle the chicken liberally with salt; you should have a nice crusty layer of it across the whole bird. Put the bird, breast side up, in an oven-safe skillet and into the hot oven for 1 hour.

About 30 minutes after putting the chicken in the oven, begin preparing the rest of the meal.

Peel the potatoes and cut them into six or eight even pieces. Put them in a saucepan, cover with cold water, and put the pan over high heat. When the water boils, reduce the heat to medium to maintain a good simmer (but not a heavy boil). Cook for 15 to 20 minutes, until you can insert a paring knife into the potatoes with little to no resistance.

Meanwhile, put another saucepan of water over high heat, for the beans. Trim the stem ends from the beans.

Scrub or peel the carrot, then cut off the ends. Cut the carrot into ribbons using a vegetable peeler (or slice it thinly; the thinner the pieces, the better the flavor of the jus). Peel and thinly slice the onion.

When the potatoes are done, drain them in a colander or strainer and set them aside. In the same pan, combine the milk, 4 tablespoons/60 grams of the butter (or more to taste), and a four-finger pinch of salt and return it to the stovetop over medium heat. When the butter is nearly melted, add the potato chunks and mash them with a masher until smooth (you can also pass the potatoes through a ricer or food mill into the pot if you want perfectly smooth mashed potatoes). Stir to combine all the ingredients, taste them, and add more salt if they need it (they usually do). Remove from the heat, cover, and set aside.

Just before pulling the chicken from the oven, put the beans in the boiling water and cook until tender, 5 to 10 minutes or as you like them. (Not sure if they are done? Do what chefs do: Taste one.)

Remove the chicken from the oven. Pull the chicken out of the pan, leaving behind any skin stuck to the bottom of the pan, and place it on a cutting board with a moat or on a plate (the bird will drop juices as it finishes cooking). Add the heart and gizzard to the pan, if using. Put the pan over high heat and allow the juices to reduce in the fat for a minute or so. Cut the wing tips and wing flats off the bird. Add them to the pan (or eat the flats as a treat while you cook; if you eat them, add the bones to the skillet if you wish). Add the carrot and onion to the pan. Stir them to coat them with the chicken fat and cook till they're tender, another minute or two.

To make the jus, add the wine to the pan and bring it to a simmer, scraping the bottom of the pan with a flat-edged spoon. Stir until all the wine has cooked off and the fat has begun to crackle again. Add 1 cup/240 milliliters of the hot water. Cook this off as you did the wine, until virtually all the liquid is gone, then add the remaining 1 cup/240 milliliters hot water, bring it to a boil, and turn off the heat.

When the beans are done (and this may happen while your jus is reducing), drain them and return them to the pot, then add the remaining 2 tablespoons/30 grams butter (or more to taste). Salt them and add the reserved lemon zest.

Reheat the potatoes if necessary by returning them to medium heat and adding a few tablespoons or so of milk until they are the consistency you like.

Cut the chicken into six pieces, taking each breast off along with the wing drumette, and each leg, then cutting them into drumstick and thigh pieces.

Serve the chicken with the potatoes and beans. Strain the sauce into a bowl for the table or simply spoon the sauce straight from the pan, without the vegetables, over the chicken.

FOUR-STAR TARRAGON SAUCE   MAKES ENOUGH FOR 1 ROAST CHICKEN

This sauce is the same jus as in the main roast chicken recipe, strained, enhanced with some shallot and tarragon and butter, and thickened slightly so that it has an appealing body. This is how the best of all possible roast chickens concludes.

1 recipe Roast
Chicken au Jus
(page 30)

2 tablespoons/
30 grams unsalted
butter, *at room
temperature*

1 ½ tablespoons
all-purpose flour

1 tablespoon finely
minced shallot

1 to 2 tablespoons
chopped fresh
tarragon

Several drops lemon
juice

Follow the roast chicken recipe through making the jus, stopping just before you add the final cup of water.

While the wine and first cup of water are reducing, make a beurre manié by combining 1½ tablespoons of the butter with the flour. Knead it till it is a uniform paste.

In a small saucepan, melt the remaining ½ tablespoon butter over medium heat. Add the shallot and cook it till it's translucent, a minute or so.

Add the final cup of water to the roasting skillet and bring it to a boil. Pour the mixture through a fine-mesh strainer into the shallot pan, pressing down on the solids to get as much liquid out as possible. Bring the liquid to a simmer, then whisk in the beurre manié. When the sauce has thickened, remove the pan from the heat.

Cut the chicken and finish the side dishes. Add the tarragon and a few drops of lemon juice to the sauce and serve.

BEURRE MANIÉ

*B*eurre manié, French for kneaded butter, is butter into which flour has been mixed—I use equal parts by volume. It is one of the best thickening agents there is, at least for relatively small quantities of liquid. There are two other traditional thickening options: roux, which is the same thing only it's cooked, and cornstarch slurry, which is cornstarch mixed with water. Both starches, flour and corn, thicken by expanding as they absorb water and heat up. Flour, though, contains the protein gluten, which, when mixed with water, tends to interlock and stick with other gluten molecules (the reason we have bread, not to mention lumpy gravy), thus the need for butter, or any fat, to coat the flour granules and prevent them from hooking up with their brethren. I believe that the enriching factor of the butter combined with the added protein makes beurre manié or a roux far superior to a cornstarch slurry, and it is always my choice for thickening (even, frankly, a Chinese stir-fry—see page 266).

The only drawback of beurre manié is that you're adding raw flour to your stock or sauce, which doesn't add the additional flavor that a cooked roux does (if you wish to cook your flour, add it after the shallot has cooked, then simply whisk in the butter after you've strained the stock). But for single batches of sauce (as opposed to a quart of gravy), beurre manié is perfect. Consider making more than you need; wrap what you don't use in plastic and refrigerate it or freeze it for when you need some last-minute thickening of a stock, soup, or sauce, or simply when you make your next chicken au jus, to thicken the jus into a sauce.

SIMPLE GRAVY   MAKES ABOUT 3½ CUPS/830 MILLILITERS

Sometimes you want a more substantial sauce than a weeknight jus. And sometimes it's Thanksgiving *Sauces* and you're in charge of the gravy. Gravy is simply thickened stock, so the quality of the gravy is directly related to the quality of the stock. This is why, if you know you want to make gravy, it's worth the effort of having good stock on hand.

Sometimes other ingredients are added, but they don't need to be for it to be a rich gravy to ladle over chicken and mashed potatoes. I like to add a little sautéed onion, which makes most savory dishes better. You can add mushrooms, chopped giblets, or whatever strikes your fancy.

While you could thicken the gravy with a slurry of cornstarch, I think a gravy thickened with flour has a better texture and is generally more satisfying (partly because of the flour and partly because the flour has to be mixed with butter or fat from cooking the bird). Smaller amounts of stock can be thickened with beurre manié, butter into which flour has been kneaded. Larger amounts benefit from a roux, in which you cook the flour in the butter rather than just kneading them together. The point of combining the fat and the flour is to coat the granules of flour so that that the flour won't clump as it expands to do its thickening work. (But I've seen chef Jean-Georges Vongerichten simply sprinkle flour directly into cold coffee to thicken a duck stew, so even the fat isn't strictly necessary.) The fat can be butter, with a roux made separate from what you're cooking, or the roux can be made in the roasting pan using the fat from the bird.

4 tablespoons/ 60 grams unsalted butter	1 quart/1 liter cold Easy Overnight Chicken Stock (page 38), Vegetable Stock (page 114), One-Hour Beef Stock (page 142), or store-bought broth
½ onion, *cut into small dice*	
Kosher salt *to taste*	
6 tablespoons/ 45 grams all-purpose flour	

Melt the butter in a small saucepan over medium-high heat. Add the onion and hit it with a three-finger pinch of salt. Stir to coat the onion with the melting butter and continue to cook until the onion is translucent.

Add the flour and stir so that it becomes coated with the fat. Continue cooking until the flour smells like pie crust.

Whisk in the stock, stirring and dragging a flat-edged spoon across the bottom to keep the flour from sticking. The stock will thicken as it comes to a simmer. Taste and, if desired, add a pinch more salt.

You can use the gravy right away or, for a more refined gravy, you can pull the pan to the edge of the burner and lower the heat till it's at a light simmer on just one side of the pan. Let it cook this way for 20 to 30 minutes, skimming the foam and skin that forms on the cool side of the pan.

BRINE

Brining is a powerful tool when you know how to use it.

There's no doubt in my mind that brining makes just about any meat juicier and has the capacity to flavor that meat as well. I don't typically brine a chicken I intend to roast because I like the texture of the unbrined skin, crusted with salt (brine dehydrates the skin, resulting in a very thin, shiny browned skin). But I always try to brine chicken I intend to fry. Pork is also a great meat to brine. Brine seasons the meat all the way through and helps keep it juicy.

The problem with brine for me is that I fail to plan and so don't have time to cook and cool the brine, then give the meat enough time in it. So I've figured out a couple of shortcuts to give me more options.

I like to cook my brine with herbs and aromatics, so that the brine is flavorful and the salt is fully dissolved. But it takes a while for this to cool, so when I'm in a hurry to get the meat into a brine, I use only half the water. Then, when I'm done cooking it, I add the other half of the water in the form of ice cubes. Brines are best measured by weight, so it's helpful to have a scale to weigh the ice as well as the salt.

The other shortcut is to double the salt concentration. A perfect all-purpose brine that won't overpower the meat is a 5 percent brine (that is, the weight of the salt is 5 percent of the weight of the water). But if you want to get that brine into the meat faster, double it to a 10 percent brine: 7½ cups/1.8 kilograms water plus 3 ounces/90 grams salt for a 5 percent brine or 6 ounces/180 grams salt for a 10 percent brine. A chicken can go 8 to 12 hours in a 5 percent brine, half that time in a 10 percent brine. (Of course, this is more accurate and much easier if you use the metric system: 1 liter of water plus 50 grams salt for a 5 percent brine or 100 grams salt for a 10 percent brine. This is why most professional kitchens use only metric measurements. You should, too, when possible.)

A brine is all about osmosis and equalizing the salt concentration between mediums, the water and the meat. If you feel you may have overbrined and the meat will be too salty, you can always put the meat in water—or, better, a 1 percent brine, which will draw out the excess salt.

A final point: If you have the time and forethought, brine your meat a day ahead; remove it from the brine and let the salt equalize throughout the meat for a day in the refrigerator.

LEMON-ROSEMARY BRINE MAKES ENOUGH BRINE FOR A 2- TO 5-POUND/ 1- TO 2.25-KILOGRAM CHICKEN; CAN EASILY BE DOUBLED OR TRIPLED FOR LARGER BIRDS

1 liter/1 quart water

50 grams/3 tablespoons kosher salt

4 garlic cloves, *smashed with the flat side of a chef's knife (OK to leave the skins on)*

1 small onion, *thinly sliced*

1 lemon, *halved, visible seeds removed*

4 rosemary sprigs

2 teaspoons whole black peppercorns, *cracked beneath a sauté pan or roughly chopped*

This is a traditional 5 percent brine. To make a 10 percent brine, keep the amount of water as is but double the amount of salt to 100 grams (about 6 tablespoons).

Combine all the ingredients in a large pot and bring to a boil. Remove it from the heat and allow it to cool to room temperature. The brine is then ready to use.

Note: To use the quick brine method, you need a scale. Use only ½ liter of water in the above recipe. Then, once you've removed the cooked brine from the heat, add 500 grams of ice and stir until chilled.

ROAST CHICKEN WITH SALSA VERDE   SERVES 4

One of our favorite New York City meals is Jonathan Waxman's roast chicken with salsa verde at his restaurant Barbuto. We like it so much we had it for our wedding-day lunch—and we returned a year later to have it again on our anniversary. Waxman's fabulous salsa recipe (widely available online) includes eight different herbs, but you can use whatever herbs are available. Parsley is almost always a good idea, and I like to include a spicy green, such as watercress. You should stick mainly to the soft herbs, but I like a little savory herb such as oregano in the mix. In the end, it's up to you—you'll want about 1¼ cups/300 milliliters total. Garlic, capers, and anchovy give it some heft and umami (I use fish sauce instead of the anchovy because I always have that on hand). It's a great sauce to have in your repertoire because it can be used on virtually any meat or fish. Add ¼ cup of red wine vinegar and it becomes a chimichurri sauce, beautiful on grilled steak.

Kosher salt *to taste*

1 (3- to 4-pound/ 1.4- to 1.8-kilogram) chicken

2 garlic cloves, *peeled*

1 tablespoon capers

1 tablespoon fish sauce or 1 or 2 anchovies, *cleaned and minced to a paste*

¾ cup/180 milliliters extra-virgin olive oil

½ cup/15 grams chopped fresh flat leaf parsley

¼ cup chopped watercress

¼ cup chopped fresh mint

2 tablespoons chopped fresh cilantro

2 tablespoons chopped fresh chives

Preheat your oven to 450°F/230°C (or 425°F/218°C if you are concerned about smoke).

Aggressively salt the chicken and put it, breast-side up, in an oven-safe skillet. Roast for 1 hour. Allow it to rest in the pan for 15 to 20 minutes before carving.

While the chicken is resting, make the sauce. Combine the garlic and capers in a mortar, along with a three-finger pinch of salt, the fish sauce, and 1 tablespoon of the oil and use the pestle to smash them to a paste (you can use a garlic press and finely chop the capers if you don't have a mortar and pestle). Transfer the mixture to a bowl, add the herbs and then the remaining oil, and stir to mix well.

Carve the chicken and spoon the sauce over the cut pieces to serve.

ROAST CHICKEN is so economical and delicious, we want to make it often. But we also don't want to get tired of it. Following are four variations on the standard roast chicken dinner.

Variations

ROAST CHICKEN WITH JALAPEÑOS, LEMON, AND GARLIC SERVES 4

This is a spicy version of roast chicken, inspired by a lovely former editor of mine, which I include for those who like bold flavors and heat. What I love about it in particular is that the lemon and chicken create abundant sauce, enhanced by the garlic (which first browns in the high heat, then flavors and helps thicken the sauce). I baste the bird with the juices several times during the second half of its cooking. Be sure to include all the seeds and white parts of the jalapeños, which is where all the heat is (these days the actual flesh of the peppers has very little heat to speak of). You should have plenty of sauce, but it will be thin. It's fine to use as is, but feel free to stir in a tablespoon of beurre manié at the end.

Kosher salt *to taste*

1 (3- to 4-pound/ 1.4- to 1.8-kilogram) chicken

2 jalapeño peppers, *cut into ¼-inch/ 6-millimeter rounds, seeds and all*

1 lemon, cut into 8 wedges, *seeds removed*

10 to 15 garlic cloves, *peeled*

1 to 2 tablespoons beurre manié *(page 32; optional)*

Preheat your oven to 450°F/230°C (or 425°F/218°C if you are concerned about smoke).

Salt the chicken aggressively and put it, breast-side up, in an oven-safe skillet. Scatter the jalapeño slices, lemon wedges, and garlic cloves around the chicken. Roast for 1 hour, basting the chicken several times during the last 30 minutes of cooking.

Remove the bird from the pan and let it rest on a cutting board for 15 minutes before carving. If you wish, add the beurre manié while simmering the sauce, or simply spoon the sauce, garlic, lemon (1 wedge per plate), and peppers over the cut-up chicken to serve.

SPATCHCOCKED CHICKEN PROVENÇAL SERVES 4

I love to spatchcock a chicken—that is, to remove the backbone of the chicken so that you can flatten it out. I use a chef's knife, or you can use kitchen shears to cut through the ribs on both sides of the backbone. (This is also the best way to halve a chicken for roasting; cut through the breast to finish halving it, removing the keel bone completely.) It's then simply seasoned with herbs, roasted with garlic, shallots, lemon, and wine, basted with the resulting juices during cooking, and served with the shallots and garlic. If you don't have herbes de Provence, make your own by combining 1½ teaspoons each of dried thyme, dried oregano, dried rosemary, and dried marjoram or savory.

1 (3- to 4-pound/ 1.4- to 1.8-kilogram) chicken

Kosher salt *to taste*

2 tablespoons herbes de Provence

5 shallots, *peeled*

10 garlic cloves, *peeled*

1 lemon, *quartered*

½ cup/120 milliliters dry white wine

Preheat your oven to 450°F/230°C (or 425°F/218°C if you are concerned about smoke).

Remove the backbone of the chicken and press down on the bird to flatten it. Salt the chicken aggressively and put it, skin side up, in a shallow baking dish or, if it will fit, a large oven-safe skillet. Coat the skin side with the herbes de Provence. Scatter the shallots, garlic, and lemon around the chicken, add the wine, and roast for 50 to 60 minutes, basting several times during the last 30 minutes of cooking.

Remove the bird from the pan and let it rest on a cutting board for 15 minutes before carving. Serve the cut-up chicken with the pan juices, shallots, and garlic. (Usually the lemon gives plenty of flavor to the sauce, but if you taste it and it could use more lemon, squeeze more lemon into the sauce.)

LIGHTNING VERSION: ROAST CHICKEN WITH MASHED POTATOES, GREEN BEANS, AND GRAVY SERVES 4

Variations

We wanted it but we wanted it fast.

My wife, Ann, my stepson, Sam, my stepdaughter, Annabelle, and I had arrived at our apartment in New York City on a cold winter night after a long journey on a clogged Merritt Parkway (George Carlin's question endures: Why do we park in a driveway and drive on a parkway?). We had eaten nothing but what was available at service stations and so were in deep need of nutrition. It was past eight, and no one wanted to trudge to a restaurant for an expensive dinner at this hour. Having just arrived, we found that the fridge was bare, but the very notion of a roast chicken dinner with mashed potatoes seemed to buoy our tired spirits.

"I can have it on the table in thirty minutes," I announced, and departed for the small grocery store around the corner. A rotisserie chicken would do the trick, with some green beans I could microwave, potatoes I could cut small for fast cooking, and a gravy from store-bought broth (get the best available, preferably organic; it's worth it).

There's no reason not to have a grand roast chicken dinner if that's what your body craves, even if you have only 20 minutes to cook it.

1 store-bought rotisserie chicken

2 russet potatoes

1 medium onion

10 tablespoons/ 150 grams unsalted butter

3 tablespoons all-purpose flour

2 cups/480 milliliters best-quality store-bought chicken broth

Kosher salt *to taste*

½ cup/120 milliliters whole milk, *plus more as needed*

1 (10- to 12-ounce/ 300- to 340-gram) package frozen, microwave-in-the-bag green beans

If you want to keep your chicken warm, hold it in a 200°F/93°C oven while you make the sides.

Peel the potatoes and cut them into large dice. Put them in a saucepan, cover them with water, put the pan over high heat, and cover the pan until it boils. Remove the lid and reduce the heat to lower the boil but keep the water solidly simmering.

Dice the onion and put it in another saucepan, along with 2 tablespoons/30 grams of the butter. Cook over medium-high heat until the onion is translucent, a minute or so after the butter has melted. Add the flour and stir until the flour is coated with butter. Turn the heat to high and add the chicken broth, stirring to make sure nothing sticks to the bottom of the pan. Add any juices from the chicken's package. When the broth has thickened and come to a simmer, reduce the heat to low.

When the potatoes are tender (after about 15 minutes), drain them. Add 6 tablespoons/90 grams of the remaining butter, the milk, and a four-finger pinch of salt to the same pan, and bring the milk to a simmer over high heat. Return the potatoes to the pan, turn the heat to medium-low, and mash the potatoes until they are uniformly mixed (it's OK to leave them chunky if you wish). Taste them and add more salt or butter as needed.

Microwave the beans according to the package instructions. Transfer the beans to a bowl, add the remaining 2 tablespoons/30 grams butter, and season with salt to taste.

Cut the chicken into quarters. (Remember to save the bones for stock!) Serve with the mashed potatoes, green beans, and gravy.

EASY OVERNIGHT CHICKEN STOCK MAKES 1 QUART/1 LITER

Make this a part of your roast chicken routine and you can enjoy the glories of fresh stock, a genuine pleasure if you're used to store-bought broths that are laced with salt, "natural flavorings," and other products not present in chicken or vegetables. What you have is clear, clean, fresh chicken broth. It takes less than a minute to prepare, then it cooks overnight in a low oven. I don't even peel the carrots or the onion—I've found that onion skin enhances the stock's flavor and color, so I just trim the root and any dirt. As has often been said, if you have chicken stock, you've got a meal.

This is beautiful for making a full-on gravy, or use it in place of water for a more intense jus. It makes a terrific soup, too, of course (see pages 39–43).

1 roast chicken carcass	1 bay leaf (*optional*)
1 onion, *root trimmed, quartered*	A few flat-leaf parsley sprigs (*optional*)
1 or 2 carrots	1 tablespoon tomato paste (*optional*)
½ teaspoon salt	1 teaspoon whole black peppercorns (*optional*)
1 leek, *green parts and all, well cleaned* (*optional*)	
4 garlic cloves, *unpeeled, lightly smashed* (*optional*)	

Combine all the ingredients in a 2-quart/2-liter oven-safe saucepan. Pour in enough water to cover the ingredients by 2 to 3 inches/5 to 8 centimeters. Put the pan, uncovered, in the oven and turn the oven to 200°F/93°C. In the morning, or after 8 hours, turn the oven off.

When you have a moment, that morning or that evening, strain the stock through a fine-mesh sieve into a clean container or pan and refrigerate it until you're ready to use it. If you won't be using it within the week, freeze it for up to a month (it will keep, frozen, indefinitely; it just may pick up flavors that you don't want). I leave this stock on the stovetop if I want to use it during the week. It will keep that long in cool weather; just bring it up to a simmer for a few minutes each day to kill any bacteria that have descended on the room-temperature, protein-rich liquid. If you're concerned about this, then by all means refrigerate until ready to use.

CHICKEN NOODLE SOUP SERVES 4

I would lay odds that homemade chicken noodle soup really does heal. I made it last for my wife, Ann, who was feeling a cold coming on. She woke the next day symptom free, certain that it had been the magic of the soup. When you make it with your own chicken stock, there is no denying that chicken noodle soup is dense with nutrition, somehow a perfect combination of vegetables, starch, and protein that leaves you completely sated but never overly full.

The secret to an excellent chicken soup is cooking the vegetables until they are just done. They should have a firm bite and a bright flavor. If they cook too long, not only do they become mushy, but they give up their flavor to the broth, having none of their own. Each component of an excellent chicken noodle soup should be distinctive, not least of all the stock itself. So, it's especially fine with Easy Overnight Chicken Stock, because the abundant vegetables and herbs will enhance.

I like the customary mirepoix, but you can add any vegetables you wish—other root vegetables or even green vegetables if it's springtime (peas or asparagus), and it's a terrific place to use ramps if they're in season where you live. Ramps are often called wild leeks, but regular leeks, the white and pale parts, thinly sliced, are excellent and really up the nutritional content. If you use leeks, save the dark green parts to add to your next batch of overnight stock.

I prefer cooking the noodles separately. Pasta cooked in the soup soaks up too much stock and thus tastes of stock rather than of clean pasta. (If you use fresh pasta, though, you can cook that in the soup.) This soup is delicious as is, but I like to finish it with some fresh parsley and lemon zest to make it even more dynamic.

Kosher salt *to taste*

8 ounces/225 grams egg noodles

1 tablespoon olive oil

2 garlic cloves, *minced*

1 medium onion, *diced*

1 large carrot, *sliced obliquely or diced*

2 celery ribs, *cut into ¼-inch/6-millimeter slices*

5 cups/1.2 liters Easy Overnight Chicken Stock (page 38) *or store-bought chicken broth*

4 to 6 thyme sprigs (*tied together with kitchen string if you have it to make them easier to remove*)

1 tablespoon fish sauce (*optional*)

1 cup/180 grams shredded or diced cooked chicken

1 tablespoon finely chopped fresh flat-leaf parsley

Grated zest of ½ lemon

Bring a medium saucepan of well-salted water to a boil over high heat. Cook the noodles according to the package instructions, then shock them in ice water to stop the cooking. Set aside.

Meanwhile, heat the oil in a saucepan over medium-high heat, then add the garlic and cook it for 30 seconds. Add the onion, carrot, celery, and a four-finger pinch of salt (if you're using store-bought broth, hold off on the salt until after you've added the broth). Cook the vegetables for a minute or two (this will enhance their flavor more than if you were to add the vegetables and stock all at once).

Add the stock, along with the thyme and fish sauce (if using). Bring it to a gentle simmer and cook for a few minutes. When the carrots are al dente (taste one to see), add the chicken and noodles. Bring the soup back to a simmer. Serve immediately, garnishing each serving with fresh parsley and lemon zest.

TORTELLINI EN BRODO   SERVES 4

You want easy and quick? Nothing could be simpler than this: Buy some ricotta-filled tortellini, cook them in your Easy Overnight Chicken Stock, and serve, garnished with some freshly grated Parmigiano-Reggiano and a drizzle of extra-virgin olive oil. A satisfying meal for breakfast, lunch, or dinner, in 10 minutes—comfort in a bowl.

You can give this soup more heft by adding cooked crumbled Italian sausage and sliced escarole along with the tortellini.

If you want to take this up a level, make your own tortellini! It's relaxing and fun when you give yourself plenty of time. Fill them with fresh ricotta mixed with the zest of 2 lemons, kosher salt, and plenty of freshly ground black pepper. You'll need 1¼ cups/300 milliliters of ricotta to fill twenty tortellini each with 1 tablespoon, to serve four.

And of course you can go all out and make it *all* from scratch: make your own sausage (see page 82), make your own ricotta (all you need is whole milk and lemon juice; see page 109), and make fresh pasta for your tortellini. I'm not going to suggest you grow your own escarole, but if you grow your own lettuces anyway, plant some escarole and do a whole from-scratch version on a Sunday afternoon.

1 quart/1 liter Easy Overnight Chicken Stock (page 38) *or store-bought chicken broth*

20 fresh ricotta-filled tortellini

1 pound/450 grams loose Italian sausage, *cooked* (optional)

1½ cups/100 grams sliced escarole (optional)

Kosher salt *to taste*

¼ cup grated Parmigiano-Reggiano, *for garnish*

¼ cup extra-virgin olive oil, *for garnish*

Tuscan bread, *for serving*

In a medium saucepan, bring the stock to a simmer over medium heat. Add the tortellini and the sausage and escarole (if using) and cook until the tortellini are cooked through. Season with salt to taste. Ladle into bowls and garnish each serving with a bit of grated Parmigiano-Reggiano and a drizzle of olive oil. Serve immediately with bread for dipping.

CHICKEN CONSOMMÉ MAKES 8 (½-CUP/120-MILLILITER) PORTIONS

The experience of making my first consommé was such a thrill, I even remember who I was standing *Soups* with, also making his first consommé: David Scott, in my first skills class at the Culinary Institute of America. We had started with standard, opaque gelatinous chicken stock, then simmered it with ground meat and vegetables and egg whites, and what we ladled out of the pot was an elixir that was clear as crystal—in fact, it was the clearest colored liquid I'd ever seen. It seemed to magnify and clarify a spoon dipped into it. David stared at his own and said, "This is *so* cool."

And I remember another of my cooking school classmates who brought his golden consommé to our instructor, Michael Pardus, for his evaluation and grade. Chef Pardus dipped a spoon into it. "Nice clarity. Nice color—really nice color." It was. It had a deeper golden cast. "If fact, I can tell from the color . . . that you *scorched* it!"

My classmate grimaced and nodded. "Yep, I scorched it."

We had been warned. The raw egg whites tend to sink and stick to the bottom of the pan. If you don't diligently drag a flat-edged spoon along the bottom as the stock comes up to heat, it sticks and burns, giving the stock excellent color but a burnt flavor.

This was the miraculous consommé, a broth that should be so clear, it was said, that you could read the date on a dime at the bottom of a gallon.

Consommé is one of the reasons I love cooking: It is a transformation. That is when you are really cooking: when you take cloudy stock, and with your skill and knowledge, transform it into an intensely flavored crystal-clear jewel. That is reason enough to make a consommé.

The other is that it is a pleasure to serve your guests such a soup, because it's both beautiful to behold and a pleasure to eat.

Here's how it works: The proteins in egg white, tight coils when cold, unravel as they heat, and they coalesce into a fine mesh that removes all impurities that could cloud a stock. It also removes flavor, however, so you must put that flavor back in by adding egg whites, ground meat, onion, carrot, and herbs.

And what you have is stock elevated to its most glorious incarnation, the consommé.

The recipe here is for chicken consommé to make with Easy Overnight Chicken Stock. But if you want an even richer, more flavorful consommé, try making a roast turkey stock (using the same overnight method) and use that for the consommé. It's a beautiful creation.

recipe continues

For the consommé:

4 large egg whites, *lightly whipped*

1 medium onion

1 small carrot

1 celery rib

2 or 3 boneless, skinless chicken thighs, *trimmed of fat, each cut into 4 pieces*

1½ quarts/1.5 liters Easy Overnight Chicken Stock (page 38)

Optional but recommended aromatics: 1 chopped plum tomato or 1 teaspoon tomato paste, fresh thyme and flat-leaf parsley sprigs, black peppercorns (cracked or roughly chopped), bay leaf

Kosher salt *to taste*

For the garnish:

1½ tablespoons finely diced carrot

1½ tablespoons finely diced or julienned celery

1 tablespoon finely minced shallot

4 shiitake mushrooms, *julienned*

Combine the egg whites, onion, carrot, celery, and chicken in a food processor. Pulse until the chicken is mainly pureed but the mixture remains a little chunky.

Transfer the mixture to a small saucepan, preferably one that is taller than it is wide (too wide a pot spreads out the clarification and allows too much reduction during cooking). Add the stock and any of the optional aromatics you choose.

Place the pot over high heat and stir with a flat-edged wood spoon, dragging it along the bottom to prevent the egg white from sticking and scorching. As the liquid gets hot, the protein will begin to coagulate and rise to the top (this is referred to as a raft, a solid disk of meat, vegetable, and egg white). Continue to stir, gently, to make sure nothing is sticking to the bottom. Once the raft has formed, stop stirring and allow it to come together. Lower the heat before the stock comes to a full boil, letting it just simmer over the raft and sink down. You should be able to see how clear the stock is at this point. Continue to simmer it for 45 to 60 minutes. Don't let it boil or the raft may disintegrate.

Meanwhile, blanch the carrot and celery garnish together in boiling water for 20 seconds, then drain under cold running water until thoroughly chilled.

Ladle the consommé through a strainer lined with a coffee filter. Your liquid should be perfectly clear. Taste and add salt if necessary. Serve immediately in warm bowls, into which you've divided your carrot-celery-shallot-mushroom garnish, or chill the consommé in the refrigerator in a covered container until you're ready to reheat and pour it over the garnish. If there are spots of oil on the surface, drag a paper towel over the surface to lift them out. If it is hot out, this consommé may be served chilled.

1. A consommé begins with pureed or ground meat and chopped vegetables to enhance the soup's flavor.

2. Stock is added to make what looks like a meat-vegetable milkshake.

3. Once the pan is on the heat, use a flat-edged spoon or spatula to continuously scrape the bottom of the pan to prevent egg white from sticking and scorching.

4. Once the stock is hot and the egg white and meat have risen to the surface in what is called the raft, you can stop stirring.

5. Allow the stock to come to a full simmer so that it bubbles over and back through the raft, then reduce the heat to maintain a gentle but steady simmer. Do not let the stock come to a boil, or the raft will break apart and the soup will be cloudy.

6. Gently ladle the finished consommé through a coffee filter. It should be crystal clear. Skim any fat that may rise to the surface.

QUICK-SAUTÉED BRUSSELS SPROUTS SERVES 4

Side Dishes

This is one of my favorite ways to prepare the nutritious Brussels sprout. Brussels sprouts are dense and need serious cooking in order to make them palatable—when whole, that is. When you tenderize them mechanically—that is, by slicing them thinly—you can cook them quickly so that they have a fresher, more dynamic flavor, and they're done in a snap. These are great cooked simply, with oil and butter. Or if you feel like adding more flavor, cook a few pieces of chopped bacon and sauté the leaves in the bacon fat.

You can use a sharp chef's knife to cut the sprouts thinly, but a Japanese mandoline makes the work go lickety-split.

2 teaspoons vegetable oil	Kosher salt and freshly ground black pepper *to taste*
1½ pounds/680 grams Brussels sprouts, *core ends trimmed, thinly sliced*	1 tablespoon unsalted butter

Heat the oil in a large sauté pan over high heat. When the oil is ripplingly hot, add the Brussels sprouts and sauté them until they're heated through. Salt and pepper them, then toss them with the butter until it melts. Taste to make sure they have enough salt and butter. Serve immediately.

ROASTED BROCCOLI WITH GARLIC SERVES 4

One of the surest ways to turn a vegetable from ho-hum into special is to roast it, giving it the complex browning flavors you get from the high heat of the oven. It's also easy, requiring little more than tossing with oil and popping them in the oven for 30 minutes or so. I also flavor them with garlic, which gets browned and mild from the high heat. This is a great way to prepare any green vegetable if you've got a lot of other dishes happening at the same time because they require so little attention. The only danger is overcooking them—they can dry out and become too crispy and brown. So, pull them from the oven while they're still bright green and return them to the oven to reheat just before you need them.

If you have time and the desire, trim off the woody exteriors of the broccoli stems from the tender white inner stems, then cut these into coin-size pieces and add them during the last 5 minutes of cooking. They're delicious.

2 tablespoons olive oil	10 to 15 garlic cloves, *peeled*
2 to 3 heads broccoli, *cut into florets and, if desired, inner stems sliced*	Kosher salt *to taste*

Preheat your oven to 425°F/218°C.

Put the oil in a large bowl, then add the broccoli florets and garlic cloves, tossing to coat them with the oil.

Transfer the broccoli and garlic to a roasting pan and roast for 25 to 30 minutes, or until the tips of the florets are lightly browned and somewhat crisp and the floret stems are crispy. Add the sliced white stems during the last 5 minutes of cooking, if you're using them. Season with salt to taste and serve.

MEDITATION ON THE BAKED POTATO:
Baked, Baked and Mashed, Twice-Baked

When my wife, Ann, told me that she didn't like baked potatoes, I couldn't believe it. Until, that is, she described what a baked potato was: a lump wrapped in foil, its skin soft and wrinkled, its flesh still hard. I promised that this was not, in fact, a proper baked potato, and that I would make her one: a potato with a skin so crisp you couldn't not want to eat it, the interior fluffy, steamy, buttery.

She was so impressed she turned it into an essay, the ultimate flattery from the writer to the cook.

To me, a well-made baked potato is one of the greatest things to eat because this buttery, salty creation is ultimately so humble, and inexpensive, and simple to prepare, and nutritious. That's a combination one needs to recognize and revere, as one does properly scrambled eggs or a perfectly roasted chicken.

As I thought more about the simple baked potato, I began to imagine other things that can be done with them. After a recent lightning chicken dinner (page 37), wherein I cut the potatoes very small to cook them quickly, I noticed I needed less milk than I do when I cut them large. The small pieces had retained considerably more liquid, and the resulting mashed potatoes were less flavorful because of it than potatoes cooked when I have more time.

One thing I have always remembered about Thomas Keller, a chef I have worked with extensively on half a dozen books: When he boils potatoes, he does so "in their jackets." (I love that old verbiage.) Potatoes boiled thus have a dry, fluffy interior, perfect for a potato puree or hand-rolled gnocchi.

Returning my thoughts to the baked potato then, it occurred to me that cooking the potato in the dry heat of the oven would let them absorb no water at all, so there would be nothing to dilute their flavor. These, then, would make the most flavorful mashed potatoes of all, if you prefer mashed to baked. And that is what I would recommend if you have the time, or if you are making a roast chicken dinner and have the oven on anyhow. Best mashed potatoes, ever, eh-ver, provided you use enough butter and salt.

And don't throw those skins away: They make terrific potato skins with cheddar cheese and scallions. Make them with the same meal or store the skins in the refrigerator to make a treat for the next day's breakfast, lunch, dinner, or even casual hors d'oeuvres.

And, finally, this brief meditation would not be complete without a discussion of the twice-baked potato. I love these, as they are a delicious extension of the standard baked potato, a chance to give any flavors you want to the humble potato. You can get imaginative, adding caramelized onion, sautéed mushroom, leftover roast beef or ham, or unusual cheeses, such as smoked gouda or smoked mozzarella or goat cheese. But I like them simple because I love the potato: diced onion and cheese, plus chopped crispy bacon if the mood strikes and there's bacon in the fridge.

What's not often said about the twice-baked potato is that it's a great way to feed big groups. You can fit twenty or thirty halves on a big baking sheet, make them well ahead of time (you can keep them at room temperature for up to 4 hours), and reheat when you need them.

BAKED POTATOES FOR ANN
MAKES 4 POTATOES

4 medium russet potatoes, *well washed*

Kosher salt *to taste*

8 tablespoons/ 115 grams unsalted butter, *or more to taste, cut into 2-tablespoon chunks, at room temperature*

Preheat the oven to 425°F/218°C.

Place the potatoes directly on the center oven rack and bake for 1 hour. Squeeze one. If the skin is soft, not crunchy, continue to bake until the shell is distinctly hard, perhaps 15 minutes more.

Remove the potatoes from the oven, immediately cut a slit down the middle lengthwise, and squeeze from both ends to open them up and allow the steam to escape (steam will otherwise soften the shell). Using a fork, chop up the potato within the shell to break it all up and separate it from the skin without removing it.

Add 2 tablespoons butter to each potato, along with a solid pinch of salt, and chop the butter into the flesh of the potato until it is completely melted. If you would like to add more butter, I would encourage you. Add more salt if you wish, too.

Serve immediately, with more butter on the table to put on the skins before you eat them as well.

MASHED BAKED POTATOES
SERVES 2 TO 4

Side Dishes

These make arguably the finest mashed potatoes because they retain all the potato flavor with no dilution. Cook 2 potatoes as for Baked Potatoes for Ann for 1 hour. When they are nearly done, melt 8 tablespoons/115 grams unsalted butter with ½ cup/120 milliliters whole milk. Halve the potatoes lengthwise and scoop the flesh into a pan with the butter and milk. Mash the potatoes as little as possible so that they remain light and airy, and season with salt.

If you intend to reserve the skins for Potato Skins with Scallions and Cheddar Cheese (page 48), try to leave a thin layer of potato on them. Return the skins to the oven for 5 minutes to crisp them up, then prepare the skins or refrigerate them in a covered container for up to 2 days until ready to use.

POTATO SKINS WITH SCALLIONS AND CHEDDAR CHEESE
SERVES 4 TO 8

This is a wonderful mixture based on an hors d'oeuvre my mom served at cocktail parties in my boyhood (put it on crispy round crackers and broil; serve with gin and tonics!). Of course, you can simply sprinkle grated cheddar on the skins and melt it under the broiler if you want to keep it simple, but I love the tangy deliciousness the mayonnaise gives to the cheese. If you love spicy heat, add sliced jalapeños, seeds and all. Or sprinkle with piment d'Espelette before baking.

4 scallions

½ cup/60 grams grated sharp cheddar cheese

2 or 3 slices bacon, *cooked and roughly chopped (optional)*

¾ cup/180 milliliters mayonnaise

Kosher salt *to taste*

4 baked potato skins *from Mashed Baked Potatoes (page 47)*

Preheat your oven to 425°F/218°C.

Chop the white and pale green ends of the scallions and put them in a bowl. Slice the green ends as desired for garnish and set aside. Add the cheddar, bacon (if using), and mayonnaise to the bowl and stir until the cheese and mayo are evenly distributed.

Salt the potato skins, then spread the mixture evenly over them. Put the filled skins on a rimmed baking sheet and bake for 10 minutes, or until the cheese is melted. Garnish with the scallion greens and serve.

TWICE-BAKED POTATOES
SERVES 4

Twice-baked potatoes are the same as regular baked potatoes, but the flesh is removed and mashed with butter and other ingredients as you wish (use your imagination; anything you might put in an omelet will work in a potato), then stuffed back into the skins and baked. These are a great do-ahead style of potato when you're feeding a lot of people; they also make a satisfying meal for one or two.

2 large russet potatoes, *well washed*

4 to 6 tablespoons/ 60 to 90 grams unsalted butter

Kosher salt and freshly ground black pepper *to taste*

⅛ to ¼ teaspoon cayenne pepper *(optional)*

2 slices bacon, cooked and chopped *(optional)*

3 scallions, *thinly sliced, some chopped greens reserved for garnish*

½ cup/60 grams shredded cheddar cheese

Preheat the oven to 425°F/218°C.

Place the potatoes directly on the center oven rack and bake for 1 hour. Squeeze one. If the skin is soft, not crunchy, continue to bake until the shell is distinctly hard, perhaps 15 minutes more.

Remove the potatoes from the oven and immediately cut a slit down the middle lengthwise. Scoop the flesh into a mixing bowl. Mash the butter into the potato with a fork. Season with salt and pepper, add the cayenne and bacon (if using), and add the scallions. Place the potato skins on a rimmed baking sheet and divide the potato mixture among them. Top with the cheese. (These can be made and held at room temperature, uncovered or loosely covered with a towel, for up to 4 hours.)

Return the potatoes to the oven for 15 to 20 minutes, until hot inside. Garnish with the reserved scallion greens and serve.

LEFTOVERS

Chicken cooked for an hour in a hot oven is so good (and so easy), it's almost worth roasting it only for leftovers. Or to make chicken soup. Having guests over? Roast a chicken the day before. When it's cool enough to handle, remove all the meat from the bones (snacking on the wings is almost impossible to avoid) and reserve it. Put all the bones in a pot with a big onion and a couple of carrots and cover with water to turn into stock while you sleep (see page 38). The next day, you can quickly and easily turn this into a pot of chicken soup with vegetables, a healing gift. All of which is to say that it's worth roasting a chicken simply to have it all on hand—no special dinner required.

Sometimes you will have devoured the chicken in its entirety; other times you will have enough leftover meat to create a full second meal. The following are a few different ways to put roast chicken meat to use, no matter how you happen to come by that chicken—whether it's leftovers from a rotisserie bird or from your own dinner, or cooked expressly for this purpose.

(These are also all excellent ways to put leftover turkey to use at Thanksgiving time, when the entire country has an abundance of leftover roasted birds.)

CHICKEN SALAD THREE WAYS

Whenever I make chicken salad, I always ask myself why I don't make it more often. It's delicious, satisfying, and nutritious, and its flavor can be shaped to your desire. Do you feel like the gentle elegance of a summer afternoon? Tarragon. Or perhaps you want a more dynamic look and bold flavors? Then curry it. Or, for an even bolder and more unusual take, spike it with jerk paste.

These three recipes are only suggestions. The base is always the same, with flavors of your imagination determining the result. Mayonnaise is always a part of the recipe. If you make your own (see page 286), you instantly elevate the chicken salad by a factor of ten. And if you have an immersion blender with a whisk attachment, there's really no excuse not to if you can spare four or five minutes. I always like to add acidity to the chicken salad, usually in the form of lemon (or, for the jerked chicken salad, I use the even-more-dynamic lime). Including the aromatic shallot, cooked, as it were, in that acid, is what I consider to be the true secret to this dressing's awesomeness. If you want other flavors, add them. Perhaps some piquant mustard, or a dash of cayenne for some heat. I don't think bacon has ever hurt anything, and could add not only smoky, salty, umami flavor but also crunch, which is the final component of an excellent chicken salad. Some form of crunch should really be a part of the mix, as the chicken is so soft. For that, I often go to celery, for its salty flavor as well as its texture. But perhaps with the curried salad, that crunch could come from papadums.

My preference for how to serve is on a lightly toasted baguette. But this stuff is amazing between slices of Wonder Bread. Toasted, of course. Or held between the knees, in homage to Jack Nicholson's performance in *Five Easy Pieces*. (If you want to avoid bread, it can be served in a bowl of crunchy head lettuce.)

CHICKEN SALAD BASE

The way to begin a great chicken salad is as follows. If this is all you do, you will have an excellent chicken salad on your hands.

1 tablespoon minced shallot

1 tablespoon lemon juice, *plus more to taste*

½ teaspoon kosher salt, *plus more to taste*

¼ teaspoon freshly ground black pepper, *plus more to taste*

1 cup/240 milliliters mayonnaise

2½ cups/450 grams shredded or medium-diced cooked chicken

2 celery ribs, *cut into small dice*

Combine the shallot, lemon juice, salt, and pepper in a large bowl and let the mixture sit for at least 10 minutes and up to 1 hour. Stir in the mayonnaise and mix until it's uniformly combined. Fold the chicken and celery into the mixture. Taste and season with more lemon juice, salt, and pepper as desired. Add more mayonnaise if you wish.

CHICKEN SALAD WITH FINES HERBES   SERVES 4

Try this hugely herbaceous, tarragon-themed chicken salad using the French classic combination of tarragon, chervil, parsley, and chives. I've made the chervil optional because it can be hard to find. But if it is available, I can't recommend an herb more highly, for an anise flavor even more delicate than tarragon. Even the shape of this herb is uncommonly elegant and beautiful.

Leftovers

1 tablespoon minced shallot

1 tablespoon lemon juice, *plus more to taste*

½ teaspoon kosher salt, *plus more to taste*

¼ teaspoon freshly ground black pepper, *plus more to taste*

1 cup/240 milliliters mayonnaise

¼ cup finely chopped fresh tarragon

2 tablespoons finely chopped fresh flat-leaf parsley

2 tablespoons finely chopped fresh chives

2 tablespoons finely chopped fresh chervil (*optional*)

2½ cups/450 grams shredded or medium-diced cooked chicken

2 celery ribs, *cut into small dice*

Combine the shallot, lemon juice, salt, and pepper in a large bowl and let sit for at least 10 minutes and up to 1 hour. Add the mayonnaise and stir to combine. Add the herbs and mix until the herbs and mayonnaise are uniformly combined. Fold in the chicken and celery. Taste and season with more lemon juice, salt, and pepper as needed. Add more mayonnaise if you wish.

CURRIED CHICKEN SALAD
SERVES 4

Leftovers

If you're looking for dynamic flavors and a vividly colored chicken salad, this is the one I would choose. I love curry generally, and it works beautifully with chicken. It also gives me an excuse to fry papadums, which offer the perfect crunch for the soft chicken salad.

1 tablespoon minced shallot

1 tablespoon lemon juice, *or more to taste*

1 garlic clove, *minced*

1 teaspoon grated ginger

½ teaspoon kosher salt, *plus more to taste*

¼ teaspoon freshly ground black pepper, *plus more to taste*

1 cup/240 milliliters mayonnaise

1 tablespoon curry powder

1 teaspoon ground cumin

½ teaspoon ground turmeric

¼ to ½ teaspoon cayenne pepper or piment d'Espelette

2½ cups/450 grams shredded or medium-diced cooked chicken

2 celery ribs, *cut into small dice*

½ cup/10 grams fresh cilantro leaves

Combine the shallot, lemon juice, garlic, ginger, salt, and pepper in a large mixing bowl and let sit for at least 10 minutes and up to 1 hour. Add the mayonnaise and stir to combine. Add the curry powder, cumin, turmeric, and cayenne and mix until everything is uniformly combined. Fold in the chicken and celery. Taste and season with more lemon juice, salt, and pepper as needed. Add more mayonnaise if you wish. Garnish with the cilantro.

JERKED CHICKEN SALAD
SERVES 4

Jerk paste, with its heavy notes of allspice and heat from the chiles, adds some of my favorite flavors to chicken salad. It's both simple and dramatic. I like to serve it on toasted baguette, but you can also serve it with crisp head lettuce or, in keeping with its Caribbean vibe, top with crunchy, deep-fried black beans.

1 tablespoon minced shallot

1 tablespoon lime juice, *plus more to taste*

½ teaspoon kosher salt, *plus more to taste*

¼ teaspoon freshly ground black pepper, *plus more to taste*

1 cup/240 milliliters mayonnaise

1 tablespoon jerk paste

2½ cups/450 grams shredded or medium-diced cooked chicken

2 celery ribs, *cut into small dice*

Combine the shallot, lime juice, salt, and pepper in a large bowl and let sit for at least 10 minutes and up to 1 hour. Add the mayonnaise and jerk paste and stir to combine. Fold in the chicken and celery. Taste and season with more lime juice, salt, and pepper as needed. Add more mayonnaise if you wish.

WHAT "OPTIONAL" MEANS TO ME

I married a recipe follower. She can't help herself; I suspect it's a congenital condition. It manifested early in perfect comportment at school and straight A's. It meant never breaking curfew as a teenager and nothing below the pearls at the drive-in. I, on the other hand, am a rules questioner. Who made the rule? Why? Toward what end? I am a lifelong B student, the sort who would say, as my wife's son sensibly remarked, "Why study to get an A when I can get a B without studying?"

All of this is to say that, when cooking with my wife, if I suggest doing something that is not in the recipe she is working on, it evokes from her a look of grave concern, followed by bafflement and the words, "But that's not what the recipe says." To which I acquiesce. Because I sense that for one who embraces rules, the fear would be that if you can stray willy-nilly from a recipe, what other rules, in life generally, might you not follow? And from there we slip inevitably into complete anarchy. Simply because I wanted to thicken a Chinese stir-fry with beurre manié rather than a cornstarch slurry.

When I am cooking alone, the only thing that is not optional in my world is any ingredient listed in the name of the recipe. In other words, if the recipe is for chicken salad with fines herbes, it must contain chicken and fines herbs, but everything else, including how you get there, is optional. This is why I try to use "optional" as rarely as possible. When I do use it, I do so mainly to indicate that you shouldn't bend over backward trying to find it or spend a fortune on a spice you may use only once (such as kala jeera, for the dal on page 245), or simply don't like the idea of putting fish sauce in chicken soup, good as it is. If I put what was truly optional—the mind boggles—I'd have to say everything that's not in the title of the recipe.

This is because recipes are not, and cannot be, instruction manuals. A chicken salad, a pot pie, beef with broccoli—these are not put together the way a chest of drawers from IKEA is. Recipes are like sheet music. The pages can be played with nuance and grace, or not so much—"Ode to Joy" by the Cleveland Orchestra versus the same sheet music performed by a high school band.

Of course, knowledge and experience determine the degree of nuance in a given dish. And they also determine how well or badly you are able to play with the rules. I can change the cornstarch slurry to beurre manié (page 32) because I know that both thicken with starch, and that the butter that separates the granules of flour and allows them to thicken a sauce would also enrich the sauce. So why don't Chinese recipes call for beurre manié or roux for thickening? Because when and where those cuisines were developing, wheat flour and butter weren't staples, as they were in Europe.

Thus, I would have good justification to stray from a recipe in this way. And I encourage such straying, even as my wife shakes her head nervously, because even if your improvisation fails, you've learned something, and that only improves your overall skills as a cook.

CHICKEN POT PIE   SERVES 4 TO 6

Leftovers

I grew up thinking these things came in a Swanson box. It was a customary dinner on a Saturday night when my parents were going out and a babysitter was on her way. In fact, pot pie is one of the best ways to create a meal out of leftovers. Use the chicken carcass to make stock that will become the base for your sauce, but only after picking it clean of meat. If you have a couple cups of chicken left over, this recipe—with basic vegetables, a thick creamy sauce, and crisp crust—is wholesome and hearty, nourishing and economical.

Of course, I encourage you to make your own crust, so that it's all from scratch, but a pre-made dough is fine for this recipe, which is all about the chicken and its sauce. The crust is tastiest if you blind bake the bottom crust before filling it, which is what I suggest—but this, like so much else in the kitchen, is up to you. Alternatively, you can do what many restaurants do: Fill individual oven-safe dishes or ramekins with the chicken mixture, cover with store-bought puff pastry, and bake.

1 recipe All-Purpose 3-2-1 Dough (page 81) or 2 sheets store-bought pie dough

4 tablespoons/ 60 grams unsalted butter

1 onion, *cut into medium dice*

4 garlic cloves, *roughly chopped*

Kosher salt *to taste*

2 carrots, *cut into medium dice*

2 celery ribs, *cut crosswise into ¼-inch/6-millimeter slices*

6 tablespoons/ 45 grams all-purpose flour

2½ cups/600 milliliters Easy Overnight Chicken Stock (page 38) or store-bought chicken broth

2½ cups/450 grams shredded or medium-diced cooked chicken

½ cup/70 grams fresh or frozen peas

¼ cup heavy cream

1 tablespoon fish sauce

½ teaspoon freshly ground black pepper

1 large egg mixed with 1 tablespoon milk

Preheat your oven to 350°F/175°C.

Roll out half of the dough and line a pie plate with it. Cover it with aluminum foil or parchment paper and fill the plate with dried beans or pie weights. Bake for 25 minutes, then remove the beans and foil and bake for 5 more minutes to brown the crust.

Meanwhile, in a large saucepan, melt the butter over medium-high heat. Add the onion and garlic, hit them with a four-finger pinch of salt, and cook till tender, about a minute. Add the carrots and celery and cook till they are heated and brightly colored. Add the flour and stir to cook the flour and ensure it's well coated with butter. Add the stock, whisking to ensure the flour doesn't clump. Bring the mixture to a simmer, then add the chicken, peas, cream, fish sauce, and pepper. Stir to mix all the ingredients. Remove the pan from the heat.

Roll out the top of the pie dough to your desired thinness. Fill the baked pie shell with the chicken mixture. Cover it with the remaining dough, pinch the edges around the rim to seal it, and cut plenty of steam holes. Brush the top with the egg wash and bake until the mixture is piping hot and the crust has browned, about 45 minutes. Let it rest for 5 to 10 minutes, then serve.

CHAPTER 2

The Omelet

How do I travel along the omelet continuum and find myself standing on planet meat loaf? I hope it's immediately clear how an omelet (refined scrambled eggs) and a quiche are related. One includes dairy, one does not; one is sautéed, the other is baked. But what does an omelet have to do with a bread pudding? Or with pastry cream? Or with meat loaf? A quiche is simply scrambled eggs turned into a custard with dairy. What that custard holds can be anything—such as sausage, which gives one an excuse to make that wonderful creation of meat, fat, salt, and seasonings.

For quiche, the custard is baked in a crust, and that crust, like custard, is a versatile, all-purpose preparation that can hold anything from blueberries to chicken and gravy. Rather than baking a custard in a crust, you can pour it over bread—the leftover bread from one of your own loaves, perhaps—and bake the mixture into a savory or a sweet bread pudding. So, starting from blended eggs cooked, we touch on custard, crust and sausage, and dessert.

Ultimately, these are all simply expressions of the nature of the egg, the one ingredient that ultimately connects all things in one way or another.

I've written about the egg before in various articles and in one whole book that explored the egg's astonishing reach. It is of course a symbol of life (containing all the stuff required to generate life) and an aesthetically beautiful object, both delicate and sturdy. In the kitchen, it is an ingredient of unsurpassed versatility, a miracle of economy, utility, nutrition, and flavor. And yet it is an ingredient so common we rarely stop to consider it.

What better way to celebrate the egg, I ask, than with the omelet, that simple yet elegant creation that needs no adornment beyond a pat of butter and fresh herbs? Set a glass of champagne beside it and you have a proper celebration of the egg, of life.

So, this is how I shall begin this chapter, with an utterly simple meal: eggs with herbs, bread, and fermented grapes.

But this is just the beginning, for this meal is so simple it is more or less a doorway leading to a world of recipes and techniques that use blended eggs. In my book about the egg, I followed the egg along all its possible permutations—cooked in the shell and out, cooked whole or cooked blended, separated and then cooked, and so on. Here I focus on a single tributary, blended, to convey a sense of and to appreciate both the egg itself, unadorned, and the egg as a device, a custard, a binder, and several preparations that we use when the custard is our focus. We will also make a crust for the quiche, and explore other preparations that you can do with that crust.

Sausage, ground and seasoned meat, is contained in the quiche custard, but you can also add those blended eggs to bind and enrich ground and seasoned meat for meat loaf, which, if you season it as thoughtfully as you do a sausage, gives you not simply meat loaf but the best meat loaf, or exquisite meatballs that might go with the homemade pasta and tomato sauce in the next chapter. Because in the end cooking is all one thing; all preparations are interconnected.

There's almost no place you can't reach when you begin with the egg. This first meal is simply a stepping-off point, but it is, in itself, uncommonly grand.

This is all about the miracle that is the EGG, and the omelet is the finest example of its beauty and deliciousness. Are you the sort who want to do it from scratch? If you don't already raise laying hens (66), see the brief primer on getting started. Growing your own herbs (66) is easy and, for some, the only way to taste that very delicate herb chervil. Make your own bread. (282) Making your own BUTTER (67) is actually really worthwhile if you have access to great cream, and so easy. Want to make your own sparkling wine? see page... Just kidding! Even I don't aspire to that and leave it to the pros. But however you get your ingredients, there is no finer meal than a FINES HERBS OMELET with TOAST AND CHAMPAGNE (65). The omelet is a more structured version of SCRAMBLED EGGS (63), which are every bit as delicious if you know how to cook them properly (gently). Goes just as well with herbs, toast, and champagne! there are a million variations

on scrambled eggs — try this quirky CHINESE-AMERICAN EGG FOO YONG (68), and consider how garnishes and seasonings in the eggs themselves transform the eggs. A CUSTARD (71) = egg + liquid. An omelet with twice the amount of liquid, usually milk and cream, is custard. You can use this custard to hold tasty ingredients for a SAUSAGE AND SPINACH QUICHE (72) or SAUTÉED MUSHROOMS (77) (which are amazing if you know how to cook them).

The omelet

But for this you'll want a crust to carry it, and a 3-2-1 DOUGH (81) should be a go-to crust for all shells. But you could also toss that sausage and spinach with dried cubed bread and pour the custard over it for a BREAKFAST STRATA (78), basically a VANILLA BREAD PUDDING WITH BOURBON CARAMEL SAUCE (79) made savory. Did I mention

it's great to make your own sausage for these dishes? you control the seasoning for a standard BREAKFAST SAUSAGE (83) or an ITALIAN SAUSAGE (83), heavy on the sage and black pepper — now imagine how many different kinds of sausages are at your command. Or mix ground pork and beef for a MEAT LOAF (85) — and add a small amount of that bread pudding, custard soaked into bread, here called a PANADE (86) to make an extra moist loaf with a great bite, or just make MEATBALLS (84), for that matter. Wrap that meat loaf in crust (try a different one, the HOT-WATER DOUGH (87), and bake it into a BEEF AND PORK RAISED PIE (85). All this from the humble omelet, blended eggs, which, when thinned with an equal amount of liquid, like a custard with twice the amount of egg (or half the amount of liquid), and given a little structure with some flour, become CRÊPES (87), which are delicious on their own with a bit of sugar and butter but can also be used as a container to hold tasty ingredients, sweet or savory (say, the sausage and spinach, or leftover chicken with thickened overnight stock, to keep with the themes and also show how its all interconnected).

FINES HERBES OMELET WITH TOAST AND CHAMPAGNE SERVES 2

When a chef tries out a prospective cook, the chef will often ask the cook to prepare an omelet. This is a valuable indicator of a cook's skills, beginning with simply knowing what pan to use. But we now have a variety of excellent nonstick pans available, so egg sticking should no longer be an issue. I do admire those chefs who have carefully seasoned and maintained their black, carbon steel pans so carefully that they have created a nonstick surface—these pans are reserved for omelets. My breakfast cookery chef at the Culinary Institute of America was said to actually sleep with her omelet pans, so revered were they. Now they are practically impossible to find because of the ubiquity of nonstick pans. (And don't get me started on those silly, American-invented pans with two semicircles hinged together to fold one on top of the other.)

I encourage you to buy one good 8-inch/20-centimeter nonstick pan and use it only for eggs, fish, and certain potato dishes. At all other times, keep it by itself, either hanging from a hook or with a kitchen towel covering it to protect its valuable surface. Too many home cooks reach reflexively for the nonstick pan. In fact, food that sticks is usually a good thing—when it sticks, it turns brown and delicious, and then it releases from the pan on its own. For this, a cast-iron skillet is best.

But there was another reason chefs asked prospective hires to make an omelet: If a cook could bring the chef a perfect omelet, one with fine, uniform curds so that it was beautifully smooth, its color a bright sunny yellow, shining with a coat of butter, not a trace of browned egg on the exterior and yet cooked all the way through, still moist inside, then this cook had something referred to in the kitchen as finesse. In French kitchens, the cook who delivered such an omelet might be called *soigné*—a word roughly translating as an expression of impeccable care and refinement.

There are only a few steps involved in the perfect omelet, all of them optional (see page 53); that is, if you disregard them all you may still have an omelet, it just won't be as good.

First, of course, is the egg itself—they do vary in quality. If you have access to very fresh eggs, use these. Eggs laid by hens that have a rich organic diet of bugs, grasses, seeds, and flowers, pecked as they freely range, are likely to have densely nutritious and brightly colored yolks, which, in addition to the nutrients, will give your omelet a lovely bright color.

The eggs should be completely blended. This means you can see no opaque whites floating in the yellow egg. I once observed a culinary competition team practicing for a competition, and one of the judges regarded blended egg that would be used in a standard breading mixture (flour/egg/breadcrumbs). Albumen pooled among the otherwise yellow egg mixture. The judge looked to me sadly, having made a mark on his clipboard, and said, "I expected better craftsmanship from these guys." I will never forget the sadness and disappointment in his eyes.

A fork works, but it takes longer than a whisk. The easiest and quickest method of blending eggs is with an immersion blender. If I'm making a two-egg omelet for myself, I use a fork. If I'm making scrambled eggs for eight people, I use an immersion blender.

Then, season the eggs with salt. Some chefs insist that salting eggs before they go into the pan makes them tough—this is nonsense. Salt dissolves in the egg mixture and seasons them uniformly; heat is the primary determiner of texture for the egg. It doesn't really matter when you salt them, before or after blending, so long as you give the salt time to dissolve. I usually wait till they're blended. How much salt? I usually give 4 large eggs about ½ teaspoon salt, measured in my fingers and by sight. If you are uncertain and would like to know what properly seasoned eggs taste like, weigh them and add 1 percent of that weight in salt (that is, the weight of the blended eggs multiplied by 0.01). Most foods benefit from this level of salt.

Next, cook them in butter, gently, over medium heat, stirring rapidly at first so that the egg develops fine curds, then lowering the heat and allowing them to cook very slowly, just till the center is a little liquidy but will finish cooking as you roll it out of the pan and onto a plate.

Finally, finish the omelet by rubbing soft butter over it so that it shines like the star that it is. Those are the steps to an excellent omelet.

I love the herb mixture called *fines herbes*—tarragon, chervil, parsley, and chives, the dominant flavor being that of tarragon. You can also use only tarragon, or only chervil, which is similar.

An important fact to know is that omelets will keep warm for a long time and are easily reheated. Just cover them with plastic wrap so they don't dry out. Keep them warm in a low, low oven or reheat for 20 seconds in a microwave.

For the toast, I use a thick slice of pain de campagne, a big country loaf. You can use Wonder Bread, but really, do this only if you have no other option. Few refined starches have less flavor than shelf-stable white sandwich bread. Of course, I encourage you to make your own bread specifically for this (see page 282). If you want your toast to be very elegant and refined, cut the crusts off before toasting. But the bottom line is to choose the best bread available.

A fine French champagne is wonderful, obviously, but America now makes some fabulous sparkling wines in the style made famous by those wineries of the Champagne region. Ever since I had my first Schramsberg blanc de blancs I never sought another—not cheap but eminently affordable. Twenty years later, I toured this winemaker's cellars with some grocers I was writing about and enjoyed an al fresco meal with the head of the company, Hugh Davies, who began the meal by sabering off the top of the first bottle using nothing more than a butter knife, all that was available in our wooded glade. (The secret, he said, was to rapidly run the knife back and forth along the seam of the bottle before thrusting the knife into the lip of the bottle to uncork it.) But any good dry sparkling white or rosé wine will suffice.

I love this meal for the ratio of its simplicity to its deliciousness and overall delight. I know of no better brunch than this, especially if you're entertaining weekend guests. The omelet always impresses. And given how well they keep warm, it's not an impossible feat to make separate omelets. Of course, from a practical standpoint, you can make it easy on your entertaining self by preparing scrambled eggs, provided you make them properly (see opposite). And for serving more than two people, that makes more practical sense.

To make this an even more substantial meal, add five spears of cooked asparagus, seasoned with lemon juice and salt, to each plate.

5 large eggs

½ teaspoon kosher salt

2 thick slices country bread, *crusts removed*

1 (750-milliliter) bottle dry sparkling wine

2 tablespoon/ 30 grams unsalted butter, plus 2 teaspoons for finishing the omelets, *plus more as needed for the toast*

1 tablespoon finely chopped fresh fines herbes or tarragon

Preheat your oven to 180°F/82°C (or its lowest setting).

In a large bowl, whisk the eggs till they are uniformly combined and no whites remain visible. Add the salt and mix it into the eggs.

Toast the bread, taking care not to overdo it—this meal is all about delicacy.

Set the table and open the champagne, refrigerating it or putting it on ice to keep it cold.

In a nonstick pan, melt 1 tablespoon of the butter over medium-high heat, swirling it to coat the pan. Add half of the eggs, reduce the heat to medium-low, and stir them vigorously with a silicone spatula. As the eggs begin to set, stop stirring and allow them to finish cooking, even raising the pan above the burner to soften the heat further. When the edges are cooked and there is just a film of uncooked egg on top, shake the pan to loosen the egg, and grip the pan's handle underhanded to make it easier to tip the pan. Slide the egg out of the pan, rolling it over itself onto the plate in a cylindrical shape. Cover the plate with aluminum foil and put the plate in the oven.

Put the toast in the oven to rewarm it as well. Wipe out your pan with a paper towel and repeat with the remaining butter and eggs. Roll this egg onto a fresh plate.

Remove the first omelet from the oven. Rub a teaspoon of butter over each omelet and garnish them with the fresh herbs. Butter the toast and serve with the omelets, as your companion pours the champagne.

ON FILLING OMELETS

Filling omelets with vegetables or cheese seems to be a bigger deal in America than in France—especially at the breakfast buffet. It can be done well, but I like the purity of a plain omelet. That said, there's no reason you can't put sautéed mushrooms, bell peppers, leeks, and/ or cheese in the center of an omelet before rolling it. If you have access to morels, those gently sautéed with some shallots and a little cream make an excellent addition to eggs. It does make the omelet considerably heavier and harder to roll. The only rule I stick to when filling an omelet is that I make sure the ingredients are hot when they go into the omelet. Another excellent strategy is to spoon the hot ingredients over the top of a rolled omelet, rather than conceal them within.

SCRAMBLED EGGS WITH TOAST AND CHAMPAGNE SERVES 2

This is the same dish as the previous except that it's easier to prepare, though it is less impressive on the plate. Also, it "eats" differently, as chefs say—that is, the experience of eating it differs. One thing that is not different is that it is equally delicious . . . provided you cook the eggs properly, which means gently! Over low heat. Take your time.

5 large eggs

½ teaspoon kosher salt, *or to taste*

2 tablespoon/30 grams unsalted butter, *plus more as needed for the toast*

2 slices bread, *toasted and kept warm*

Shredded cheese
(*such as grated cheddar or smoked Gouda, or crumbled goat cheese*), *added just before finishing* (*optional*)

1 (750 ml) bottle dry sparkling wine

In a large bowl, whisk the eggs thoroughly—they should be completely uniform, with no translucent pools of egg white floating in the yellow. Add the salt now—it will dissolve and season the eggs uniformly.

Melt the butter in a skillet (preferably nonstick) over low heat, then pour in the eggs. The heat should be so low that it takes a few seconds for the egg touching the pan to congeal. Use a silicone spatula to lift these curds off the bottom of the pan and allow other curds to set up. For even more control of the heat, turn your burner to medium or medium-high, but keep lifting the pan off the burner when the eggs begin to cook too quickly. (If you want to make it very easy, or if you're new to scrambling, cook them in a double boiler, or simply cook them in a saucepan that you allow to float in simmering water. This is the best way to scramble eggs, but it leaves a hard-to-clean pan, so I opt for direct heat).

When nearly half of the egg mixture has turned to gentle curds and the remaining third is still liquid, sprinkle on the cheese (if using). Then, when closer to two-thirds of the mixture has turned to curds and the rest is liquidy but thick, remove the pan from the heat completely. Allow the eggs to continue cooking to the desired texture, then divide between serving plates.

Butter the toast, pour the champagne, and serve.

The Seriously From-Scratch Version of
FINES HERBES OMELET
WITH
TOAST AND CHAMPAGNE

There may be no more spiritually satisfying rendition of this meal than a from-scratch version, which, practically speaking, would be to use eggs from your own chickens, grow your own herbs (the best way to have chervil on hand as it's so delicate), and make your own bread. For the challenge of it, I would also add, make your own butter from cream that has not been homogenized. If you live on a farm with cows, you're golden. The uber from-scratcher will of course attempt homemade bubbly, but that's going a bit far even for me.

To raise your own laying hens:

I have always relied on the kindness of neighbors who raise chickens (thanks, Jonathon and Amelia!), but it's not difficult to raise your own laying hens once you have the coop. Most who do say that caring for a dog is more time consuming than raising hens. In my new home of Rhode Island, I have a friend named Drake Patten who owns a store called Cluck!, serving urban and suburban agriculturalists and gardeners. She also raises chickens, ducks, goats, sheep, and lambs on her farm, Hurricane Hill Farm, in the town of Cranston.

When I spoke to her about beginning to raise chickens, the first thing she said was, "Find out what the ordinances are where you live. Know what you're allowed to do." So, the first step is to check online or call your city hall.

The next necessity is to provide a safe place for your hens. You'll need to buy or build a proper coop so that they are protected from dogs and other animals. Many people are able to retrofit an existing shed. Safety is the key issue here, not temperature. "People raise chickens in Alaska, after all," Drake said. She reminded me that chickens originated as jungle birds and still do like to roost.

Which brings up the third primary decision you need to make: What breeds thrive best in your climate?

Start with these online guides: backyardchickens.com, a large online forum; tillysnest.com, by Melissa Caughey, who is also the author of a book Drake recommends for parents, *A Kid's Guide to Keeping Chickens*; and mypetchicken.com, an excellent resource for buying what you need and finding information on and purchasing various breeds.

But before you do any of this, be sure to know *why* you want to raise chickens. Hold a grown chicken, Drake advised. "They're fidgety and can freak people out," she said. You never know.

And one last important note: Once you've committed to raising chickens, it's a good idea to let your neighbors in on it. Some may object (and most certainly will if you try to raise a rooster). Most neighbor problems go away if you're generous with the eggs!

To grow your own lettuces and herbs

Herbs are easy to grow and are a wonderful ingredient to have on hand all season long. Start them from seed in early spring in a flowerpot on your windowsill or fire escape, or buy them already started and tend them in your own garden. My favorite herbs to grow are tarragon, chervil (great but temperamental if not tended carefully), flat-leaf parsley, and chives. And I also love to grow hard herbs, those with woody inedible stems: thyme, oregano, and rosemary. The hard herbs are great to overgrow at the end of the summer and set out to dry to use all winter on roast chicken and in stews and braises.

Lettuces, too, are very easy to grow in season. If anything, I've found that the hardest part of growing them is picking them fast enough. They grow so quickly that they can easily get too big. But if you plant a variety of lettuces and stagger the planting, you can have lettuce all summer long. It's in the category of foods you really can't buy: baby lettuces picked just before serving.

Want lettuce and herbs all year round, even in a colder climate? The two key factors are light and temperature. Lettuces need about fourteen hours a day of light. Here in New England, we get only about nine hours of light in the winter. So even if you have a big, warm loft that gets tons of light, you may still have trouble with lettuces. And the area in front of windows tends to be too cold in winter—or there's a radiator that gets too hot. But, thanks to the burgeoning marijuana industry, grow lights and stands and mini greenhouses are now plentiful and affordable. You can get rolling for well under $100.

To make your own butter:

It's simple to make your own butter, but we have so much good butter available at grocery stores, it's not worth the effort unless you have access to really good cream. Whipping cream in a standing mixer or food processor will eventually cause the fat to separate from the water. Once the fat and water have separated, strain the fat (save the liquid, the buttermilk; it's refreshing to drink or to use as flavorful acidic liquid in cooking). Now you must knead any remaining water out of the butter. This is the fun part. To give it flavor, add 0.5 to 1 percent of its weight in fine sea salt or flaky salt. The salt also preserves the butter. Then toast a good piece of bread or an English muffin and slather it with your homemade butter, and you'll know what fresh butter is all about.

If you are a yogurt maker and have a dairy-friendly culture, making cultured butter. is definitely worth the effort. Add some of your culture to the cream and let it sit in a warm place (110°F/43°C is optimal) for 12 to 18 hours—in summer I set a covered pot of milk and culture in the sun; in winter, I put it in a warm oven. You can do the same for cream to make butter. Taste for the amount of flavor you're after, then proceed with the whipping and kneading process.

From Scratch

To make your own toast from your own bread, see page 282.

It doesn't take much imagination to picture how satisfying such a from-scratch meal could be: to gather your own eggs (or beg some from a friend—in summertime please, when eggs are plentiful, not in spare winter), and to cut the herbs from your garden, and to spread your own cultured butter on toast from bread you baked. It's enormously satisfying because it connects us so deeply to our food.

EGG FOO YONG SERVES 4

I want to extend the notion of omelets and scrambled eggs beyond their customary forms by including this excellent use of blended eggs cooked in a pan. Once you recognize that you can put more than chives and cheese in eggs, there seems to be little that won't work this way. Here meat and vegetables are blended into the mix to create this quintessential Chinese-American dish.

I have a deep love of the Chinese-American food I ate growing up in Cleveland in the 1970s: diced meat battered, fried, then stir-fried in a sticky sweet-sour sauce, fried noodle dishes, big fat egg rolls with a thick blistered wrapper, chicken with cashews, and fiery kung pao chicken.

Egg foo yong, an elaborate egg pancake served with a savory sauce, is this kind of classic, and it appears to have been created by Cantonese cooks who had immigrated to the United States' West Coast in the mid-nineteenth century. It got a bad name by the time it had become a staple in mediocre Chinese restaurants, but it deserves a wider audience, even a routine spot in your repertoire of dishes to prepare for friends. It's just elaborate enough to merit dinner-party treatment, but it's easy and can be prepared ahead of time.

I also love it for what it has to say about the egg—that the egg makes an ideal framework, as it were, for other ingredients and flavors. The neutral egg here takes on deep notes of oyster sauce and soy sauce, sharpened by a bit of rice vinegar. It's loaded with chopped vegetables and meat (I prefer a mixture of pork and chicken), which is really what it's all about. The egg is just there to hold everything together—egg foo yong is like a fritter in that respect—and the addition of cornstarch allows the eggs to form distinct pancakes.

The sauce was originally simply chicken stock seasoned with soy sauce and thickened with cornstarch (see James Beard's recipe in his classic *American Cookery*). But because the sauce is so prominent, it's worth giving it a little more love with aromatics. It's extraordinarily good if you use your own stock, but don't *not* make this dish just because you don't have homemade stock.

Eggs generally hold well, so these pancakes can be cooked and kept warm in a low oven for an hour or two without losing any of their deliciousness. (You can even refrigerate them and then microwave them—not perfect, but not bad either!)

This is a deeply satisfying and nourishing, dish. I prefer it served over rice to make a more substantial meal, but there's no reason you couldn't serve it with the sauce alone. Or you could even make mini pancakes and serve them with the sauce for dipping.

recipe continues

For the sauce:

2 cups/480 milliliters Easy Overnight Chicken Stock (page 38) or store-bought chicken broth

5 tablespoons/72 grams cornstarch

1 teaspoon vegetable oil

2 scallions, *thinly sliced on the bias*

1 or 2 garlic cloves, *roughly chopped*

1 (1-inch/2.5-centimeter) piece ginger, *grated*

2 teaspoons sugar

3 tablespoons soy sauce

2 tablespoons dry sherry or Shaoxing wine

For the egg pancakes:

8 ounces/225 grams boneless, skinless chicken or pork, or a mixture of the two, *finely chopped or ground*

1 tablespoon oyster sauce

1 tablespoon soy sauce

Vegetable oil *for frying*

8 large eggs

1 ½ teaspoons kosher salt

1 ½ tablespoons rice wine vinegar

1 tablespoon dry sherry or Shaoxing wine

1 tablespoon toasted sesame oil

1 carrot, shredded

1 (8-ounce/225-gram) can water chestnuts, *drained and coarsely chopped*

6 scallions, *thinly sliced on the bias*

Steamed rice (see page 270), *for serving*

MAKE THE SAUCE:

In a small bowl, whisk together 2 tablespoons of the stock and 2 tablespoons of the cornstarch to form a slurry for the sauce; while you're at it, do the same in another bowl with another 3 tablespoons of stock and the remaining 3 tablespoons cornstarch and set aside for the eggs.

In a medium saucepan, heat the oil over medium-high heat. When it's hot, add a quarter of the scallions, plus the garlic and ginger, and stir-fry for 30 or 40 seconds. Add the remaining chicken stock, sugar, soy sauce, and wine. Bring the mixture to a simmer. Add the 2-tablespoon slurry and cook for a minute or two, until the sauce thickens. Set aside.

MAKE THE EGG PANCAKES:

In a medium bowl, mix the meat, oyster sauce, and soy sauce until they're uniformly combined. Heat 1 tablespoon vegetable oil in a medium sauté pan over high heat. When the oil is hot, add the meat mixture and stir-fry until the meat is just cooked through. Transfer it to a plate.

In a separate bowl, beat the eggs until they are uniformly mixed and no clear white is visible. Add the salt and the 3-tablespoon slurry to the eggs and whisk to mix. Add the vinegar, wine, sesame oil, carrot, water chestnuts, half of the scallions, and the cooked meat. Mix well to combine.

Pour about ⅛ inch/3 millimeters of vegetable oil into a large skillet and heat over medium-high heat. When it is hot, use a ⅓-cup/80-milliliter measure to scoop the egg mixture into the skillet; make as many as you can fit without allowing them to touch. Fry, turning each egg pancake over when it is slightly brown on the bottom, about 1 minute. Continue cooking until it's cooked through and set, another minute or so depending on how hot your pan is.

Transfer the pancakes to a paper towel–lined plate as you finish each batch. (If you are holding these to serve later, cover with foil and put them in a 200°F/93°C oven until you're ready to serve.)

While you are cooking the eggs, strain the sauce through a fine-mesh sieve, return it to the pan, and bring it back to a simmer. Remove from the heat and add the rest of the scallions.

Serve the pancakes over rice, spooning plenty of sauce over them.

CUSTARD

Here's a handy ratio: Beat your eggs as for an omelet, then measure their volume and add twice that volume of milk or cream, and you now have a custard base. If you add sugar and vanilla to it, you have a sweet custard like that for crème brûlée. Add savory ingredients, and you have a quiche. Or pour it over day-old bread to make a bread pudding. It's such an easy way to make use of that bread.

This is also how I make a Thanksgiving dressing, using turkey stock instead of dairy. I mix bread and whatever seasonings and add-ins I feel like (sage, sausage, mushrooms, celery, and so on). Then I make a custard base using 2 parts turkey stock with 1 part egg and pour it over the bread mixture. If the bread soaks up all the liquid but remains dry, I add more custard base, knowing that the liquid will cook to a delicate sliceable consistency, holding all the other delicious ingredients together.

Another name for the same thing is bread pudding. This can be sweet or savory, depending on which way you take the custard. You can add sugar and vanilla for a simple dessert bread pudding or you can add onions and cheese for a savory side dish. This is an especially good technique if you are a baker, or live with one.

The custard can be cooked in a water bath, which ensures gentle heat and delicate texture throughout. This is how a traditional crème caramel is made. Or it can be baked in the direct heat of the oven, as with quiche. Add a little flour and you can cook it in a pan to make crêpes (page 87). Understanding the custard and how it works gives you more power and versatility in the kitchen—and the confidence to improvise.

SAUSAGE AND SPINACH QUICHE   SERVES 8

Custard   We have seen what happens to blended eggs cooked in a pan over direct heat. Now it's time to explore what happens when we add liquid to those blended eggs. When eggs are combined with milk and cream, seasoned, and baked, you have one of the most delectable egg concoctions there is, the custard. The custard is a delight, especially for its texture.

The quiche is savory. If we add sugar and vanilla to the eggs and cream, we have a sweet dessert custard. There's no reason you couldn't load this custard with fruit and make a dessert quiche sprinkled with crushed toffee. And you don't need to add cream. You could add chicken stock or some other liquid, which is what we do when we make a savory bread pudding. But I'm getting ahead of myself.

Here I focus on one of my favorite preparations, the quiche, which is delicious cold, hot, or at room temperature. Quiche Lorraine is simply quiche with bacon, and it was, according to Craig Claiborne writing in the *New York Times,* the way quiche arrived in America in the 1950s. By the 1970s Claiborne called the movement the "quiching" of America. Quiche was on so many menus it became maligned as girlie food, popularized in a 1982 book called *Real Men Don't Eat Quiche.*

Only recently has it seen a resurgence in popularity, and my guess is that this is thanks to Thomas Keller, who insists at his second restaurant, Bouchon, and in the book of that name, that the quiche should never be made in a pie plate. When he returned from a year in France, he found an America that believed quiche was made in a pie shell. More likely, this was simply a bastardization of the French quiche, because most Americans didn't have 2-inch/5-centimeter ring molds. This height is essential to the pleasures of a true quiche. It needs that depth to create the exquisite texture that makes it such a pleasure to eat. A custard cooked in a pie shell is almost inevitably overcooked because it is so thin.

Instead of a ring mold, you can use a cake pan with 2-inch/5-centimeter sides, lined with parchment. Crusts baked in ring molds can leak, and this is a heartbreaking loss. Use a cake pan so that even if there's a crack in your crust, you'll still have a tall, gorgeous quiche.

Recently, finding myself without a cake pan or a ring mold, I decided to do it in a cast-iron skillet. It's all the same principle, so it works great, but I especially loved the way it looked served that way. Serve hot, straight from the parchment, or cool and refrigerate it, then pop it out of the parchment and return it to the skillet. It can be served cold, at room temperature, or hot (reheat in a 350°F/175°C oven for 20 minutes).

Try this style of quiche once and you'll never go back.

The quiche gives me reason to address doughs and crusts, as well as what to fill that quiche with, here bacon or sausage (any loose sausage will work, of course, or try making your own, as on page 82) and onion for a classic quiche Lorraine.

recipe continues

Custard

Pie dough is easy—a discussion follows—but it is another preparation. There is no reason why you can't use a good-quality store-bought crust if you wish. You may need to roll it out a little more to fit the pan, and it won't be quite as satisfying to eat—but we always have to weigh the time we have against our goals.

Vegetable oil, *as needed*

1 pound/450 grams spinach

1 medium onion, *cut into medium dice*

1 pound/450 grams loose sausage, store-bought *or homemade* (page 82)

½ recipe All-Purpose 3-2-1 Dough (page 81) *or store-bought pie crust*

2 cups/480 milliliters milk

1 cup/240 milliliters cream

6 large eggs

2 teaspoons kosher salt

½ teaspoon freshly ground black pepper

Freshly ground nutmeg *to taste* (*about 5 gratings*)

1½ cups/150 grams grated Comté or Emmentaler cheese

Preheat your oven to 350°F/175°C.

Heat about a tablespoon of oil in a large skillet over medium-high heat and sauté the spinach until it is completely wilted, about 1 minute. (Alternatively, you can blanch it in a pot of boiling salted water for about 30 seconds.) Shock it in cold water, wring it out completely, and chop it coarsely.

In the same skillet, heat another teaspoon or so of oil over medium-high heat. When the oil is hot, sauté the onion until translucent, then add the sausage, breaking it up as you do, and cook until the pink is gone. Drain the fat from the pan. Add the cooked spinach and stir till it's all evenly distributed. Set aside to cool.

Roll out the dough to a thickness of about ¼ inch/6 centimeters. Place a 2-by-9-inch/5-by-22-centimeter ring mold or a 9-inch/22-centimeter cake pan on a rimmed baking sheet (line the baking sheet with parchment paper if you're using a ring mold; if you're using a cake pan, line its bottom with parchment). Lightly oil the inside of your ring mold or cake pan. Lay the dough into the mold—there should be plenty of dough overhanging the edges to help it maintain its shape.

Reserve a small piece of dough to fill any cracks that might open in the dough as it bakes. Line the dough with parchment or aluminum foil and fill it with dried beans or pie weights. Bake for 30 minutes, then remove the beans and parchment. Use the reserved dough to gently patch any cracks that may have formed, then continue baking until the bottom of the crust is golden and cooked, about 15 more minutes. Remove it from the oven and again patch any cracks that may have opened; this is especially important if you're using a ring mold, or the batter will leak out. The shell should be anywhere between cold and warm when you add the batter, not piping hot from the oven.

Reduce the oven temperature to 325°F/163°C. In a 6- or 8-cup/1.5- or 2-liter liquid measuring cup, combine the milk, cream, eggs, salt, pepper, and nutmeg and, using an immersion blender, blend until frothy. This can be done in a standing blender as well (though depending on the size of your blender, you may need to do it in batches). Or you could even mix the batter in a large bowl using a whisk—beat the eggs first, then add the rest of the ingredients. The idea is to add the ingredients in two layers, using the froth to help keep the ingredients suspended.

Layer half of the sausage mixture into the shell. Pour half of the frothy custard over the mixture. Sprinkle with half of the cheese. Layer with the remaining sausage mixture. Refroth the batter and pour the rest into the shell. Sprinkle the remaining cheese over the top. You may want to set the baking sheet with the quiche shell on the oven rack and pour the remaining batter into it there so that you can get every bit of batter into the shell without worrying about spillage. You can even let it overflow to make sure it's up to the very top. Bake for about

1½ hours, until the center is just set (it may take as long as 2 hours, but take care not to overcook it—there should still be some jiggle in the center).

Allow the quiche to cool, then cover with plastic wrap and refrigerate it until it's completely chilled, at least 8 hours or up to 3 days.

Using a sharp knife, cut off the top edge of the crust along the outer rim. Slide the knife along the edge of the ring mold or cake pan to remove the quiche.

Slice and serve cold or, to serve hot, slice and reheat for 10 minutes in a 375°F/190°C oven on a rimmed baking sheet lined with lightly oiled parchment or foil.

QUICHE VARIATIONS

It's difficult to find a food that doesn't go with eggs, part of the miracle of the egg.

Quiche Lorraine: Classics are classics for a reason. If you love bacon, this is the quiche for you. If you cure your own bacon (see page 280), that's even more reason to make this variation. Omit the sausage and spinach. Cut 1 pound/450 grams of sliced bacon crosswise into strips or cut slab bacon into ¼-inch/ 6-centimeter lardons and cook the bacon. Drain it, but save enough fat to cook the onion in. Add the bacon and onion in two frothy layers as described above.

Quiche with Morels and Ramps: Mushrooms are an excellent source of deep flavor, even white button mushrooms if you cook them properly (see page 77). And mushrooms go especially well with eggs. Many grocery stores carry wild mushrooms, which will give an even more complex flavor and texture. If you have access to morels, these are fantastic with eggs. If they are fresh morels, then it is springtime, when ramps

also appear. Like a cross between a scallion and a leek, these plants grow like weeds throughout the northeastern and midwestern United States, with a small white bulb and long wide leaves. Slice them thinly and sauté them. A quiche made with sautéed morels and ramps is an excellent spring quiche, or you can simply replace the sausage in the above recipe with mushrooms, leaving the spinach in for color, flavor, and nutrition. Or add even more color (and sweetness) by including 2 or 3 roasted, peeled, and diced bell peppers, always a good choice with eggs.

There's no end to variations to include in your quiche. You could even get creative by replacing half of the milk with, say, an asparagus puree. Blanch a bunch of asparagus stalks in hot water, then plunge them into an ice bath. Cut off the tips and reserve to use whole in the quiche. Puree the stalks well in a blender, then strain the puree. Use the strained puree in the custard and add the tips to the quiche along with the sautéed onion.

HOW TO COOK MUSHROOMS

The best way to cook most mushrooms, but especially mushrooms that don't have a lot of flavor, such as the white button mushroom, is in high, high heat. Mushrooms benefit hugely from browning, but browning doesn't happen in the presence of water, which mushrooms are loaded with. So, the key to getting a good sear on mushrooms is to sear them before they can release their water.

To do this, get your sauté pan hot, screaming hot, so hot that when you pour in the oil, the oil immediately loosens and swirls and begins to smoke. Immediately add your mushrooms, just enough to cover the bottom of the pan in one layer. Press them hard against the pan so that they hiss and squeak. When one side is browned, flip them or toss them in the pan and repeat to get as much browning done as possible before the mushrooms begin to drop their water and cool off the pan.

Now that the mushrooms are browned, you can flavor them. Add a big tablespoon of minced shallot and stir to cook, then deglaze with dry white wine. Add salt and plenty of freshly ground black pepper, and continue cooking until all the liquid has cooked off. Now you have delicious sautéed mushrooms for your omelet or quiche.

* *Add them to quiche in place of sausage for a vegetarian alternative.*

* *Add cream and brandy and more pepper for a superb mushroom sauce for steak (see page 123).*

* *Stir a couple tablespoons of butter into them to finish them off and serve them as a side to roast chicken or steak.*

* *Add them to Meat Loaf (page 85); they'll deepen the flavor and add juiciness.*

* *Transfer half of the mushrooms to a saucepan, add cream just to cover, and bring the cream to a simmer. Blend the mixture thoroughly with an immersion blender, then add the remaining whole pieces of mushroom. Reheat for some of the most luxurious cream of mushroom soup you've ever had.*

SAUSAGE AND SPINACH BREAKFAST STRATA SERVES 8

Variations

I'm using the same ingredients here as for the quiche to illustrate how interconnected dishes are. I don't look at recipes as isolated preparations, but rather preparations along a single continuum. Of course, you can swap out the breakfast sausage for Italian sausage, or bacon, or ham, or chorizo or any meat you choose. (Or you can replace the sausage with sautéed mushrooms to make this vegetarian—if you're doing this, try to find a variety of wild mushrooms.) You can throw in different ingredients, such as roasted red peppers or sautéed mushrooms. I've also added a couple more eggs, not for the custard itself but to enrich the strata and make it more nutritious and hearty.

Regardless what you put in it, the breakfast strata (or bread pudding), is a great way to feed a lot of people for brunch. And it can be assembled, refrigerated, and cooked the next day if that's more convenient. It can also be eaten cold or cut and reheated in a 350°F/175°C oven.

2 tablespoons olive oil

8 ounces/225 grams spinach, *cooked and coarsely chopped*

½ Spanish onion, *cut into large dice*

1 pound/450 grams loose Breakfast Sausage (page 83)

3 cups/710 milliliters half-and-half

8 large eggs

2 teaspoons ground mustard

1 teaspoon kosher salt

¼ teaspoon cayenne

Freshly ground black pepper *to taste*

8 cups/400 grams cubed bread, *day-old or dried in a low oven*

3 cups/340 grams shredded cheddar cheese

Preheat your oven to 325°F/163°C. Oil or spray a 9-by-13-inch/22-by-33-centimeter baking dish. In a large skillet, heat 1 tablespoon of the oil over medium-high heat and sauté the spinach until it is completely wilted, about 1 minute. (Alternatively, you can blanch it in a pot of boiling salted water for about 30 seconds.) Shock it in cold water, wring it out completely, and chop it coarsely.

Add the remaining 1 tablespoon oil to the same skillet and heat it over medium-high heat. When it is hot, add the onion and cook until soft, a minute or so. Add the sausage and cook, breaking it up as you do, until the pink is gone. Transfer the sausage and onion to a paper–towel lined plate.

In a large bowl, combine the half-and-half, eggs, mustard, salt, cayenne, and several grinds of black pepper. Whisk or blend till everything is uniformly combined.

In another large bowl, combine the sausage and onions, spinach, bread, and 1 cup/115 grams of the cheese and toss it all together. Transfer this mixture to the prepared baking dish and pour the egg mixture over it. Top with the remaining 2 cups/225 grams cheese. Allow the strata to sit for at least 15 minutes before baking, or cover and refrigerate it until you're ready to cook it.

Bake until the eggs are set, 45 to 60 minutes. Serve immediately or cool and refrigerate to serve cold.

VANILLA BREAD PUDDING WITH BOURBON CARAMEL SAUCE

SERVES 8

This recipe replaces the savory elements of the previous strata with sweet ones. It's topped with a caramel sauce rather than cheese. You can simplify this by using only vanilla extract, or you can enhance the flavor by infusing the half-and-half with a vanilla pod.

3 cups/710 milliliters half-and-half	½ teaspoon grated fresh nutmeg
1 cup/200 grams sugar	¼ teaspoon kosher salt
1 tablespoon vanilla extract or 1 teaspoon vanilla extract plus one vanilla pod	8 large eggs
	8 cups/400 grams cubed bread, *day-old or dried in a low oven*
1 teaspoon ground cinnamon	Bourbon Caramel Sauce (at right), *for serving*

Preheat your oven to 325°F/163°C. Oil or spray a 9-by-13-inch/22-by-33-centimeter baking dish. Combine the half-and-half and sugar in a small saucepan. If using a vanilla pod, cut it in half lengthwise and add that to the pan. Bring the half-and-half to a simmer over medium heat, then remove the pan from the heat. Scrape the beans from the pod, if using, and return them to the half-and-half. Add the vanilla extract (if using), cinnamon, nutmeg, and salt. Allow the mixture to cool to room temperature (it can be warm, as long as it doesn't cook the eggs when combined).

Add the eggs and blend the mixture till uniformly combined. Spread out the bread in the prepared baking dish and pour the custard over the bread. Allow the bread to soak up the custard, 10 to 20 minutes.

Bake until the custard is set, 45 to 60 minutes. Serve hot, cold, or at room temperature topped with the bourbon caramel sauce.

BOURBON CARAMEL SAUCE

MAKES ABOUT 2 CUPS/420 MILLILITERS

Variations

This is a super-easy caramel sauce, equal parts sugar and cream, flavored with bourbon. Remember to add the cream slowly to the melted sugar, the hottest thing in your kitchen; the moisture will vaporize instantly and foam violently until the sugar has cooled.

1 cup/200 grams sugar	1 cup/240 milliliters heavy cream
Water, *as needed*	¼ cup bourbon

Put the sugar in a high-sided saucepan with a few tablespoons of water—just enough to coat it all (it should look like wet sand). Put the pan over medium heat and cook the sugar until it turns a deep amber color; occasionally swirl the sugar in the pan to ensure even cooking, but don't stir it. This can take several minutes. You'll know you're getting close when the sugar around the edges begins to brown. Swirl more frequently at this point for more even cooking.

While the sugar is cooking, warm the cream in a microwave, a minute or so.

When the sugar is amber, remove it from the heat and add the warm cream slowly, whisking constantly until all the cream is added. Stir in the bourbon and serve.

CRUST AND ITS USES

When water brings together flour and fat into a dough, this dough can become a framework for virtually anything you want to serve. It carries the custard in the form of a quiche; it extends leftover roast chicken in the form of a pie. If you wrap a meat loaf in it, you have what is in effect a version of that classical creation called pâté en croûte. It's a wonderful idea to make a chicken or beef stew, divide it into individual serving dishes, and cover each dish with crust. Bake till it's bubbling inside and the crust is browned and you have individual pot pies. Or lay dough into a fluted tart pan and pour a lemon custard into it for a lemon tart. Spread that same dough with thinly sliced apples and brown sugar and cinnamon for a simple apple tart.

Crust is simple to make and uncommonly versatile in both the sweet and savory kitchens. Learning the ways to use it, and being conscious of how it helps shape dishes, extends your reach as a cook.

In my opinion, it's perfectly fine to buy and use good-quality frozen dough for its convenience. It's usually labeled pie dough, which is unfortunate, because it suggests that pie is all it's good for. You can use it for any of the applications listed above for homemade dough.

While there are many variations on basic dough—add eggs for richness, add sugar for sweetness, add milk for a variation in browning, make a hot dough by melting fat in simmering water, and so on—the fundamental 3-2-1 dough is bedrock and need never be varied. It's so simple and perfect, I don't see a reason to change it or encourage any variations here (except for possibly the Hot-Water Dough, page 87, which is pretty damn good, and comes together faster).

ALL-PURPOSE 3-2-1 DOUGH   MAKES ENOUGH DOUGH TO FILL 2 PIE SHELLS OR FOR 1 COVERED PIE

Crust and Its Uses

This dough works every time if you weigh your flour; if you measure flour by the cup, you may need to add a little extra beyond the 2 cups recommended. But as long as it rolls out nicely without too much sticking, that's all that matters.

"3-2-1" refers to the proportion of flour to fat to liquid, in that order. Thus, 12 ounces flour, 8 ounces fat, and 4 ounces water, an easy ratio if that fat is in the form of lard or shortening (or in a close metric version, which is even easier and shows the beauty of metrics as well as of ratios: 300 grams flour, 200 grams fat, 100 grams water). If those 8 ounces/200 grams of fat are butter, you need to take into account that butter contains roughly 15 percent water, a little more than an ounce, so you need to add less water, roughly 2½ ounces/70 grams, or just enough to bring the flour and fat together.

Doughs happen because of the gluten in flour, the protein that extends into long elastic strands, which link up to form bread dough and pasta dough. Fat shortens those strands, preventing the gluten from linking up, to give us something tender rather than chewy, crust rather than bread. Working the dough is necessary because you need some gluten formation so that it holds together; this is why dough must be so thoroughly kneaded. But work this dough too much, create too much gluten, and you can toughen the crust. Using ice water helps keep the fat in a solid rather than a liquid state.

But it's really as simple as 1, 2, 3.

15 ounces/450 grams all-purpose flour

10 ounces/300 grams unsalted butter, lard, shortening, or any combination thereof, *cut into small pieces, cold or even frozen*

5 ounces/150 grams (¼ to ½ cup) ice water (*see the headnote; this quantity depends on the fat— whole butter has water in it, so you need only 2½ ounces/70 grams; shortening and lard do not contain water so you need the full 4 ounces/100 grams*)

½ teaspoon kosher salt

Combine the flour and cold fat in a mixing bowl and rub the fat between your fingers until you have small beads of fat and plenty of pea-size chunks. (If you're making a bigger batch, this can be done in a standing mixer with a paddle attachment, but remember not to paddle too much after you add the water, just enough so that the dough comes together.) Add the ice water gradually, and the salt, and mix gently, just until combined—if you work the dough too hard it will become tough. Shape into two equal-size disks, wrap in plastic, and refrigerate for at least 15 minutes or up to 2 days, until you're ready to roll.

MAKING YOUR OWN LOOSE SAUSAGE

Making sausage is easy and, if you have the right recipe (keep reading!), it is superior to most sausages you can buy—at the very least, you can customize your sausage to fit your own taste.

Sausage is best if you're able to grind the meat yourself because you have more control over the flavor. You can determine the amount of fat in the sausage, remembering that fat is flavor, and you can control the seasoning. But don't let not having a meat grinder prevent you from making sausage. Grocery stores sell ground pork or, even better, you can probably request it freshly ground from the meat department of your grocery store. Sausage should be about 30 percent fat, and that's what you should request when ordering it. Also request that it be ground through a large die, or coarsely ground, which results in a better bite.

I've made a lot of sausage since my colleague Brian Polcyn and I published *Charcuterie* in 2005, a book that devotes a central chapter to the power and the glory of sausage. And little has changed since then beyond my ever-increasing respect for and love of sausage. How can this most humble of creations, ground meat and fat, be among the most satisfying and exciting things to eat? *Because* we control the fat, the salt, and the seasonings.

Fat is what makes sausage juicy and succulent. Salt is what gives it flavor. And seasonings are what distinguish one sausage from another. The first recipe below uses seasonings associated with breakfast sausage: sage, black pepper, and a hint of nutmeg. That is followed by a recipe for Italian-style sausage, which would be appropriate for lasagna (see page 89). But once you get the hang of it, you can season a sausage mixture any way you wish, provided you include the right amount of fat and salt.

Salt is dependent on your personal taste to some degree, though it's not optional. And it's best measured with a scale for precision, because it's so important. I like a sausage to include at least 1.5 percent of its weight in salt and as much as 1.75 percent. That is, to determine the amount of salt, multiply the weight of the meat in ounces or grams by 0.015 and that will give you the number of ounces or grams of salt. If you don't have a scale, use Morton's kosher salt, which is about ½ ounce/14 grams per tablespoon. You'll need a scant teaspoon of salt for every pound of meat (or 6 or 7 grams of salt per 450 grams meat). This assumes, of course, that the weight of your meat is accurate. If you don't have a scale, it's best to have your meat and fat weighed and ground by a butcher. This is a perfectly reasonable strategy for making great sausage at home.

BREAKFAST SAUSAGE
MAKES 1 POUND/450 GRAMS

This is a customary breakfast sausage seasoned with sage, pepper, and nutmeg. It's sweetened with regular granulated sugar, though you can use twice the amount of sugar in the form of maple syrup. It's great in Sausage and Spinach Quiche (page 72), or add a cup or two of béchamel to it to make sausage gravy, or form it into patties and cook it that way.

- 1 pound/450 grams pork shoulder, *ground*

- 1 scant teaspoon Morton's kosher salt or fine sea salt, or 2 teaspoons Diamond Crystal kosher salt (*1.5 percent of the weight of the meat*)

- 2 teaspoons ground sage

- 2 teaspoons sugar

- 1 teaspoon ground mustard

- 1 teaspoon freshly ground black pepper

- ¼ teaspoon grated fresh nutmeg

- 3 tablespoons cold dry white wine

Combine the pork, salt, and seasonings in a mixing bowl. Mix thoroughly by hand (or you can use a standing mixer fitted with a paddle attachment—just don't overmix or let the meat get warm). Add the cold wine and continue to mix until everything is uniformly combined.

ITALIAN SAUSAGE
MAKES 1 POUND/450 GRAMS

This is a spicy sausage adapted from my book Charcuterie *for smaller portions. It's a great all-purpose Italian-style sausage to have on hand, and works especially well in lasagne (page 89). If you like, form the sausage into patties and sauté in a teaspoon of oil until browned and cooked through, 5 to 10 minutes depending on the thickness of the patties.*

Crust and Its Uses

- 1 pound/450 grams pork shoulder, *ground*

- 1 scant teaspoon Morton's kosher salt or fine sea salt, or 2 teaspoons Diamond Crystal kosher salt (*1.5 percent of the weight of the meat*)

- 1 tablespoon dried oregano

- 2 teaspoons fennel seeds, *coarsely chopped*

- 2 teaspoons paprika (*preferably hot Pimentón de la Vera paprika, but sweet is OK, too*)

- 1 teaspoon sugar

- 1 teaspoon ground coriander

- 1 teaspoon red pepper flakes

- ½ teaspoon freshly ground black pepper

- Pinch cayenne pepper

- 2 teaspoons red wine vinegar and/or apple cider vinegar

- 3 tablespoons cold dry red wine

Combine the pork, salt, seasonings, and vinegar in a mixing bowl. Mix thoroughly by hand (or you can use a standing mixer fitted with a paddle attachment—just don't overmix or let the meat get warm). Add the cold wine and continue to mix until everything is uniformly combined.

MEAT LOAF AND MEATBALLS

Meat loaf differs from sausage in two ways: flavor and texture. Sausage typically uses only pork, that flavorful, fatty meat. The pork is seasoned with salt and mixed thoroughly, and both the seasoning and the mixing cause the meat to bind to itself, creating a dense, springy texture. Meat loaf (and meatballs, which are in the same family) usually contains a good amount of beef, which gives it a different flavor from an all-pork mixture. And most meat loaf contains egg and dairy (a custard base!—see page 71) along with bread, a mixture often referred to as a panade. This helps keep the meat moist but, importantly, it makes the meat loaf tender rather than dense by preventing the meat from binding with itself the way sausage is encouraged to do. So: sausage = porky and springy; meat loaf (and meatballs) = beefy and tender.

Kenji López-Alt, in his excellent book *The Food Lab*—highly recommended reading for those curious about the whys of cooking—discusses the science of both kinds of mixtures. In his discussion of meat loaf, he added one important bit of information to my understanding: the impact of veal on meat loaf. Veal is useful both for its neutral flavor (tending to enhance the other flavors it's mixed with) and for its moisture-retaining gelatin, two reasons veal bones make such extraordinary stock. But rather than go out of his way to track down veal, López-Alt simply retrieves a couple packets of gelatin from his pantry, as I do for my One-Hour Beef Stock (page 142).

The meat mixture in the following recipe can be baked in a loaf pan and finished with the traditional ketchup glaze, or shaped into balls and pan-fried. And as long as you measure out the right amount of salt relative to the amount of meat you use, you can add anything else—pepper, fresh parsley, mushrooms, garlic, or other aromatics—for your personal take on meat loaf.

BEEF AND PORK RAISED PIE (OR, WITHOUT THE CRUST, MEAT LOAF)
SERVES 6

I've just completed a third book with my friend and colleague, Brian Polcyn, exploring pâté, typically ground and seasoned meat baked and served cold. In the book, Brian wanted to include something he referred to as a raised pie, common in British cookery. I've long made my Uncle Bill's pork pie, ground pork around which dough is formed free-style, which is a version of raised pie, a recipe that hails from Shropshire. But Brian created a similar effect that's much easier to shape and cook and serve: rolling dough around the meat rather than creating a traditional pie shape. *Crust and Its Uses*

Here is a deep, rich meat loaf, with beef and pork and an egg panade (plus egg wash for the dough, if you're using it). The 3-2-1 dough will work for this preparation, but I prefer a hot-water dough (see page 87); cooked this way, it's especially crisp and flaky, plus it's a snap to make. It should rest for 20 to 40 minutes, so consider making the dough after you get the vegetables sautéing and before you begin the meat loaf.

Of course, you can shape this into a loaf and bake it as a traditional meat loaf (see the instructions for this in the Note below). Either way, make a beef gravy (page 33) and serve with peas and mashed potatoes for a classic Americana dinner. This is one of those preparations that's even better the following day, either cold (see page 298 for a Bánh Mì version of the classic meat loaf sandwich) or reheated in the microwave or oven.

2 tablespoons vegetable oil	1 cup/240 milliliters dry white wine	½ cup/35 grams panko bread crumbs	2 tablespoons tomato paste
1 medium onion, *cut into medium dice*	1 tablespoon powdered gelatin	8 ounces/225 grams ground beef (*70 to 80 percent lean*)	1 recipe Hot-Water Dough (page 87)
1 teaspoon kosher salt	2 large eggs	8 ounces/225 grams fatty ground pork	10 to 12 thin slices bacon
½ teaspoon freshly ground black pepper	½ cup/120 milliliters heavy cream	¼ cup chopped fresh flat-leaf parsley	Egg wash: 1 large egg mixed with 1 tablespoon milk
1 carrot, *coarsely grated*	1 tablespoon Worcestershire sauce	2 teaspoons dried thyme	
5 garlic cloves, *coarsely chopped*	1 tablespoon fish sauce		

Heat the oil in a large skillet over medium-high heat. When it's hot, add the onion and stir. Add ½ teaspoon of the salt and the pepper. Stir to cook for a minute or two, then add the carrot and garlic, reduce the heat to medium, and sauté until the vegetables have cooked down and browned slightly, about 10 minutes. Add ½ cup/120 milliliters of the wine to deglaze the pan. When the wine has cooked off, transfer the vegetables to a plate and refrigerate, uncovered, until you're ready to mix them with the meat. It's best if they are thoroughly chilled before mixing.

Preheat your oven to 425°F/218°C. Line a rimmed baking sheet with parchment paper.

Pour the remaining ½ cup/120 milliliters wine into a wide, shallow bowl and sprinkle the gelatin over it so the gelatin can bloom (absorb the liquid). When it has bloomed and no white or dry particles remain, microwave the gelatin mixture for 20 to 30 seconds, just until the gelatin has dissolved. If you don't have a microwave, put the gelatin in the oven until it has melted, 5 minutes or so, depending on how fast it heats up. When the gelatin has melted, transfer it to a clean bowl so that it's not too hot when added to the meat.

In a medium bowl, combine the eggs, cream, Worcestershire sauce, fish sauce, bread crumbs, and remaining ½ teaspoon salt in a bowl and whip with a fork till the ingredients are uniformly combined into a panade.

Put the beef and pork in a large bowl or the bowl of a standing mixer fitted with the paddle attachment (this can be mixed using a sturdy wood spoon or spatula if you don't have a mixer). Add the parsley, thyme, and tomato paste. Add the panade and the chilled vegetable mixture and paddle for 1 minute, adding the wine-gelatin mixture as you do, until all the ingredients are combined and the meat has taken on a furry or tacky appearance.

Roll out the dough into a rectangle ¼ inch/6 millimeters thick; it should be about 14 inches/35 centimeters by 12 inches/30 centimeters. Lay the bacon across the center of the dough, up and down rather than side to side—slightly overlapping. The idea is to wrap the meat loaf in the bacon completely so that the bacon creates a barrier between the meat's moisture and the surrounding dough.

Shape the meat mixture into a log along the length of the bacon strips—it should be about 10 inches/25 centimeters long and the diameter of a soup can. Fold the bacon over it to encase the meat. Fold the top of the dough up and over the meat, then fold the bottom up, trimming as necessary so that you can then pinch the edges together to seal the dough. Roll the meat pie onto the prepared baking sheet, seam side down. Use scissors or a paring knife to cut steam holes across the top, brush it with the egg wash, and bake to an internal temperature of 150°F/65°C, about 45 minutes. Allow it to rest for 10 to 15 minutes before cutting into 1½-inch/4-centimeter slices.

Note: If you prefer a traditional meat loaf, you won't need the bacon, though you might consider cooking 4 ounces/110 grams of it, then cooking the onion, carrot, and garlic in the fat and adding the bacon, chopped, to the meat mixture. Combine the cooked vegetables, meat, cream, bread crumbs, and panade in the mixer and mix as above, adding the wine and gelatin. Pack the meat mixture into a greased loaf pan or shape it free-form on a rimmed baking sheet and bake to an internal temperature of 150°F/65°C, about 45 minutes. To make a glaze, combine ½ cup/120 milliliters ketchup, 2 tablespoons brown sugar, 2 tablespoons red wine vinegar or apple cider vinegar, and 1 tablespoon Worcestershire sauce and use a pastry brush to paint the mixture on the top of the meat loaf two or three times before it's done. Allow the meat loaf to rest for 10 to 15 minutes before slicing into 1½-inch/4-centimeter slices.

HOT-WATER DOUGH MAKES ABOUT 1 POUND/450 GRAMS

This very easy dough recipe, created especially for baked meat pies, was introduced to me by my partner in charcuterie, Brian Polcyn. It is made by melting fat (Brian uses lard; I use butter) in water, then adding the water and fat to the flour while still warm, reminiscent of pâte à choux dough. It results in a lovely, crispy crust. This dough can also be used for Chicken Pot Pie (page 54).

10 ounces/285 grams (about 2 cups) all-purpose flour

6 tablespoons/ 90 grams unsalted butter

¼ teaspoon/3 grams kosher salt

½ cup/120 milliliters water

Put the flour in a bowl, then make a well in the center.

Combine the butter, salt, and water in a small saucepan and bring to a simmer over high heat. When the butter has melted, pour the warm mixture into the well in the flour and mix to a paste. It should come together easily.

Cover and let rest in a warm spot for 30 to 45 minutes before rolling.

CRÊPES MAKES 8 (8-INCH/ 20-CENTIMETER) CRÊPES OR 16 (4-INCH/10-CENTIMETER) CRÊPES

Crêpes are so easy to make that there's no reason you shouldn't have them in your cooking arsenal, and the ratio is simple: equal parts by volume eggs, milk, and flour. For a small batch for two people on a Sunday morning, that would be a scant ½ cup/60 grams flour, ½ cup/120 milliliters milk, ½ cup/120 milliliters beaten eggs (2 large eggs), a pinch of sugar, and a dash of vanilla. They make a lovely quick breakfast. They can be filled with anything savory—indeed, they're the perfect solution to making an elegant meal out of leftovers (chicken and gravy, for instance). That's how Thomas Keller used leftover lobster knuckle meat at the French Laundry; knuckle meat was too inelegant to serve on its own, but wrapped like a pillow in a chive crêpe, it was gorgeous. And crêpes can make any number of desserts. Reheat in butter with some sugar and Grand Marnier for a classic crêpe suzette, or use any other sweet filling. Layer them with pastry cream or jam to make a crêpe cake (page 318).

Crust and Its Uses

4 large eggs (1 cup/ 240 milliliters)

1 cup/240 milliliters milk

1 scant cup/120 grams all-purpose flour

Pinch kosher salt

1 tablespoon sugar (*optional; don't use if making a savory dish*)

½ teaspoon vanilla extract (*optional; don't use if making a savory dish*)

Unsalted butter, *for cooking*

In a medium bowl, whisk together the eggs and milk till they are uniformly blended. Add the flour and salt (and sugar and vanilla if making a sweet dish) and gently whisk to incorporate. It's best to let the mixture rest for 20 to 30 minutes but not strictly required. Make sure there are no lumps.

In a small nonstick pan, melt 1 teaspoon butter over low heat. Pour in just enough batter, tilting the pan around, until you have a thin layer coating the bottom of the pan. Let it cook just until the top has solidified. Slip it out of the pan onto a plate. Repeat with the remaining batter and more butter as needed, stacking the crêpes as you go and leaving some overlap of the edges so they're easy to separate.

Crêpes can be made up to 8 hours in advance; cover the plate until ready to serve.

CHAPTER 3

Lasagne

As a child, I don't think I was ever so happy as when I was eating buttered elbow macaroni. As an adult, I still find pasta to be a great comfort to eat. It is infinitely variable and goes with just about anything. When I see orecchiette with sausage and broccolini or broccoli rabe on a menu, I don't think I've ever not ordered it. Penne baked with garlic and olive oil and mozzarella, discovered in New Haven visiting a girlfriend in college in 1981, remains a private and personal joy. And I grew up eating Mom's spaghetti with meat sauce (we wouldn't call it Bolognese until the 1990s), which we were all convinced was the best meat sauce on the planet. Her "secret" was starting the sauce with a few pieces of cut-up bacon, plenty of red wine, and—wait for it—Open Pit barbecue sauce.

Looking back on it, the reason this odd bottled sauce worked so well in a tomato sauce is that the number-one ingredient in it is high-fructose corn syrup, followed by water and vinegar. And sugar is indeed an excellent addition to tomato sauces. By the 1990s, much of America had made Marcella Hazan's wonderfully simple tomato sauce with fresh Roma tomatoes and onion and butter. That was a revelation. What isn't possible when you put pasta in the center of a meal?

In its very embryonic days, this book had two chapters, "Roast Chicken" and "The BLT." At the time, I didn't even know if the conceit would work—were there nine to twelve great meals that would teach the gamut of culinary fundamentals? My wife, Ann, and I had been discussing possibilities in bed one morning, and, as I remained to peruse the *New York Times*, she stepped into a shower. As I recall, moments later I heard metal shower curtain rings scrape violently across the bar, and a voice from behind the closed door shouted, "LASAGNA!"

I knew even without thinking that she was right.

My wife's Neapolitan roots run so deep she grew up calling all pasta "macaroni" and all red sauce "gravy," among the myriad grandparents and aunts and uncles, the eldest of whom spoke no English. For Ann, lasagna was a Christmas Day tradition, made by Gogo, her mother. And it was a great dish to serve the steady stream of relatives who came and went on Christmas Day, following the previous night's Feast of the Seven Fishes. Lasagna can be made ahead and serves a gang of people, and everyone loves it. Surprisingly, in my half century of eating, I had never had a homemade lasagna until I'd had Gogo's that first Christmas with her. I'd had plenty of Stouffer's throughout my childhood, and I'd had lasagna from steam tables, but homemade was a great pleasure I waited fifty-three years for.

Lasagna would make a perfect pasta-focused chapter. As if to underscore its value, we discovered a favorite Italian restaurant on our street in New York City, Don Angie, run by Angie Rito, which has a family-style platter of lasagna that's fabulous (Angie spreads the meat and sauce on large sheets of handmade pasta, rolls them when it's cold and set, cuts it in thick, pinwheeled pucks, covers them with cheese, and bakes them—ingenious).

Lasagna, which denotes a layered pasta, has so many lessons built into it that its tributaries seem boundless. And, yes, regarding the title of this chapter, "Lasagne," plural, because you can put anything between these silken sheets of pasta (Hazan includes four in her classic book, including one with ham and mushrooms, one with artichokes and béchamel, and one with ricotta and pesto).

Pasta, as I said, is one of the great pleasures of eating, period. Pity those with celiac or gluten sensitivity, who cannot go near it, and pity those avoiding carbs altogether for weight maintenance. For pasta is truly one of the finest culinary concoctions devised by *Homo sapiens*. It is delicious. It is convenient. It can be made ahead. It is satisfying. It is nutritious. It is inexpensive. It is infinitely variable. And leftovers can be better than straight from the oven.

And another important attribute of pasta: Even the most inexpensive, mass-produced boxed versions are good to eat, unlike premade hollandaise sauce (yes, it exists) and other products that are mere imitations of the foods that inspired them.

But you can also buy excellent fresh or fresh-frozen pasta. Most grocery stores stock a variety of frozen ravioli and tortellini. And pasta is also easy to make at home (and talk about inexpensive—homemade pasta works out to about 35 cents per portion). Making your own pasta takes a little time, but like homemade mayonnaise, homemade pasta has a texture and flavor that are like nothing you can buy.

I've been making pasta since I was in high school. Homemade spaghetti seasoned only with really good olive oil is a transporting pleasure. But usually I buy and cook dried pasta—indeed, there are many pasta dishes I think are better with boxed dried pasta rather than homemade. Where lasagna is concerned, being able to control the thickness is one of the great benefits of using homemade pasta. Plus the sheer fun of working with noodles that size. The Italian market near me sells sheets of fresh pasta dough, with which one can make pappardelle, ravioli, lasagna—but rolling out fat sheets to make lasagna is its own kind of pleasure. Not only is the texture noticeably different, with a distinctive bite, but the layer on top also gets crispy in a way that boxed pasta simply does not. In this chapter, I offer two recipes—whole-egg pasta and yolk-only pasta.

Moreover, lasagna offers the opportunity to explore different sauces, and not just white versus red versus green, but different kinds of red sauces. I'm thrilled to discuss three different kinds of red sauces, as well as a red sauce combined with a white sauce. A good lasagna often calls for three, even four, different kinds of cheeses—all are worth mentioning, and two are worth making yourself.

For all these reasons, lasagna is an iconic and instructive meal—or lasagne, plural, as I want to offer two variations, a quick and easy one and a totally from-scratch version.

Making lasagna from scratch, and even making lasagna using boxed pasta and store-bought sauce, is a project. But every time I've made it, I've found myself feeling that, yes, it's a lot of work, but it's also the starting point for so much fun. As always, if you're making it from scratch, spread out the work—if you make the Bolognese a day or two ahead, homemade lasagna from scratch is a snap. I never once asked myself why I was doing this. Marshal all your components—consider making the sauces a day or two ahead—and start assembling. And once you're done, with the lasagna is bubbling and browning in the oven, pause to consider that you've made probably the most difficult pasta dish there is.

And for me, personally, it's now a connection to the past and will forever carry with it a sense of loss. For it was Ann who made the lasagna this year. And I hope next year, Ann will let me do a completely-from-scratch lasagna, in honor and memory of beloved Gogo.

make fresh **MOZZARELLA CHEESE** (109)

TRY making your own **RICOTTA CHEESE** (109) surprisingly easy and so tasty when fresh! and for the more ambitious —

you will also need to make BÉCHAMEL SAUCE (103) one of the great "mother" sauces in the home kitchen

the long-simmered, deeply flavored **NEOPOLITAN TOMATO SAUCE** (102)

NOW you are seriously ready to make **SERIOUSLY FROM-SCRATCH FIVE-LAYER LASAGNA** (105)

LASAGNE

if you really want to start FROM SCRATCH,

WINTER TOMATO SAUCE (101)

With your leftover Bolognese, try **PAPPARDELLE with CREAMY BOLOGNESE SAUCE** (110) and with leftover pasta scraps, I recommend the

BROKEN PASTA with POTATOES (111) which requires making an extremely versatile and delicious —

to flavor in a pasta dish, I've provided a recipe for **SPAGHETTI WITH GARLIC TOMATO BASIL AND BEURRE TOMATE** (116) great when summer tomatoes are bursting with juices —

a excellent —

VEGETABLE STOCK (114)

Last, for a novel way to

GROW your own **PLUM tomatoes.**

NOW get ready to MAKE **fresh Pasta** (45-99) FOR YOUR LASAGNE

SUMMER TOMATO SAUCE (101) (this uses whole plum tomatoes)

next you'll need to make **BOLOGNESE SAUCE** (102) which will require a simple tomato sauce for the base —

TRY ONE OF THESE

CLASSIC FIVE-LAYER LASAGNA WITH BOLOGNESE, BÉCHAMEL, AND MOZZARELLA   SERVES 12 TO 15

This is the simpler of the two lasagna variations presented here, but it's every bit as delicious—pasta layered with a Bolognese-béchamel sauce and topped with mozzarella. For this recipe I used a 10-by-15-inch/25-by-38-centimeter pan, because I began this book after marrying a woman who had a lovely Le Creuset baking dish of that size. Otherwise I would have used my standard 9-by-13-inch/22-by-33-centimeter pan, and I might have been able to build the lasagna higher with the same amount of pasta. Everyone has pans of different sizes, so use your common sense.

      The lasagna can be assembled ahead, refrigerated, and then baked. Or it can be baked and kept for 4 to 6 hours at room temperature and reheated. Or it can be baked, cooled, and refrigerated, then reheated. Regardless, it's important to let it rest at least 45 minutes before cutting into it, or it will be too runny. This recipe will serve at least twelve. Because I rarely cook for that large a crowd, this means half can be frozen and reheated for a great last-minute weeknight meal.

2 pounds/900 grams
lasagna noodles,
dried, fresh, or
homemade
(see page 99)

6 cups/1.5 liters
Bolognese Sauce
(page 102)

2 cups/480 milliliters
Béchamel Sauce
(page 103)

1 cup/240 milliliters
plain tomato sauce
(*a good store-bought
version is fine*)

1 pound/450 grams
mozzarella, *shredded*

1 cup/80 grams
grated Parmigiano-
Reggiano

Preheat your oven to 400°F/205°C.

      Cook the pasta until it's al dente, according to the type you're using (fresh pasta needs only a few minutes). Drain and chill in an ice bath or in plenty of cold running water.

      In a large bowl, combine the Bolognese and béchamel sauces (if they are cold and stiff, heat them to ensure they mix uniformly).

      Spread a layer of tomato sauce evenly across the bottom of your baking dish. Put a layer of pasta on top, cutting the sheets as needed to fit the pan. Spread a quarter of the Bolognese-béchamel mixture across the pasta. Repeat three more times, then cover the final layer of pasta with the mozzarella and then the Parmigiano.

      If your baking dish is filled to the brim, put it on a rimmed baking sheet to catch any sauce that might bubble over. Bake the lasagna for 1 hour, or until piping hot.

      Allow to cool for at least 45 minutes before cutting and serving. The longer you wait, the better. Room-temperature lasagna can be cut, and individual slices can be reheated in a hot oven.

DISCOVERING FRESH PASTA

I was fifteen, the summer before my junior year of high school, when I first made pasta, and I thought it was the coolest thing. This stuff I thought only came from a box, you could actually make it! But in 1978, that's what most people thought about everything. Butter came from a butter factory, vinegar from a vinegar factory, same with Cheerios and Pop-Tarts and pretzels. Reading as an even younger teenager a recipe for homemade pretzels, I asked my dad if he could get me the ingredients at the grocery store. My dad, incredulous, looked at the last ingredient and said, "Lye is poisonous! I'm not buying lye!" We have, happily, come a long way (see the pretzel recipe on page 290).

There is a long tradition of making yolk-only pasta (see page 99), but usually I make whole-egg pasta. It results in a silky-smooth, firm dough that's very easy to work with. Raw pasta freezes very well, so you should make plenty and freeze it. And when you make a large batch, you can do most of the mixing in a standing mixer using the paddle first, then the dough hook. Mixing is the most important part of making pasta. It needs to be very elastic and so smooth that you just want to keep touching it.

WHOLE-EGG PASTA SERVES 4

All the recipes in this chapter that call for pasta can be made successfully with a box of dried pasta, or store-bought fresh pasta. But the results will be just a little different with homemade pasta, and this is one good reason to make it yourself. Another reason to make it is that it's fun. Just be sure you have enough time, because if you've got time constraints, you won't enjoy yourself. (This is true of any cooking that takes a little time.) And by time, all I mean here is an hour or so start to finish, from the time you pull your eggs from the fridge to pouring the oil on a steaming bowl of noodles.

When I learned to make pasta in Italy, they had a simple ratio: 100 grams flour, 1 egg, a dash of olive oil. And we mixed it right there on a plastic tablecloth. For my book *Ratio: The Simple Codes Behind the Craft of Everyday Cooking* (and for my Ratio app, which makes all the calculations on your smartphone for you), I give a ratio of 3 to 2, by weight; 3 parts flour to 2 parts egg is almost the same as the Italian version. And if you're playing fast and loose, I'd follow the late Marcella Hazan's rule of 2 eggs per cup of flour (depending on how you measure your flour, this could be a little wet; for 2 eggs you'd need 6 ounces of flour, and a cup of flour can weigh that or less). Hazan wouldn't have measured by weight, but I prefer to use a scale: Set a bowl on the scale and tare it off. Crack 1 egg per person into the bowl, then calculate the flour (1.5 times the weight of the eggs) and add it to the bowl. Then just give it a quick drizzle of flavorful olive oil.

Many teachers and cookbooks instruct you to form a well of flour on your board and crack the eggs into it, but I always wind up with egg running over the well and off the counter onto my foot, so I always begin the mixing in a bowl and finish by kneading it.

Kneading the dough is the most time-consuming part of making the pasta. You need to knead it by hand until it is luxuriously smooth, which takes about 15 minutes by hand. If you're making a larger amount, you can use a standing mixer to get at least half of the mixing done, but you almost always need to knead by hand to some degree.

Next, the dough needs to rest. All that kneading has developed the gluten and gotten it in line for such smooth dough. If you try to roll it right away, it will resist you. It's telling you to be patient. You can't rush gluten formation any more than you can rush a pot of water to boil. Cover the dough with plastic wrap or a towel and let it rest for at least 15 minutes at room temperature or up to 4 hours in the fridge.

Now you can roll it. Using a rolling pin is possible, but it's difficult to get it thin enough. I used to own a pasta rolling pin, which was about 3 feet long and tapered (you can get one online from Vermont Rolling Pins), and this worked well for hand-cut noodles; there are some good YouTube videos of old Italian women rolling it by hand this way. But a hand-cranked machine or standing mixer attachment is the most common and best choice for everyday pasta making.

This recipe makes enough pasta to serve four people; see the instructions below if you're making pasta for Classic Five-Layer Lasagna (page 94).

12 ounces/360 grams all-purpose flour (*about 2 cups*)

8 ounces/240 grams egg (*about 4 large eggs*)

1 tablespoon extra-virgin olive oil

Combine all the ingredients in a bowl and stir with your fingers or a pair of chopsticks until it all comes together. Pour the dough out onto a clean counter and knead it for 15 minutes, or until it is so smooth you don't want to stop kneading because what was

Keep portioned pasta covered with plastic or a cloth towel as you work so the surfaces don't dry out.

Use plenty of flour as you roll to prevent sticking.

I roll each portion vertically through the largest setting,

then fold the resulting piece into thirds, like folding a letter,

then reroll the folded pasta through the largest roller again, horizontally.

The idea is to make the pasta as wide as the rollers.

Also, roll your pieces through successively thinner settings, one after another. That is, roll each piece through the second setting, then change the roller to the third setting and roll all the pieces through this setting, and so on. This is more efficient, and it also gives the pasta a little rest before being stretched thinner. Sheets of pasta should be kept fairly thick for lasagna—the penultimate setting, if not the antepenultimate setting.

once shaggy and dry is indescribably smooth and wonderful to touch.

Cover the dough or wrap it in plastic and let it rest for at least 15 minutes. If it will rest for more than an hour, refrigerate it. Always make the dough the day you intend to roll it. When you're ready to roll, cut the dough into quarters.

If you're using a pin, roll it out till it's very thin, using plenty of flour to keep it from sticking, then roll it up and slice the roll crosswise into noodles of whatever thickness you wish. Toss the noodles on a board with some cornmeal to prevent sticking. This is what I would do if I wanted nice, thick pappardelle.

If you're using a pasta machine, put the dough vertically through the roller once on the thickest setting. Then fold the dough into thirds and run it horizontally through the machine, again on the

thickest setting. The idea is to make each piece as wide as the roller is. Repeat with the other three pieces, dusting with flour as often as needed.

Roll the dough through successively thinner settings till you have the desired thickness. I find that the thinnest setting on my machine makes the dough so thin that it sticks and doesn't cut well, so I usually stop at the penultimate setting. All machines are different; experiment with your roller and use what works best.

If you're cutting the pasta for noodles, it's a good idea to let the pasta sheets dry for 10 or 15 minutes before sending them through the machine's cutter. If you're making lasagna, cut the pieces to size.

TO MAKE FRESH PASTA FOR CLASSIC FIVE-LAYER LASAGNA

This will give you enough pasta for five layers in a 10-by-15-inch/25-by-38-centimeter pan. Save all the scraps, refrigerate them, and use later in the week for Broken Pasta with Potatoes (page 111), or simply reheat them with garlic in olive oil, perhaps with some halved cherry tomatoes and basil chiffonade.

15 ounces/425 grams flour	2 tablespoons extra-virgin olive oil
4 large eggs, plus 2 large egg yolks (*save the whites for Whiskey Sours, page 120*)	

Mix and knead as described above. Roll the pasta as wide as possible.

EGG YOLK PASTA SERVES 2 TO 4

I first began to think about pasta seriously while working on The French Laundry Cookbook *with Thomas Keller and listening to his stories about learning to make pasta with an old grandmother he met and worked for in a restaurant in a small town in Italy. In those days, the early 1990s, he said the talk centered on who could get the most yolks into a kilo of flour. The more yolks the better, but too many and the dough would become too sticky and difficult to work with. The consensus was that the ideal was 30 yolks per kilo, or 50 percent more yolk than flour (1.5 kilos yolk per 1 kilo flour). This makes a very rich, yellow, flavorful pasta. I think adding one whole egg and a little water makes it easier to work with, with little difference in richness. I serve it as is, with just a little butter or delicious olive oil. If I am lucky enough to have some truffle, I'd put shavings on top, but little else.*

Pastas

1⅓ cups/200 grams flour	1 tablespoon water
4 yolks	2 teaspoons extra virgin olive oil
1 egg	

Combine all the ingredients in a bowl and mix to form a sticky dough. On a floured surface, knead the dough until it's delightfully smooth and pleasant to the touch.

Roll and cut as desired.

SUMMER TOMATO SAUCE
MAKES ABOUT 4 CUPS/1 LITER

Take advantage of fresh plum tomatoes when they're in season and make this simple sauce. I love it as is on pasta—so fresh and delicious and nutritious.

1 onion, *roughly chopped or minced*	Kosher salt *to taste*
8 tablespoons/ 115 grams unsalted butter	2 pounds/900 grams whole plum tomatoes, *halved*

Method 1: In a high-sided pot, sweat the onion in a little of the butter until softened, seasoning with salt. Put the onion, remaining butter, and tomatoes in a blender and puree. Pour the sauce into the pot and simmer over low heat for 1 hour.

   Method 2: Preheat the broiler. Put the tomatoes, cut-side down, on a rimmed baking sheet and broil till they're charred. Meanwhile, in a high-sided pot, sweat the onion in a little of the butter until softened, seasoning with salt. Put the charred tomatoes in a blender, along with the sautéed onion and remaining butter, and puree; be sure to remove the circular insert in the blender lid and put a towel over the hole to keep the steam from blasting the blender open. (Alternatively, if you have an immersion blender, you can simply add the charred tomatoes to the pot with the onion, along with the remaining butter, and puree.) Simmer over low heat for 1 hour.

WINTER TOMATO SAUCE
MAKES ABOUT 4 CUPS/1 LITER

Tomatoes are a seasonal ingredient in most parts of the United States. If they aren't seasonal where you are, then you live in southern California and are lucky! For the rest of us, I want to give a simple tomato sauce for winter, when canned whole peeled tomatoes should be used. If making this to use for Bolognese Sauce (page 102), double this recipe and refrigerate or freeze what you don't use.

Sauces

1 onion, *roughly chopped or minced*	Kosher salt *to taste*
6 tablespoons/ 85 grams butter	2 (28-ounce/ 794-gram) cans whole tomatoes

In a high-sided pot, sweat the onion in a little of the butter until softened, seasoning with salt.

   Puree the tomatoes with their juices in a blender. Add them to the pot, along with the remaining butter. (Alternatively, if you have an immersion blender, you can puree the tomatoes in the can, or dump the tomatoes into the pot with the onion, along with the remaining butter, and puree.) Simmer over low heat for 1 hour.

Sauces

NEAPOLITAN TOMATO SAUCE
MAKES ABOUT 8 CUPS/2 LITERS

This is the sauce most often associated with Italian pasta dishes—deep, dark, red, and rich. This particular version has been passed down in my wife's family ever since her great-great-grandmother arrived from Naples in 1884. It's surely gone through all kinds of permutations, but it now uses the canned tomato products familiar to all home cooks. When Gogo made this, she would brown her sausage in the pan first and use the rendered sausage fat to start the sauce (adding the sausage and also meatballs back at the end). A good practice!

¼ cup olive oil	2 cups/480 milliliters dry red wine
1 onion, *thinly sliced*	4 (6-ounce/170-gram) cans tomato paste
3 or 4 garlic cloves, *roughly chopped*	1 (28-ounce/794-gram) can tomato puree
Kosher salt and freshly ground black pepper *to taste*	1 (28-ounce/794-gram) can diced tomatoes
2 teaspoons red pepper flakes	1 tablespoon sugar
¼ cup chopped fresh flat-leaf parsley	

In a large pot, heat the oil over medium-high heat. When it is hot, sauté the onion and garlic until soft and translucent, salting aggressively as they cook. Add a few grinds of black pepper, the red pepper flakes, and the parsley. Add the wine and deglaze the pan. Add the tomato paste, stirring as you add. Add the tomato puree, diced tomatoes with their juices, and sugar and stir to combine.

Simmer, uncovered, for 3½ to 4 hours, stirring occasionally. Using one of the empty cans to capture any remaining tomato juice, add water as needed if the sauce looks too thick.

BOLOGNESE SAUCE
MAKES 7 TO 8 CUPS/1.75 TO 2 LITERS

This is a delicious meat sauce, enriched by milk, which is cooked off so that the solids brown and deepen the flavor. It's great as is on spaghetti, and will make enough for one big pan of lasagna. Hell, why not add some chili powder and serve it on buns as sloppy Joes? This recipe can be halved.

For a vegetarian version, sauté 2 pounds/ 900 grams diced cremini mushrooms, as described on page 77. Make the sauce without the meat, then add the mushrooms about 5 minutes before serving and allow them to simmer in the sauce.

2 tablespoons olive oil	1 cup/240 milliliters dry red wine
1 onion, *diced*	6 cups/1.5 liters plain tomato sauce (*a good store-bought version is fine*)
1 carrot, *grated*	
2 celery ribs, *diced*	
Kosher salt to taste	1 tablespoon dried oregano or 2 bay leaves
2 pounds/900 grams coarsely ground meat (*preferably a mix of pork, veal, and beef*)	1 tablespoon fish sauce (*if you have it on hand; optional, needless to say*)
2 cups/480 milliliters milk	

In a large pot, heat the oil over medium-high heat. When it is hot, add the onion, carrot, and celery and cook until softened, 5 minutes or so. Hit them with a four-finger pinch of salt as they cook.

Add the meat, and cook, breaking it up as much as possible. When it has lost all its pinkness, add the milk and simmer until all the liquid has cooked off and the milk solids begin to brown.

Add the wine and stir. When the wine has come to a simmer, add the tomato sauce, oregano or bay leaves, and fish sauce (if using). When it has resumed a simmer, taste it and add more salt if needed. Simmer the sauce for 45 to 60 minutes, until thick.

BÉCHAMEL SAUCE   MAKES ABOUT 3 CUPS/720 MILLILITERS

Béchamel sauce is one of the great sauces, and it's not used nearly as much as it could be. It's essentially milk thickened with flour, but I always include onion, which adds flavor, sweetness, and umami. Brown the onion first for an even richer sauce. I also usually season it with nutmeg, which is traditional but not always necessary—it depends how you want to use the béchamel. It can be used for gravies, for gratins, for myriad sauces (add mushroom, add cheese). Add ground Breakfast Sausage (page 83) for biscuits with sausage gravy. Béchamel is also the beginning of fabulous homemade mac and cheese: Take it off the heat, add grated cheddar, and stir till it's melted, maybe add some white vermouth, toss with cooked macaroni, and bake. (Gosh, thinking of this now, I realize that same variation without the cheese would also make a beautiful sauce to nap lobster tails with.) If you're using the béchamel for a savory dish, such as mac and cheese or lasagna, I recommend the savory seasonings, bay leaf, cayenne, and fish sauce. For something sweeter, use only the pepper and nutmeg. But it's up to you—use that thing on the top of your neck.

As a rule, 1 tablespoon of flour will lightly thicken 1 cup of milk, but it will be fairly thin, like a stock-based sauce. For a thicker gravy, as for sausage and biscuits, add 1 ½ to 2 tablespoons per cup of milk.

4 tablespoons/
60 grams unsalted
butter

1 small onion, *cut into
small dice*

Kosher salt *to taste*

6 to 8 tablespoons/
45 to 60 grams
all-purpose flour

1 quart/1 liter milk

1 bay leaf (*optional*)

¼ teaspoon freshly
ground black
pepper

2 teaspoons fish
sauce (*optional*)

Cayenne pepper *to
taste* (*optional*)

Grated fresh nutmeg
to taste (*optional*)

Combine the butter and onion in a saucepan over medium-high heat, stirring to coat the onion with the melting butter. Add a four-finger pinch of salt. When the onion is translucent and tender, add the flour and cook for a minute or so.

Whisk in the milk (and add the bay leaf if you're using it), then stir continuously with a flat-edged wooden spoon or spatula until the milk comes to a simmer, making sure no flour sticks to the bottom of the pan and scorches. Add the black pepper. Add the fish sauce, cayenne, and/or nutmeg (if using). Cook very gently for 15 minutes or so. Taste it—if you can taste raw flour, cook it a little longer, skimming any foam that gathers on one side of the pan.

Seriously From-Scratch
FIVE-LAYER LASAGNA

SERVES 12 TO 15

To call your lasagna "seriously from-scratch," you must by definition make your own ricotta and mozzarella—neither of which is hard, but I recommend making them a day or two ahead of making the lasagna. You can make and cook the pasta ahead as well. The Bolognese can likewise be made several days ahead of assembling the lasagna. So, if you want to go at it, I recommend having a good plan and a prep list, and giving yourself plenty of time—this is a great weekend project for those who love to cook. This is an enormously satisfying experience if you take the time to appreciate the steps. Have fun making the cheese; take time to appreciate the texture of fresh pasta as you roll it out.

But if you want to forgo the cheese making and still call this from-scratch, this is perfectly reasonable—here's why. There's no question that making cheese is itself a worthwhile endeavor; this kind of knowledge helps us better understand our food and where it comes from. That said, I still consider this lasagna from-scratch if you buy your cheeses, because you can usually buy better fresh cheeses than the ones you can make at home on an occasional basis. I make things like pasta and mayonnaise from scratch, because they are of a quality you can't buy anywhere. You can buy a roast chicken, but it's nowhere near as good as one you roast at home. That's the ultimate factor when deciding how deep into the cooking I want to go.

Do make your own tomato sauce (because it's so easy) and add it to ground meat and onions and herbs for the Bolognese. And it really isn't that hard to make your own pasta. But use store-bought pasta if you prefer—you know your own comfort level and time constraints. I want you to enjoy this project.

2 pounds/1 kilogram lasagna noodles, *dried, fresh, or homemade (see page 99)*

1 pound/450 grams ricotta, *store-bought or homemade (page 109)*

3 large eggs

¼ cup minced fresh flat-leaf parsley

Grated zest of 1 lemon

½ teaspoon kosher salt, *plus more to taste*

½ teaspoon freshly ground black pepper

1 cup/240 milliliters plain tomato sauce *(a good store-bought version is fine)*

6 cups/1.5 liters Bolognese Sauce *(page 102)*

1 pound/450 grams fresh mozzarella, *store-bought or homemade (page 109), cut into ¼-inch/ 6-millimeter slices*

1 pound/450 grams scamorza *or good-quality provolone, cut into ¼-inch/ 6-millimeter slices*

2 cups/120 grams grated Parmigiano-Reggiano

Preheat your oven to 400°F/205°C.

Cook the pasta until it's al dente, according to the type you're using (fresh pasta needs only a few minutes). Drain and chill in an ice bath or in plenty of cold running water.

In a large bowl, combine the ricotta, eggs, parsley, lemon zest, salt, and pepper and stir or whisk till uniformly combined.

Spread a layer of tomato sauce evenly across the bottom of a 9-by-13-inch/22-by-33-centimeter or larger baking dish. Put a layer of pasta on top, cutting the sheets as needed to fit the pan. Spread half of the Bolognese evenly on top of the pasta. Cover the Bolognese with another layer of pasta. Spread the ricotta mixture evenly over it. Cover the ricotta with another layer of pasta. Spread the remaining Bolognese sauce on top of the pasta. Cover this with another layer of pasta. Fan the slices of mozzarella and scamorza across the pasta, interspersing them. Sprinkle a third of the Parmigiano on top. Cover the cheese with a final layer of pasta, then sprinkle the remaining Parmigiano over the top.

If your baking dish is filled to the brim, put it on a rimmed baking sheet to catch any sauce that might bubble over. Bake for 1 hour, or until piping hot.

Allow to cool for at least 20 minutes before cutting and serving. The longer you wait, the better. Room-temperature lasagna can be cut, and individual slices can be reheated in a hot even.

SIMPLE CHEESES AT HOME

"Why do you make your own ricotta?" I asked the novelist Jane Hamilton. Hamilton lives on an apple farm in Wisconsin and is an avid cook.

"Because it tastes so good!" she said immediately.

Indeed, tasting cheese as you make it is all the reason you need. There is a freshness and clarity to ricotta you make yourself from good milk. We do it not just because it's easy, but because it's one of those preparations that you can't really buy. Fresh, homemade ricotta is invariably different from store-bought versions. And it tastes better, as Jane said. You can also season it to taste; I like to give it some floral notes with fresh thyme.

You can make fresh ricotta in 20 minutes, and mozzarella in 45 minutes. The most difficult ingredient to find may be the milk itself. It's important to use milk that has not been ultra-pasteurized. And if you have access to whole milk that has not been homogenized, use that. If you have a farmer or dairy near you, this is often the best choice, though Whole Foods sells organic milk that has not been ultra-pasteurized. Check the labels or ask for the dairy manager at your local grocery store.

Milk, lemon juice, and salt is all you need for ricotta. To make mozzarella, you also need rennet, an animal-based enzyme, which helps make a tighter curd that can be stretched and folded to make soft mozzarella. Most mozzarella recipes call for powdered citric acid, which allows for more precision than lemon juice. If you're going to the trouble of buying rennet, it's a good idea to get the citric acid as well. Both are inexpensive and easily found online. You'll also need cheesecloth or a clean straining cloth to separate the curds from the whey. And finally, you'll need an instant-read thermometer.

Acid denatures the proteins in milk—that is, uncoils them, especially given enough heat, just as heat and acid uncoil the protein in egg whites when making a consommé (page 41). This is why half-and-half that's on its way out, while still tasting OK, will curdle when poured into hot coffee; the half-and-half has developed enough acid to separate from the whey when heated by the coffee.

When the milk proteins uncoil, the whey separates from the casein, which collect around the fat, forming curds and tasty, yellowish whey. When strained, these curds are ricotta. How well you drain them will determine the texture of your ricotta. Sometimes it's best loose and moist, for use on pizza and pasta or on toasted slices of baguette, drizzled with extra-virgin olive oil. You can drain it overnight if you want it more solid, and you can even salt it and press it to create ricotta salata, which will allow you to keep the cheese for longer in the refrigerator.

A gallon (about 4 liters) of milk should yield about a pound (about 450 grams) of cheese, and plenty of whey left over, a tangy liquid that's good to drink on its own or to cook with instead of buttermilk.

RICOTTA CHEESE
MAKES ABOUT 2 CUPS/480 MILLILITERS

2 quarts/2 liters whole milk (*preferably not ultra-pasteurized*)

1 teaspoon kosher salt

5 tablespoons/ 75 milliliters lemon juice

Combine the milk and salt in a medium saucepan and heat over medium-high heat until it reaches 200°F/93°C, just before a boil. Give it a stir now and then to make sure the solids aren't sticking to the bottom.

Remove the pan from the heat and gently stir in the lemon juice. Let the milk rest while the curds form, 10 to 15 minutes. Strain through cheesecloth. Serve immediately or store in a jar with plenty of whey to keep it moist. The sooner you use it, the better, but it will keep in the refrigerator for up to 5 days or so.

MOZZARELLA CHEESE
MAKES 12 TO 16 OUNCES/340 TO 450 GRAMS

Cheeses

1 gallon/4 liters milk

2 teaspoons citric acid

¼ teaspoon rennet mixed into ¼ cup water

½ teaspoon fine sea salt, *or to taste*

Combine the milk and citric acid in a large saucepan and heat over medium heat until it reaches 90°F/32°C. Give it a stir now and then to make sure the solids aren't sticking to the bottom. Curds should be starting to form. Take the pan off the heat and gently stir in the rennet water until you feel it's well distributed. Cover the pot and let it sit for 10 minutes.

A solid curd will have formed. Cut a 1-inch/2.5-centimeter crosshatch pattern into the top of the curd. Return the pot to medium heat and bring the curds and whey to between 105°F/41°C and 110°F/43°C. Remove the pan from the heat and give it a few more gentle stirs.

Scoop the curds into a strainer lined with cheesecloth. Reheat the whey to 180°F/82°C. Either work with the whole batch of curds at once or divide it into portions. Put the curds in the whey and let them heat for 30 seconds. Then, using rubber gloves, lift the curds out and pull and stretch and fold the mozzarella over on itself repeatedly so that it becomes smoother and smoother, returning it to the warm whey when it becomes too cool to stretch. In the middle of the stretching, season it with the salt, folding the salt in so that it becomes evenly distributed. Repeat until it's the consistency you like, but try to stretch it as little as possible or it can become rubbery.

Store in room-temperature whey for up to a day or refrigerate and bring to room temperature to serve or use for cooking.

PAPPARDELLE WITH CREAMY BOLOGNESE SAUCE   SERVES 4

Now that we have both a Bolognese sauce and homemade pasta, the easiest meal is to combine them. I love to add béchamel to the Bolognese, as well as some mozzarella for a truly comforting bowl of pasta. Of course, it's fine to use store-bought pasta and hard mozzarella. It's just different. It's really the sauce that's the star here.

A note on cooking pasta: Most basic recipes describing how to cook pasta suggest boiling it in salted water. What does that mean? It does not mean putting a pinch of salt in a huge pot of water. It means *seasoning* the water. The proper way to cook pasta is to add enough kosher salt that the water tastes pleasantly seasoned. Not salty (as you should make it when cooking green vegetables), but seasoned. If you want to know a correct level of seasoning, for most people it's 1 percent. So, measure out 1 liter of water and add 10 grams of salt. Or measure out 1 gallon of water for your pasta and add 1.28 ounces salt (roughly 2¼ tablespoons).

Kosher salt *to taste*

1 pound/450 grams pappardelle

4 cups/1 liter Bolognese Sauce (page 102)

2 cups/480 milliliters Béchamel Sauce (page 103) *or more to taste*

1 pound/480 grams mozzarella, *grated*

¼ cup minced fresh flat-leaf parsley or julienned fresh basil, *for garnish (optional)*

Bring a large pot of salted water to a boil over high heat. Cook the pappardelle until al dente.

While the pasta is cooking, combine the Bolognese and béchamel sauces in a large saucepan and heat just to a simmer. Cover and remove the pan from the heat.

When the pasta is done, drain it and transfer it to a large bowl. Add half the sauce and half the mozzarella and toss. Serve immediately, topping each serving with the remaining sauce and more cheese as desired, finishing it with fresh parsley or basil (if using).

BROKEN PASTA WITH POTATOES   SERVES 6

This is a classic preparation in southern Italy, highlighting the fact that Italians are masters of economy. When I saw "broken pasta" on the menu at Trattoria da Nennella in Naples, I wondered why on earth broken pasta would warrant its own dish. Once I tasted it, I only wanted to make it myself. A few days later, in a small grocery store on the island of Procida, I actually found boxed broken pasta on the shelf—a variety of pasta scraps marketed just for this reason. My guess, though, is that Italian kitchens of old stored a variety of pastas in specific containers. By the end of the year, the containers would be littered with broken bits of pasta. Of course they would find a way to put this perfectly good, if irregular, pasta to work. And they would supplement the smallish amount of pasta with potatoes.

No matter its origin, it remains a staple of the southern Italian kitchen and is one of the most comforting meals I know. For me the key is using a good vegetable stock, so I've provided a simple recipe following this one. This is a very wet pasta dish; you should need a spoon to eat it. It's finished with hard cheese; in Italy the choice would be scamorza; use that if it's available. But a good-quality provolone also works great.

A variation of this recipe was given to me by the fifth-generation Neapolitan and food photographer Luciano Furia, to whom I'm grateful! I like to save time by cooking the bacon in one pan while the vegetables sweat in another, but if you want to use (and clean) only one pan, feel free to cook the bacon first, then remove it and cook the vegetables in the bacon fat with extra olive oil. In either case the bacon, cooked and roughly chopped, along with its rendered fat, should wind up in the pot. As for the potatoes, I don't peel them, but you can if you wish.

4 ounces/110 grams sliced bacon	½ teaspoon freshly ground black pepper	1½ to 2 quarts/1.5 to 2 liters Vegetable Stock (page 114)	¾ cup/60 grams grated Parmigiano-Reggiano
¼ cup olive oil	1 teaspoon red pepper flakes (*optional*)	4 cups mixed dried pasta (*or 1 pound/450 grams leftover scraps from making lasagna*)	8 ounces/225 grams scamorza, good-quality provolone, or fresh mozzarella, *diced*
2 celery ribs, *cut into small dice*			
2 carrots, *cut into small dice*	1 to 1¼ pounds/ 450 to 680 grams russet potatoes, *peeled if desired and cut into large dice*	1 pint/300 grams cherry tomatoes (*2 dozen or so*)	¼ cup minced or sliced fresh flat-leaf parsley or chives, *for garnish*
1 medium onion, *cut into small dice*			
½ to 1 teaspoon kosher salt, *or to taste*			

In a large skillet, cook the bacon over medium-high heat until crisp. Remove the bacon and roughly chop it, then return it to the fat in the skillet and set aside.

Heat the olive oil in a large pot or Dutch oven over high heat. Add the celery, carrots, and onion and season with the salt and pepper. Add the red pepper flakes here if you like a little heat. Lower the heat to medium. Cook the vegetables, stirring frequently, till they're tender, 10 minutes or so. Add the reserved bacon and bacon fat.

Raise the heat to high and add the potatoes. Cook until they get some color, 5 minutes or so, adjusting the heat as necessary. Add just enough stock to cover the potatoes, then add the dried pasta (if using fresh lasagna scraps, add them later, with the tomatoes). Bring the stock to a simmer, then lower the heat to medium to keep it at a gentle simmer. Cook for 10 to 12 minutes, until the pasta is cooked, adding more stock as needed to keep the potatoes and pasta just covered.

Add the tomatoes, first crushing them in your hand to release their juices. (If you're using fresh pasta, add it now, too.) Simmer for another few minutes to cook the tomatoes. Stir in the Parmigiano.

Remove the pot from the heat. Scatter the diced scamorza evenly over the surface, then press the pieces below the surface, cover the pot, and let it sit for 5 to 10 minutes to allow the cheese to soften.

Garnish with the fresh parsley or chives and serve.

Other
Pasta
Preparations

VEGETABLE STOCK   MAKES 2 TO 3 QUARTS/2 TO 3 LITERS

Vegetable stock is probably the most valuable stock in a home kitchen because it's so quick, versatile, and flexible. It falls into the category of preparations not to buy at the store because it's so much better than any boxed product that they can't really be compared. I highly recommend making it a regular part of your repertoire. Make it on a Sunday afternoon and use it throughout the week for sauces and as a braising liquid.

You can use any sweet vegetables you wish. Onions and carrots are the stock's backbone—never skimp on them. Fennel and thyme give it great anise and floral notes. Mushrooms and bay leaves give it savoriness. Tomato and tomato paste balance the sweetness with acidity and add color. I don't use celery because Thomas Keller told me that celery can make stocks bitter, and I've found that he's right. (The only stock I like celery with is beef stock; beef and celery are a terrific pairing generally.)

Slice everything thinly. You can sweat the vegetables for a deeper flavor, or even caramelize the vegetables for deep sweetness. But simply combining everything raw and covering with cold water will do very nicely. Always be thoughtful about adding salt to a base preparation; if you know you'll be using this for a soup base, you can add salt at the beginning. But don't add salt if you're making a dish like Broken Pasta with Potatoes (page 111), which is finished with a salty cheese.

The only danger here is cooking the stock for too long or too hard, so cook at a low-low simmer, barely bubbling. After about an hour the vegetables can fall apart, and those fragments absorb the stock, which means some of your stock will get thrown out when you empty your strainer.

1 leek, *halved lengthwise, well cleaned, and thinly sliced*

3 carrots, *thinly sliced*

1 Spanish onion, *brown papery skin and all (though discard any skins with dirt that won't rub off), thinly sliced*

1 small fennel bulb, *greens trimmed, thinly sliced*

8 ounces/225 grams white button or cremini mushrooms, *thinly sliced*

1 medium tomato, *thinly sliced*

1 tablespoon tomato paste

1 bay leaf

4 or 5 thyme sprigs

3 quarts/3 liters water

Combine all the ingredients in a large pot. Bring to a boil over medium-high heat, then immediately turn the heat to low and simmer gently for 50 to 60 minutes. Strain through a fine-mesh sieve or through cheesecloth.

Taste the broth. If you would like the flavor to be more concentrated, reduce it by as much as one-third, to about 2 quarts/2 liters. Store in the refrigerator for up to 3 days or in the freezer for up to 2 weeks.

PASTA E CECI   SERVES 6 TO 8

This pasta and bean soup variation is an excellent way to put leftover pasta scraps from lasagna to use, but it's also a good excuse to use the nourishing chickpea (see page 256). Please use dried chickpeas, not canned, as these give the broth much better flavor.

Often, the soup is made with white beans, such as cannellini, and the very small ditalini pasta (pasta e fagioli). Because I'm using the larger and more assertive chickpea, the legume favored by my late mother-in-law, Gogo, whose family hailed from Naples, I'm also using a larger shell pasta.

I love the flavor that salt pork lends to this dish, and I also add a little more backbone to the broth with chicken stock. If you want to make this a vegetarian dish, omit the salt pork and chicken stock.

1 ½ cups/300 grams dried chickpeas

6 ounces/170 grams salt pork or bacon, *cut into medium dice*

1 large onion, *cut into medium dice*

4 garlic cloves, *roughly chopped*

2 celery ribs, *sliced*

1 large carrot, *diced*

½ cup/15 grams chopped fresh flat-leaf parsley

2 cups/480 milliliters Easy Overnight Chicken Stock (page 38) or store-bought chicken broth

1 (28-ounce/794-gram) can whole peeled tomatoes

1 (4-inch/10-centimeter) Parmigiano-Reggiano rind, plus ½ cup/60 grams grated Parmigiano-Reggiano

2 bay leaves

½ bunch thyme, *tied with string*

2 teaspoons kosher salt

1 teaspoon freshly ground black pepper

1 tablespoon fish sauce (*optional*)

1 pound/450 grams shell pasta *or fresh scraps reserved from pasta making*

Put the chickpeas in a large bowl and add 5 cups/1.2 liters water. Soak overnight, then drain, reserving 2 cups/480 milliliters of the soaking liquid. Set aside.

Heat the salt pork and 1 cup/240 milliliters fresh water in a large soup pot over high heat. When the water has cooked off, lower the heat to medium and continue to cook until the pork is browned and has rendered its fat. (If you're making this vegetarian, simply heat 2 tablespoons of vegetable oil over high heat.)

Add the onion and garlic and cook until the onion is tender, a few minutes. Add the celery and carrot and cook for a few more minutes. Stir in half of the parsley, then add the reserved chickpea soaking liquid, chicken stock, and 2 cups/480 milliliters fresh water (or 4 cups/950 milliliters fresh water if you're not using chicken stock). Add the tomatoes with their juices, crushing each one by hand as you put them in. Add the Parmigiano rind, bay leaves, thyme, salt, pepper, and fish sauce (if using). Simmer for about 2 hours, until the chickpeas are tender.

About 10 minutes before serving, taste the broth. Add more salt if it needs it. Add the pasta and bring the pot to a boil for a minute, then reduce the heat to a simmer and cook until the pasta is tender.

Serve in bowls, garnished with plenty of grated Parmigiano and the remaining parsley.

Note: If you are short on time, you can use 2 (15-ounce/425-gram) cans chickpeas, rinsed and drained, plus 2 additional cups/480 milliliters water in place of the dried chickpeas and soaking liquid. Simmer for about 1 hour.

SPAGHETTI WITH GARLIC, TOMATO, BASIL, AND BEURRE TOMATE
SERVES 2 TO 4

*Other
Pasta
Preparations*

This is one of my all-time favorite dishes in summer, when tomato and basil are abundant and I can also usually find really good garlic at the farmers' market. Freshness is everything here, but the very concept of the sauce is also gratifying, and delicious. I've been making a version of this since I read about it in an obscure paperback cookbook in 1984. At the time, I hadn't heard of fresh basil, so I used dry, assuming that's what the recipe called for, and still it was good enough to make again. I moved to New York City in 1985, where I discovered fresh basil at my local bodega. Ah! Now I get it, I thought. This dish became a staple in my penurious city days.

Maybe fifteen years later, I began to notice that when I salted the tomatoes early, they released a lot of liquid. I knew there was a ton of flavor in that liquid, but how to get at it? It was the consistency of water, and you wouldn't want to put water on your pasta. By then I'd learned about beurre blanc (whisking butter into white wine to make a sauce) and beurre monté, a restaurant term for melting butter while keeping it homogenous, by whipping it into a small amount of water.

I figured the same could be done with the tomato water, making what in effect is not a beurre blanc, but a beurre tomate. It worked like a dream. The tomato water emulsifies into the butter so that it all clings lovingly to the pasta. Combine it with the tried-and-true combination of garlic and basil and you have a sublime pasta dish.

This makes for a genuinely satisfying meal in itself, or a terrific "primo" dish before the main course, Italian-style. It is best cooked as you need it—it shouldn't take longer than it takes a pot of water to boil and spaghetti to cook. But if you want, everything can be made ahead and combined quickly *à la minute*.

Make your own spaghetti (see page 96), and this one is out of the park.

4 large ripe tomatoes, diced (*if tomatoes are plentiful, use a mix of red and yellow*)

1½ to 2 teaspoons kosher salt, *plus more for the pasta water*

1 cup/15 grams fresh basil chiffonade

12 ounces/340 grams spaghetti

6 tablespoons/ 90 grams unsalted butter

8 garlic cloves, *minced*

Put the tomatoes in a bowl and sprinkle the salt over them to encourage them to give up their water. Take a pinch of the basil chiffonade and mince it. Add it to the tomatoes and toss to combine. Set aside.

Bring a large pot of salted water to a boil over high heat. Cook the spaghetti until al dente.

Meanwhile, melt 1 tablespoon of the butter in a sauté pan over medium heat. Add the garlic and cook till it's tender, then turn the heat to high. Working quickly, hold a basket strainer or colander over the pan with the garlic. Pour the tomatoes into the strainer so that the tomato water goes into the pan. Return the tomatoes to the bowl and set aside. When the tomato water comes to a simmer, add the remaining 5 tablespoons/75 grams butter and swirl the pan continuously over the heat until it's completely melted. Remove the pan from the heat.

When the pasta is done, drain it and toss it with the beurre tomate. Serve in pasta bowls, topped with the tomatoes and basil.

1. Cook the garlic gently in a little butter over medium heat, just till softened but not browned.

4. When the tomato water comes to a simmer, add the pats of butter and swirl the pan continuously until all the butter is melted and has been incorporated into the sauce, which should be uniform and creamy-looking. This is essentially a beurre blanc sauce made using tomato water instead of wine.

2. Dump the diced, salted tomatoes into a colander over the pan so that the juice falls into the pan.

3. When the juice has drained, put the colander with the tomatoes on the plate that held the tomatoes and turn the heat to high.

5. I add about half the tomatoes to the pasta, tossing them with the pasta to warm the tomatoes and make the pasta more juicy.

6. Serve this pasta and top with the remaining tomatoes and basil.

WHISKEY SOUR   SERVES 1

Leftovers   This is one of my favorite drinks, period, and I include it here as a way to make excellent use of the egg whites from egg yolk pasta (page 99). The better the whiskey, the better the cocktail. These can be made in batches in a large measuring cup and poured as needed for multiple guests; use an immersion blender for thorough mixing. I prefer an equal mixture of lemon and lime juice for the citrus. To make simple syrup, combine 1 cup/240 milliliters sugar and 1 cup/240 milliliters water in a Pyrex measuring cup and microwave for 2 to 3 minutes, until the sugar is dissolved. This will keep for a month refrigerated. Simple syrup can be enhanced by loading the sugar water with lemon and lime zest before heating. Good thing you saved those egg whites.

1 large egg white,
whipped till frothy

1 ounce/30 milliliters
lemon and/or lime
juice

1 ounce/30 milliliters
simple syrup
(*see headnote*)

2 ounces/60 milliliters
bourbon or rye

3 Luxardo maraschino
cherries (*preferably
on a toothpick*), plus
1 teaspoon of the
cherry syrup

Combine the egg white, juice, syrup, and whiskey in a mixing glass and mix thoroughly. Pour over ice. Garnish with the cherries and cherry syrup.

CLASSIC, NO-FRILLS BLOODY MARY SERVES 1

I've never liked Bloody Marys that come with more garnish than drink, so I garnish this simply. But the real treat of this cocktail I discovered by accident. When relatives were visiting, they requested Bloody Marys. We had no Bloody Mary mix, which is loaded with stuff I don't like anyhow. But I had a can of tomatoes on hand and used them. Everyone remarked how fresh and clean it tasted. And so here it is, yet another kind of tomato sauce! This recipe will give you about 3 cups of juice; save any leftovers for a simple tomato sauce (page 101).

Leftovers

1 (28-ounce/794-gram) can whole peeled tomatoes

2 ounces/60 milliliters vodka

1 to 2 teaspoons Worcestershire sauce

1 to 2 teaspoons prepared horseradish (*or home-cured; see Note below*)

Squeeze of lime

Squeeze of lemon

Several dashes Tabasco

Pinch of celery salt

1 lime wedge, *for garnish*

Using an immersion blender, blend the tomatoes with their juices in the can till they are thoroughly pureed. Pass them through a fine-mesh strainer; discard the pulp or save it to add to a Winter Tomato Sauce (page 101).

In a mixing glass, combine 4 ounces/120 milliliters of the tomato juice with the vodka, Worcestershire sauce, horseradish, lemon and lime juices, and Tabasco. Pour over ice into a tall glass, sprinkle with celery salt, and garnish with a lime wedge.

Note: To make your own prepared horseradish: Grate a horseradish root and ferment it in a 5% brine, as with the pickled vegetables (page 296). Once it's pickled thoroughly, puree it in a food processor and store it in the pickling liquid, adding a little fresh water if it's too salty. Store it in the refrigerator for 3 to 6 months (or longer; obviously, discard it if it develops mold).

CHAPTER 4

Steak Frites

Whenever I am asked the Last Meal question, which chefs like to discuss and debate among themselves (there's even a fun portrait book about it called *My Last Supper*), I have my own unvarying response. And as it is for most chefs, that meal is a simple and familiar one. Not thousand-dollar-a-pound-Kobe-beef or otoro tuna heaped with the finest caviar (though I once had both at Masa in New York City and they were pretty stunning). Chefs can get that kind of stuff because of the nature of their work. Chefs want the simplicity and deep emotional connection not always available in their uncommonly busy days. Cooking accessible food is how they connect to life and to the past. They often want food from the mother or grandmother in their life (sometimes, but rarely, the father or grandfather, I've noticed). I too want simple and familiar.

My answer to the question over the years, and the reason for it, hasn't changed: Since the only thing we *can't* know is when, as Brendan Gill put it, "the inescapable catastrophe of death" will strike, I want to be able to have my Last Meal as many times throughout my life as possible. And so, mine begins with a dozen oysters from Duxbury, Massachusetts, along with a dry, sparkling Schramsberg blanc de blancs. A bottle of it, shared with my family. This would be followed by the bistro classic, steak frites: a flat iron steak—a rich but chewy cut of beef—sautéed until medium-rare and topped with butter and shallots, served with crispy fries and a big fat California zinfandel from nearby Sterling Vineyards, and plenty of it. If it's not literally my last meal, I will add an arugula or watercress salad for balance, acidity, pepperiness, and fiber, dressed with lemon juice and Greek extra-virgin olive oil. And to conclude: Blanton's bourbon, one large ice cube, and a chunk of the darkest Mast Brothers chocolate.

So, when I thought about the meals for this book, I knew steak frites had to be among them. And of course, I'd relish the lessons and variations that come along with the meal—the finer points of sautéing, making compound butter and a quick pan sauce for steak au poivre, plus other quick sautés and sauces. There are different ways to make French fries depending on your circumstances—parcooking them so they can be finished while the steak rests, for instance. And then simple, acidic salads that balance rich dishes.

You can go all out for a great steak frites, but it can also be a last-minute meal. The father of one of my best friends once looked me dead in the eye and said, "Tell me a great meal I can make in 15 minutes." He said it aggressively, as if there weren't such a thing. My response to Mr. Loomis was, "Steak and salad." What could be simpler or more delicious? Cook the steak for 6 minutes while you make the salad. Let the steak rest while you set the table. An 11-minute meal, in fact. Rather than make a compound butter, I'd just smear some soft butter on top. If I had time to mince a shallot, I'd throw that into the pan toward the end of the cooking. Squeeze some lemon and drizzle extra-virgin olive oil over arugula or watercress. If it's summertime, put some fresh ripe tomatoes, salted in advance, on the side.

Steak frites, in the end, demonstrates how simple a great meal can be—even the Last Meal before the great unknown. Because for me that dish would be an occasion to look back not only at all the steak frites I'd had throughout my life, but all the selves I'd been when I had those meals, and then, with bourbon and some chocolate to sweeten the way, I could prepare to sail off triumphantly into the hereafter, happy.

If I could choose my last meal it would be Steak Frites, (129) one of the simplest meals and most delicious. It also packs all kinds of lessons, such as the power of the COMPOUND BUTTER (132) flavored with parsley and lemon or chipotle and lime — and always some minced shallot, THE PRINCE of the ONIONS (139)

Of course you need the frites to go with that steak, and these FRENCH FRIES (134) can be cooked a number of different ways.

swap out that butter for a STEAK au POIVRE (138) or a STEAK WITH SAUCE BORDELAISE (140) simple pan sauces (serve some roasted BONE MARROW, 141, with your steak — it's fabulous).

I begin with butter, cream, and wine sauces; we also have to discuss stock-based sauces for which you need... stock. Just as I've simplified chicken stock, I've simplified BEEF STOCK (142) into a concoction that takes just 1 hour, rather than 4 to 8 hours. But not everything can be simple → →

for restaurant-caliber sauces, begin with CLASSIC BROWN VEAL STOCK (146).

You've got to roast the bones, but you can leave it in the oven overnight, just like the CHICKEN STOCK (chapter 1, 38) OR make a ONE-HOUR BEEF STOCK (142) on the stovetop for amazing PHO BO (144) or even a cocktail, THE BULL SHOT (149)

or, using pho treatment, a THAI BULLSHOT (149) and make the most out of your veal bones by learning to make a REMOUILLAGE (148)

Steak benefits from simple sides— in summertime, simply sliced tomatoes, salted (150), or some greenery, here salad, and can be as simple as ARUGULA SALAD (150) with lemon and olive oil, a CLASSIC CAESAR (151) one of the world's greatest salads (make your own crontons!), but you should also have the COMPOSED SALAD (152) in your arsenal, here exemplified by one comprising GREEN BEANS, POTATO, CORN, FENNEL, and RADISH, with a Balsamic Vinaigrette. (152)

WHAT CUTS OF MEAT
CAN BE USED FOR STEAK FRITES?

Steak frites is said to have been invented in Belgium, but how anyone can claim to have invented steak with fried potatoes escapes me. What is likely true is that whatever bistros served it, they were not using expensive tender cuts, such as filet mignon or a strip steak (though the latter would be perfectly fine here). A thrifty bistro would have used an inexpensive cut from the sirloin, the rump, or even a slice of top round. Today we have a range of cuts available to us, and they're often called by different names depending on the butcher. The flat iron has become the traditional cut for a classic bistro-style steak frites because, while chewy, it's got a rich, almost minerally flavor. This cut comes from the shoulder of the cow, sitting on the shoulder blade in a larger collection of muscles called a blade roast, top blade roast, or sometimes Spencer roast. The flat iron is right in the middle of it, divided by a layer of gristle. If your butcher doesn't offer the flat iron, you can usually ask them to cut it for you (if they don't know, tell them it's that muscle in the middle of the blade roast; if that doesn't help, find a new butcher).

A hanger steak is especially rich and delicious to prepare for steak frites. But you can use many kinds of cuts—top sirloin, a blade steak, or what's sometimes called a petite filet. The only cut I would not use is a ribeye, which is more fatty and rich and delicious. Many restaurants use the ribeye, but it seems contrary to the ethos of the dish; ribeye is best grilled in my opinion and is so succulent and fatty it doesn't need a sauce.

And of course, if it's summer, go ahead and grill that steak. It will still be a great classic steak frites.

CLASSIC BISTRO STEAK FRITES   SERVES 2

Here it is, in all its simplicity: the perfect Last Meal steak frites, for two (though it could be doubled or tripled depending on your kitchen and equipment). The recipe includes a traditional compound butter for the steak (but this is happily and infinitely variable) and builds in the frites and arugula salad as well, so it's all one recipe. It cuts not one corner, but I'll offer notes on simplifying it for when you have only a half hour, or only 11 minutes.

2 (6-ounce/170-gram) flat iron steaks (*¾ inch/2 centimeters thick*)

Kosher salt *to taste*

1 tablespoon minced shallot

1 tablespoon lemon juice (*about ½ lemon*), *plus ¼ lemon for the salad*

8 tablespoons/ 115 grams unsalted butter, *at room temperature*

1 tablespoon minced fresh tarragon

1 tablespoon minced fresh parsley

1 quart/1 liter vegetable oil, *for deep-frying, plus more for sautéing*

2 russet potatoes, *peeled and held in water to prevent browning*

Freshly ground black pepper *to taste*

2 handfuls fresh, tender arugula

Extra-virgin olive oil, *as needed*

Fine sea salt *to taste*

At least 3 or even 6 hours before you intend to cook the steaks, generously season them on both sides with kosher salt. Put them on a paper towel–lined plate, cover them with plastic wrap, and leave at room temperature until you're ready to cook them.

To make the herb butter, in a small mixing bowl, combine the shallot and lemon juice and add a pinch of kosher salt. Let the shallot macerate for 10 to 15 minutes.

Add 6 tablespoons/90 grams of the butter. Mash it into the shallot with a fork, then add the tarragon and parsley. Using a stiff rubber spatula, mix it all together till the ingredients are uniformly combined and the butter is soft and creamy. (For a restaurant-style presentation,

spread a 12-inch/30-centimeter sheet of plastic wrap on your counter. It helps to sprinkle the counter with water to hold the plastic wrap flat. Spatula the butter into the center of the plastic wrap. Fold the top of the plastic wrap over the butter and press your hand into the base of the butter to begin creating a log shape. Holding the plastic wrap at either end of the butter, roll the butter toward you, using enough tension to force the butter into a tight log about 5 inches/13 centimeters long. Twist and tie both ends and lower the butter into an ice bath to chill it and preserve its shape. Remove it from the ice bath before cooking the steaks so that it softens; you don't want to put freezing-cold butter on your hot steaks.)

Heat the vegetable oil in a large pot or Dutch oven until it reaches 275°F/135°C on a deep-fry thermometer. Meanwhile, cut the potatoes into ¼- to ⅜-inch/6- to 9-millimeter fries. (If you want them perfectly uniform, use large potatoes and square off all six sides so that they are perfectly rectangular, then cut the fries from this block. If you are super type-A, use a ruler and Sharpie to draw a 3-inch/8-centimeter line on your cutting board, marked at ¼-inch/6-millimeter intervals as a guide, and pay attention to the angle of your knife. Most people have a left or right slant to their grip, so be aware of this so that you slice straight down. Take your time. Make them as uniform as possible. This is most easily accomplished if your knife is sharp. Make your first slice. Feel the sliced side. If it is rough, your knife is dull; if it's smooth you're working with a good knife.) The fries can be cut as much as a day ahead of time; store them in a bowl of water in the fridge. Some chefs even think this results in better fries as exterior starch granules fall off.

When the oil has come to temperature, add the fries. (If you've soaked them, spread them out on a towel to dry first; excess water can cool down the oil too much). Cook the fries until tender, 10 to 15 minutes or so, depending on your pot and the oil. They should remain pale. Carefully spread them out on a baking sheet lined with paper towels. These can be refrigerated or even frozen if you'd like to parcook them in advance.

Raise the temperature of the oil to 350°F/175°C (if there are a lot of potato fragments remaining in the oil, consider straining the oil so that the fragments don't burn, then return the oil to the pot).

While the oil for the fries comes up to temperature, uncover the steaks and give each side several grinds of black pepper. Put a heavy skillet over high heat and let it sit for 3 to 5 minutes. If you have a grill pan, this is an even better choice. Not only do you get appealing grill marks, but the smoking fat rising from the grooves lightly smokes the meat for an actual grill flavor. When the pan is smoking-hot, add enough vegetable oil to coat the bottom of the pan. If you're using a grill pan, just wipe the ridges with a couple of oil-soaked paper towels. When the oil is hot, lay the steaks in, pressing them down hard with a spatula (especially if using a grill pan). Then leave them alone. Don't touch them or check to see if they're sticking; they'll release from the pan when they're browned.

Once the steaks are in, return your potatoes to the Dutch oven to finish their cooking, 3 to 5 minutes, until golden brown.

Cook the steaks for 2 to 3 minutes. Turn them over, add the remaining 2 tablespoons/30 grams butter, and continue cooking for another 3 minutes, basting them occasionally with the butter. Push a finger into the steaks. They should give some and not offer much resistance for medium-rare (125°F/52°C if you want to use an instant-read thermometer). If they're very squishy, they're still rare (in which case, if you like rare, they're done). When they are done to your liking, transfer them to a plate, where they will finish cooking as you complete the meal.

Put the arugula in a bowl. Drizzle it with olive oil. Squeeze the lemon quarter over it and toss. Gently season with fine sea salt. Taste to see if it needs more seasoning or oil. You can plate the salad now.

Stir the potatoes. When they are gorgeous and tantalizingly browned, use a skimmer to transfer them to a wide bowl lined with paper towels. Shake them in the bowl while seasoning them with kosher salt; this helps shake off excess oil and coat them evenly with the salt.

Put some fries on each plate. Add the steaks, topping them with a couple of tablespoons of the herb butter. (Save any leftover butter to toss with hot green vegetables or use it as a sandwich spread.)

SEASONING AND SAUTÉING MEAT

It's difficult to do a good job sautéing a boneless cut of meat—whether it's beef, chicken, pork, or fish—when it's just been pulled from the fridge. That's because dense protein is slow to change temperature. Likewise, when it's hot out of the pan or oven, it stays hot longer than you would intuit. A roasted chicken will stay hot inside for a half hour or more. A thick steak will stay hot for a good 10 minutes as it rests, and rest it should. Alain Ducasse, the Michelin-starred chef, said his rule is that meat should rest for as long as it took to cook, which is a good general rule (it doesn't hold for a huge cut, such as standing rib roast, though that should rest 30 to 45 minutes).

So plan ahead (*always* plan ahead) by pulling the meat from the fridge, giving it plenty of time to temper. Once you salt it, it's better to err on the side of leaving it out for too long. If it's not too hot in your kitchen, you can leave fresh, clean, salted meat covered at room temperature for 10 to even 12 hours without worry. That might be pushing it for most people's comfort zone, but certainly 3 to 6 hours at normal room temperature is fine. (If your kitchen is brutally hot, you'll want to adjust that accordingly.)

It's a great practice to salt your meat as soon as you bring it home from the store, wrap it, and refrigerate it until you want to cook it one, two, even three days later. Salt reduces spoilage bacteria on the surface of the meat and penetrates it to season the meat throughout. If you wait and salt the meat moments before cooking it, half the salt can wind up in the pan. So, you can't salt meat too early, but you can salt it too late (an exception is if you want a crust of salt on the exterior—this is how I like chicken and why I salt it just before cooking). And of course you can oversalt meat—this is a matter of learning. Use the same kind of kosher salt every time, pay attention, and learn the optimal amount of salt for your tastes.

Once your steak is salted and brought to the right temperature, then you can add black pepper or cayenne or any other seasoning you like.

Then, for boneless or minimally boned cuts of tender meat, you want to put it into a pan that's already blazing hot to get the complex flavors of browning. First get the pan hot, then add oil and let that get hot, then add your room-temperature meat. If you put a cold piece of meat into a hot pan, when it's perfectly cooked on the outside it can still be cold in the middle.

COMPOUND BUTTER

"Butter, butter, butter. Give me butter." So said the icon of contemporary French cuisine, Fernand Point of the landmark restaurant La Pyramide.

Butter is one of the great ubiquitous ingredients available to all cooks. We now have all kinds of high-end butter at the grocery store. If you like them, use them. I buy what's least expensive for daily cooking. Butter can become stale and even rancid if it sits too long in the fridge; freeze it if you won't be using it within a couple of weeks or so.

If you have a good dairy near you, buy their cream and try making your own butter (see page 67) to see what super-fresh butter really tastes like.

Butter smooths and enriches every sauce. Chef Jean-Georges Vongerichten uses butter to meld equal parts soy sauce and lime to create a wondrous *à la minute* sauce for fish or chicken. And of course, butter is a finished sauce all on its own. Serve a roasted chicken breast and butter it: transformative. My beloved father routinely buttered his steaks.

The compound butter takes this idea a step further by incorporating seasonings and aromatics that, when they melt on hot meat, enhance that meat in beautiful ways as you eat it.

The traditional compound butter is called maître d' butter, likely because it was a standard finishing sauce in French restaurants. It is traditionally butter mixed with lemon juice, minced parsley, salt, and pepper. But it can include anything you think will taste great. Shallot, macerated in citrus to remove its harshness, is always a great aromatic addition to compound butters. Tarragon is my favorite herb and goes great with beef, fish, and chicken. You could even make a bacon compound butter for pork chops. Flavored butters are limited only by your imagination. Make a curried butter for chicken, or a garlic and mint butter for lamb chops. And you can use them on anything—toss hot cooked vegetables with them, or use them as a sandwich spread. You could even do a sweet version with sugar and cinnamon for pancakes and French toast. It's limitless.

My favorite butter for steak frites is essentially maître d' butter that has plenty of tarragon. But my favorite butter for grilled steaks, such as a fat strip steak, is a chipotle-lime butter, which follows the same rules for all compound butters—an aromatic (shallot, garlic, ginger, onion, chiles—use your imagination!), acid, and minced herbs.

CHIPOTLE-LIME BUTTER
MAKES 4 SERVINGS

- 1 tablespoon minced shallot

- 1 tablespoon lime juice

- Kosher salt

- 8 tablespoons/115 grams unsalted butter, *at room temperature*

- 2 chipotles in adobo sauce, *seeded and minced*

- 1 tablespoon minced fresh cilantro

In a small bowl, combine the shallot, lime juice, and a pinch of salt and let sit for 10 minutes. Add the butter and mash it into the shallot with a fork. Add the chipotles and mix with a rubber spatula, then add the cilantro and continue mixing until everything is uniformly combined. It's ready to serve, or you can roll it in plastic wrap into a tight cylinder and chill it in an ice bath, then refrigerate it till you are ready to use it.

HOW TO COOK A FRENCH FRY: THREE TECHNIQUES FOR THREE DIFFERENT SITUATIONS

How much discussion French fries stir up! They are a nationally beloved dish, and yet half the fries served at restaurants . . . well, to be blunt . . . suck. They're soggy and flavorless. I love a restaurant that cares about its fries. McDonald's arguably became the success it is because of its fries, which were a staple of my 1970s youth. In-N-Out Burger, by contrast, makes far superior burgers, but their fries . . . well, to be blunt . . . The fries at Thomas Keller's bistro Bouchon, a restaurant with which I've worked, became so popular they were forced to either employ a single person to cut fries all day or find a quality brand of frozen fries—and they did the latter. The truth is, frozen fries can be excellent. Tony Bourdain thought this was nonsense. Then, having dinner at Bouchon Las Vegas, he was served the fries and had to admit they were excellent—but the revelation so upset him he knocked over a glass of wine, apparently in anger. (Watch it on his *No Reservations* Vegas episode!) Theoretically, this means that you can buy frozen fries from the grocery store and deep-fry them and they'll be pretty good. But in practice, I find most of the commercial ones at the grocery store are ultimately lacking in flavor, so I recommend taking the time to seek out a high-quality brand.

I think we can all agree that the qualities that make a French fry delicious are these: delicately but definitively crisp and beautifully browned on the outside, fluffy and hot inside, gently salted, with a rich, fresh, clean potato flavor. Starting with the latter first: You need a good-quality potato, a fresh russet you cut yourself, or high-quality frozen russet fries, and a good neutral oil. The best salt to use is a fine sea salt, which will cling more uniformly than heavy grains of coarse kosher salt (Diamond Crystal is just fine and light enough; I find Morton's too heavy for fries).

Now, the two biggies: crispy outside, fluffy inside. There is no reason you can't cut a potato into fries, dunk them in hot oil until they're the color you want, then salt and serve them straight away. That's how my grandma made them and they were delicious. But they weren't all that crisp. The advantage of buying, say, Ore-Ida shoestring fries, besides convenience, is that they are uniformly cut. This is important, as uniformly cut fries cook uniformly. If they're cut haphazardly, in most cases a third will be undercooked and a third overcooked. But again, I find the flavor of most frozen fries insipid, so if you do cook them, serve them with an aioli or a strong sauce. (I like ketchup as a utility ingredient in other sauces or in combination with other sauces, but I don't care for ketchup on French fries—though who can denigrate such a deeply American pairing? I do urge you to introduce your kids to the French custom of using mayo or aioli as a dipping sauce for fries.)

As far as I can tell, no one has covered the subject of achieving French fry perfection more thoroughly and accurately than Kenji López-Alt in his book *The Food Lab*, and I am in complete agreement with him. If you are curious about the finer points and all the variations he made to test French fries, I urge you to read his book. I believe there are three best ways of achieving French fry perfection at home. These depend on my circumstances, which are (in order from least ideal to most): (1) I don't have a ton of time but I need to get fries on the table 45 minutes from now; (2) I've got some time but not a full day; (3) I'm planning ahead and have time to parcook my fries 6 hours or more before I want to finish them.

To Peel or Not?

I don't care. I prefer peeled, because they're more refined. But I like skin-on as well, and if I'm shy on potatoes, I definitely don't peel so I can take advantage of using every scrap I do have. If you want perfect fries and are going all out, buy the biggest russets you can find and don't peel them; just square them off into perfect rectangles (save the trimmings in cold water in the fridge and use for roasted potatoes or chop them and add to roasted root vegetables).

Oil

Use a neutral vegetable oil, and plenty of it: You'll need about 3 quarts/3 liters to fill a 7-quart/6.6-liter Dutch oven about halfway. If money is no object, the best oil for deep-frying is peanut oil, for its high smoke point and flavor. I find that peanut oil is not just a little better but considerably better, resulting in a crisper, cleaner fry. So, on those occasions when I want to pull out all the stops, I splurge on peanut oil, although it can be twice as expensive as vegetable oil.

Freshly cut fries, especially if they've come out of a water bath, can cause hot oil to bubble furiously. If you have too much oil in your pot, it can boil over as the water vaporizes and make a serious mess on your stove. So, dry your potatoes as well as possible. If you're concerned, add damp fries slowly to avoid the mess.

Also, don't crowd your pot. Too many fries will cool the oil and they won't cook well. The higher the oil-to-fry ratio, the better.

CAN YOU REUSE OIL?

YES!

In writing his book *How to Read a French Fry*, the writer Russ Parsons discovered that oil that has previously been used to cook something else in it actually cooks the potatoes better. Cooking food in oil breaks down the oil (which is why you can't use it indefinitely). One of the breakdown components is a surfactant, Russ explains, that lowers the surface tension between the oil and the vapor (water) bubbling out of the fry. If there are too many bubbles, the surface tension is such that the oil has a hard time contacting the potato itself and browning it. This is why you may notice that if you save a batch of oil (as you should) and use it for the next batch, the second batch browns even better.

But I was reusing deep-fry oil even before I knew about Russ's discovery. Because I try to save money whenever possible, I always strain and save oil I've fried potatoes in. You should be able to make three, four, or even five batches of fries from the same oil, especially if you supplement it with fresh. Eventually the oil will break down to the point that it tastes bad and saturates the food you're cooking. And always try to discard your oil in containers—don't pour oil down the drain, as it can clog the outgoing pipes of your plumbing system.

FRENCH FRY SITUATION 1

*You have very little time,
45 minutes or so.*

In this scenario, you start the potatoes in cold oil. This method is perfectly fine and can give you crisp, fluffy fries. The drawback here is that they cook a little less evenly than the other versions, and they tend to stick to the bottom of the pot.

Cut your fries as desired, ideally into ¼-inch/6-millimeter matchsticks. (If you have a Japanese mandoline, such as a Benriner, use it. I encourage you to make the small investment in this invaluable tool, especially if you make fries often. Cut the potatoes on the thickest setting, which is about ¼ inch/6 millimeters. Grip the potato with a sturdy towel so you don't worry about turning your thumb into a fry, then stack half of the slices and cut the fries that same width. Then do the other stack. I reserve the oddly shaped edges for mashed or scalloped potatoes.)

Fill a large Dutch oven halfway with vegetable oil; you'll need 2 to 3 quarts/2 to 3 liters. Add the fries and put the pot over high heat. Stir the fries regularly as the oil heats to keep them from sticking to the bottom. Once it's hot and bubbling, let the fries cook until they're golden brown, stirring frequently so they don't stick to the bottom. The moisture leaving the potatoes will keep the oil temperature low for most of the cooking. As soon as the temperature begins to rise above 250°F/121°C, they cook very quickly. It will take about 40 minutes total, from the time you put them in the oil until they're nice and crisp.

Use a skimmer to transfer the fries to a wide bowl lined with paper towels. Shake them in the bowl while seasoning them with kosher salt. Serve immediately.

FRENCH FRY SITUATION 2

*You've got some time
but not hours and hours.*

I most often find myself in this situation when I decide to cook fries. This calls for the blanch first, finish later method, the method used by just about every restaurant serving fresh-cut fries. It results in the most even cooking and uniformly crispy exterior. When I was on the grill station at the American Bounty restaurant at the Culinary Institute of America, this was how I cooked the fries we served with grilled steak. It works, and it has the great advantage of giving you flexibility in the kitchen. You can blanch the fries up to 3 hours ahead of time. Then, when you're ready for them, just cook them in hot oil. They'll be brown and perfect in 5 to 10 minutes.

Cut your fries as described in Situation 1 and hold them in cold water.

Heat your oil over high heat until it reaches 275°F/135°C on a deep-fry thermometer. Pat the fries dry with towels and add them to the hot oil. The temperature will drop considerably, so keep the flame on high. After 3 to 5 minutes, they should be completely tender and completely pale, though they may have the minutely bubbled beginnings of a crust (usually about the time the oil has returned to a temperature of 250°F/121°C or 275°F/135°C). The point is that they should be completely tender but not browned. Carefully remove them with a skimmer (they're very delicate, so try not to break them). Spread them out on a rimmed baking sheet lined with paper towels. Set aside at room temperature for up to 3 hours.

When you're ready to finish them, heat the same pot of oil to 425°F/218°C. Add the room-temperature blanched fries. Cook them until they're golden brown, 5 minutes or so depending on your pot, how much oil you have, how long you blanched them for, and how many fries are going into that oil.

Use a skimmer to transfer the fries to a wide bowl lined with paper towels. Shake them in the bowl while seasoning them with kosher salt. Serve immediately.

FRENCH FRY SITUATION 3

*You've planned ahead
and have hours, if not days . . .*

. . . before you want to serve perfect homemade French fries.

This method results in the best fries of the three. It's the same as Situation 2, except that you freeze the fries after blanching them. Freezing alters the cell structure, resulting in an especially crispy fry. The only other difference is that you're adding frozen stuff to hot oil, dropping the oil temperature precipitously. So, start the oil hot, 450°F/230°C, and monitor from there after the iced potatoes are added.

Cut and blanch the fries as described in Situation 2.

After you've drained the fries on paper towels, transfer them to another rimmed baking sheet, this one lined with parchment or waxed paper. Put the baking sheet in the freezer. If you plan to cook them within 24 hours, there's no need to cover them. If you would like to cook them a day or a week or 3 weeks later, transfer the frozen fries to a zip-top plastic bag.

To finish them, bring your oil to 450°F/230°C over high heat. Add the frozen fries, stirring well as you do. Keep the flame on high; it won't likely return to 425°F/218°C before the fries are beautifully browned and cooked. They should finish in about 10 minutes from frozen.

Use a skimmer to transfer the fries to a wide bowl lined with paper towels. Shake them in the bowl while seasoning them with kosher salt. Serve immediately.

STEAK AU POIVRE   SERVES 4

Variations   Steak au poivre is traditionally made with filet mignon, but because the cut has little taste of its own and is also one of the most expensive cuts, I recommend using a good strip steak for this recipe, which features a cream-based sauce flavored with cognac and plenty of black pepper. I'm suggesting using two large strip steaks, halved, to serve four. But feel free to go traditional with a 4- to 6-ounce/110- to 170-gram filet mignon, cut from the tenderloin. (This recipe works great with chicken breast as well, if that's your thing.)

This is best with fresh whole black peppercorns, toasted and then coarsely ground in a mortar. If you don't have a mortar and pestle, crack the toasted corns beneath a heavy sauté pan, then finish chopping them by hand. Of course, you can just shake pepper out of a McCormick tin—but if you do, it's worth purchasing a fresh can.

For a little added flair, add a couple of tablespoons of brined green peppercorns to the sauce as the cream is reducing. Or, if you want to switch it up a little, add a teaspoon of Szechuan peppercorns to the black pepper.

2 (12-ounce/340-gram) strip steaks (1 to 1¼ inches/2.5 to 3 centimeters thick), *trimmed of excess fat and gristle, then halved crosswise to make four steaks*

Kosher salt *to taste*

2 tablespoons whole black peppercorns

2 tablespoons vegetable oil

2 tablespoons/ 30 grams unsalted butter

2 large shallots, *finely minced (about ⅓ cup/80 milliliters)*

½ cup/120 milliliters cognac

1 cup/240 milliliters heavy cream

1 bunch thyme

Remove the steaks from the refrigerator and give them a nice coating of salt on all sides. Cover with plastic wrap and let sit at room temperature for 4 to 10 hours. (If you forget to do this, it's not the end of the world. But do try to leave the steaks out for at least an hour before cooking them.)

Heat your oven to 200°F/93°C, then turn it off.

Put the peppercorns in a large skillet (cast iron is best) over high heat. Swirl them around to heat them. When you can smell them, after about a minute, transfer them to a mortar and grind them with the pestle until they're coarse. (Or put them on a cutting board, crack them with a heavy sauté pan, and chop them with a knife until they're coarse.) Press them into both sides of the steaks. (Save any pepper that doesn't adhere to the meat to put into the sauce.)

In the same skillet, heat the oil over high heat. When it's smoking hot, add the steaks. Press down hard to give them a good sear and to press the pepper into the meat. Turn them after 3 to 4 minutes or as you wish (depends how thick they are, the heat of your pan, how you like your steak). Add the butter and continue cooking, basting the steaks occasionally. When they're medium-rare

(125°F/52°C if you want to use an instant-read thermometer) or offer only mild resistance to an index finger pressed into the meat, transfer them to a plate and put them in the warm oven.

Add the shallots to the pan and cook them over medium-high heat till tender, a minute or so. Add any leftover pepper on the plate to the sauce. Add the cognac. If you want, you can ignite the cognac for fun (but it's not necessary). Cook until the cognac is reduced to a few tablespoons. Add the cream and 3 or 4 thyme sprigs and reduce the sauce by half.

Remove the thyme sprigs. Serve the steaks, spooning the sauce over them. Garnish each plate with 2 fresh thyme sprigs.

Variations

THE PRINCE OF THE ONIONS

I've written a lot about shallots, because the onion generally is one of the great underappreciated workhorses of the kitchen, and the shallot is the most powerful onion in the whole family in terms of its varying uses. There are now so many onions available in grocery stores. So-called sweet onions, such as Vidalia, have fewer sulfurish and acidic compounds, so they aren't as harsh when raw as regular Spanish, yellow, white, and red onions. Shallots are also quite sharp when raw. But once you cook them, all onions are pretty much the same because cooking eliminates those volatile compounds. So, the rule for me is that if I'm cooking an onion, I buy the biggest (fewer to peel) and the cheapest onion available. Sometimes the big sweet onions are less expensive than the small yellows. If you do want to use sweet or red onion raw, it's a good idea to salt it ahead of time and also give it a soak in water to reduce the harsher effects.

Shallots make any sauce better, especially if the base of your sauce is neutral, as with a cream sauce. I use shallots almost exclusively for sauces, though they're terrific roasted and served whole, and they make killer onion rings just dipped in flour and fried. I don't know what it is about them, but they seem to make everything better.

Sauté a cup of minced shallot until browned and smear it on a steak—that alone is a great sauce. When using shallots raw, always macerate them in acid. For instance, avocado becomes an amazing guacamole when mixed with shallot macerated in lime juice.

When buying shallots, look for the biggest ones you can find; they should be firm and the skin tight around the bulb.

What can I say? I love shallots.

STEAK WITH SAUCE BORDELAISE   SERVES 2

Variations

Everyone should know how to make a wine reduction sauce. This preparation also uses reduced beef stock, because I wanted to slip in my One-Hour Beef Stock method (page 142). Which of course required that I discuss bone broth (page 148), which has become such a fad there are whole retail stores devoted to it in my New York City neighborhood. Sauce bordelaise includes sautéed mushrooms, so it's great with any sautéed steak cut—strip, hanger, rib—and it's especially good with sautéed or grilled filet mignon, if you like this mild, very tender cut. If you want this to be a true bordelaise, use a cabernet sauvignon from Bordeaux, but any reasonably priced big cabernet or zinfandel will work. You're going to be using a cup—which will leave you a generous two-thirds of the bottle to share with whoever is helping you in the kitchen while you cook!

2 (6-ounce/170-gram) flat iron steaks (¾ inch/2 centimeters thick)

Kosher salt and freshly ground black pepper *to taste*

Vegetable oil, *as needed*

7 tablespoons/ 100 grams unsalted butter

¼ cup minced shallot (*about 1 large shallot*)

1 cup/70 grams medium-diced white button or cremini mushrooms

1 cup/240 milliliters cabernet sauvignon *or other big red wine*

2 cups/480 milliliters One-Hour Beef Stock (page 142)

1 or 2 dashes red wine vinegar

1 tablespoon minced fresh flat-leaf parsley or finely sliced fresh chives

At least 3 or even 6 hours before you intend to cook the steaks, generously season them on both sides with kosher salt. Put them on a paper towel–lined plate, cover them with plastic wrap, and leave at room temperature until you're ready to cook them.

Uncover the steaks and give each side several grinds of black pepper. Put a heavy skillet or grill pan over high heat and let it sit for 3 to 5 minutes. When the pan is smoking-hot, add enough vegetable oil to coat the bottom of the pan. (If you're using a grill pan, just wipe the ridges with a couple of oil-soaked paper towels.) When the oil is hot, lay the steaks in, pressing them down hard with a spatula. Then leave them alone. Don't touch them or check to see if they're sticking; they'll release from the pan when they're browned.

Cook the steaks for 2 to 3 minutes. Turn them over, add 2 tablespoons/30 grams of the butter, and continue cooking for another 3 minutes, basting them occasionally with butter. Push a finger into the steaks. They should not offer much resistance for medium-rare (125°F/52°C if you want to use an instant-read thermometer). When they are done to your liking, transfer them to a plate, where they will finish cooking as you make the sauce.

Melt 1 tablespoon of the butter in a medium saucepan over medium-high heat. Add the shallot and a pinch of salt and cook till tender, about a minute. Add the mushrooms and several grinds of black pepper and stir. Cook the mushrooms until they're tender and browned and the liquid has mostly cooked off, 3 to 5 minutes.

Add the wine and simmer until it has reduced to a wet syrup (not too thick), 5 to 7 minutes. Add the stock and bring to a simmer. When the stock has reduced by about half, 5 to 10 minutes, add the vinegar, then swirl or whisk in the remaining 4 tablespoons/60 grams butter until it's completely melted.

Serve the sauce over the steak, garnishing with the minced herbs.

Note: If you want to take this to the professional level, it's not that difficult. (Nothing in cooking is that difficult—some dishes just involve more steps than others.) So, if you want to up your dinner game for special friends or for that man or woman you'd eventually like to bed, here is how I would do it.

Instead of 2 cups/480 milliliters beef broth, use 1 cup/240 milliliters beef broth plus 1 cup/240 milliliters Classic Brown Veal Stock (page 146), which you've made ahead and kept frozen. Add sprigs of thyme along with the stock (but be sure to remove them before finishing the sauce). Instead of white button or cremini mushrooms, use chanterelles.

Variations

Steak bordelaise often includes a garnish of bone marrow, or poached bone marrow is added to the bordelaise sauce. This is an over-the-top garnish that is absolutely delicious. Find a butcher that will sell you four 2-inch/5-centimeter bones for marrow (often called pipe bones) so that whole pieces of marrow can be pushed out of the bone intact. Or simply use what you can find. It's best to soak the marrow for a day in salt water to draw out any blood. Then give them each a pinch of salt, toss them in flour and, while the sauce is kept warm and the steaks are resting, pan-fry them in vegetable oil until browned. Serve the steaks, sauce them, garnish with fresh herbs, and top with the marrow.

Alternatively, you can dice the marrow and add it to the sauce as you're whisking in the butter. (Traditionally, marrow is poached first, but I find you lose too much this way; better to cook it in the sauce.)

After that special dinner for two, offer a single-malt whiskey with a chunk of good chocolate, put on Miles Davis's *Kind of Blue,* and see what happens.

COOKING AND SERVING BONE MARROW

If you love bone marrow, here are two great ways to cook and serve it. The second-best bone marrow I've ever had was at the old Union Pacific under the talented Rocco DiSpirito. He seasoned big pieces, 2 or 3 inches/5 or 8 centimeters tall, with salt, pepper, and coriander and roasted them for 15 minutes in a 350°F/175°C oven. He served them with a little teaspoon and toasted baguette slices.

But the best marrow—and I mean the best by far—was created by Derek Clayton, aka Powder, former executive chef at Michael Symon's Lola in Cleveland, using marrow he'd removed from the bone in cylinders. Taking his cue, he said, from *The French Laundry Cookbook* (simply dusting boneless marrow with flour and sautéing it), he served delicately crispy, melty chunks of marrow with grilled bread—"grilling it is really important," he told me, for that charred flavor—and parsley, shallot, and lemon.

ONE-HOUR BEEF STOCK   MAKES ABOUT 2 QUARTS/2 LITERS

Generally, all meat stocks comprise three fundamental elements: meat, which gives the stock its flavor; bones, joints, and skin, which give the stock body in the form of gelatin; and aromatic flavors from vegetables, herbs, and spices. Stock takes time because water extracts and converts the collagen in the bones, joints, and skin very slowly. The most gelatin-rich stock, veal stock, takes many, many hours at a gentle temperature. Happily, this can be done in your oven while you sleep if you wish. So, veal stock is no more difficult than Easy Overnight Chicken Stock (page 38).

To speed up the process of making beef stock without diminishing its quality, it's simply a matter of adding gelatin that has already been extracted from bones and joints, in the form of powdered gelatin. Water will extract the flavor of ground meat and vegetables in about an hour, then you strain and add the gelatin. That's all there is to it.

Beef stock is a perfect base for soups. Reduced, it can become a traditional beef sauce. It's also an ideal poaching medium for beef, whether filet mignon (my favorite way to cook this cut; I wrote about it in *Ruhlman's Twenty* and serve it with a lemon-coriander vinaigrette). In the 1970s, my beloved mom was fond of the cocktail called a Bullshot, beef broth and vodka (page 149).

The quality of the gelatin is important. I'm not a fan of the most commonly available brand, Knox. To me it tastes too boney. Try melting some Knox gelatin in plain water and smell it—you'll see what I mean. My preferred brand is Great Lakes. But there are many good ones available, including non-GMO and hormone-free gelatins.

I'm not usually a fan of the super lean beef sold these days at grocery stores, but in this case, choose the leanest beef available. For the vegetables, remember that the finer you cut them, the faster the water will extract their flavor.

2 pounds/900 grams
lean ground beef

1 large Spanish
onion, diced
(*root and tip discarded,
brown papery skin
reserved*)

6 carrots, *cut into
thin disks*

3 celery ribs,
chopped

2 bay leaves

2 tablespoons
tomato paste

2 quarts/2 liters
water, *or as needed*

3 tablespoons
powdered gelatin

Combine the beef, onion, carrots, celery, bay leaves, and tomato paste in a large pot. Pour in the water; add more if it's not enough to cover everything. Bring the water to a simmer over high heat, breaking up the ground beef as you do. When it reaches a gentle simmer, reduce the heat to maintain that simmer. Cook for 1 hour, then strain it, discarding the solids.

Pour about 1 cup/240 milliliters of the stock into a wide, shallow bowl or pie plate—the more surface area you have, the easier it is to bloom the gelatin. (You can do this halfway through the cooking: Press a fine mesh strainer into the stock and ladle the reverse-strained stock into a bowl.) Allow it to cool to room temperature or put it in the refrigerator to cool. Sprinkle the gelatin slowly and evenly over the cooled stock to bloom it (soak up the liquid). When it has bloomed and no white or dry particles remain, microwave the bowl for 30 to 60 seconds to melt the gelatin. Add it to the stock. (Alternatively, you can simply put ¾ cup/180 milliliters cold tap water in a bowl, bloom and melt the gelatin as described above, and add it to your stock. This saves the step of cooling a cup of beef stock but dilutes the stock a bit.)

Taste the stock. If you'd like it to be stronger, simmer and reduce by as much as half.

Store in an airtight container in the fridge for up to 5 days or in the freezer for up to 3 months.

*Sauces,
Stocks, and
Broths*

PHO BO SERVES 4 TO 6

One morning not too long ago, I began thinking about pho, virtually the national dish of Vietnam. Typically, it is a beef soup with rice noodles and loads of aromatic garnishes. Such was the power of imagination that I determined to have it for dinner that night. Like most people, I don't have enough hours in the day to do everything I'd like to do, but as a self-employed writer I'm flexible in how I chose to organize those hours. So, when the urge for pho struck, I knew I could make a one-hour beef stock at lunchtime and have a complete traditional pho on the table at dinnertime.

For traditional pho, the cook simmers meaty beef bones to make a stock (seasoned with charred ginger, onion, and sweet spices), then slices off the tough meat and includes it in the finished soup. But by then, the flavor will have cooked out of the meat. Better to use an inexpensive cut raw, slice it thin, and barely cook it. Or even serve it raw in the bowl and ladle hot broth over it and the noodles.

The traditional flat linguine-like rice noodles used for pho will say "bánh pho" on the package. In the spirit of this book, I looked into making them from scratch but decided against it after consulting with my friend Andrea Nguyen, a Vietnamese food expert who tried it herself and said even she would not go to the trouble. (If you're curious, she does have a good video on her site of how they're made: vietworldkitchen.com.) They're typically soaked in hot water, like rice paper wrappers, but then they need to be quickly dunked, using a strainer, in the simmering stock.

The rest is garnish, of the heady aromatic kind: scallion, mint, basil, cilantro, culantro (thick, long, broad leaves that taste like cilantro; sometimes called thorny cilantro), bean sprouts (similarly dunked in the hot stock or quickly blanched), sliced Thai chiles, and Sriracha, that much-loved Southeast Asian–inspired hot sauce. The larger herbs are typically torn by hand, then added to the soup. Serve the pho with toasted baguette slices.

This is easily one of the best uses of quick beef stock I know. And if you have any pho left over, there is yet another use for this versatile broth (see the Thai Bullshot, page 149).

2 quarts/2 liters
One-Hour Beef
Stock (page 142)

1 medium onion,
*peeled if desired and
halved through its
equator*

1 (3-inch/8-centimeter)
piece ginger,
halved lengthwise

Vegetable oil, *as
needed*

2 cinnamon sticks

3 or 4 star anise

5 whole cloves

12 to 16 ounces/
340 to 450 grams
bánh pho *or rice
noodles of your choice*

1 cup/90 grams bean
sprouts

1 (1- to 1½-pound/
450- to 680-gram)
boneless eye round
or top loin, *thinly
sliced and seasoned
with salt, at room
temperature*

Raw garnishes,
to taste:

Fresh herb leaves: mint
and/or spearmint,
culantro and/or
cilantro, Thai basil

Scallions, *thinly sliced*

Lime juice

Fish sauce

Sriracha

In a large saucepan, bring the beef stock to a simmer. Meanwhile, rub the cut sides of the onion and ginger with a little oil and sear them in a dry sauté pan over high heat till they are charred, 3 to 5 minutes. Transfer them to the stock. Toast the cinnamon, star anise, and cloves in the same pan for a minute or so, until they're fragrant. Add these ingredients to the stock and gently simmer for about 45 minutes.

While the stock is simmering, put the noodles in a large bowl or saucepan and pour boiling water over them. Let them soak for 10 to 20 minutes, then strain them.

Scoop out the aromatics from the stock (or strain it). Cook the noodles and then the bean sprouts either in the stock (use a strainer) or separately. Stir the beef into the simmering stock, then serve the soup, beef, and noodles immediately, garnishing to your taste.

*Sauces,
Stocks, and
Broths*

CLASSIC BROWN VEAL STOCK MAKES ABOUT 2 QUARTS/2 LITERS

The most powerful stock in the kitchen is brown veal stock. It's the one thing you can make that will give you restaurant-caliber food at home. Include it in braises and stews, reduce it in sauces, and you will be amazed.

In the past, the finest restaurants all used brown veal stock, but that's not the case today. I know that Jean-Georges Vongerichten doesn't use it, even in his four-star eponymous restaurant. But he's Jean-Georges and has other tricks up his sleeve. Joe or Jane Cook, at home in the suburban heartland, well, if they sauté mushrooms (as on page 77), then toss in two or three frozen veal stock cubes, they will have a four-star sauce worthy of Jean-Georges in the time it takes to bring the liquid to a simmer. It's a marvel.

I've been told that my chili (pork shoulder, chuck roast, no beans, page 228) is "the best." In fact, the secret is not my concoction of seasonings, it's the veal stock. Try braising anything, even something as basic as beef stew—and it will be ten times better if you include veal stock than without it. If you like to cook and love great food, you must make brown veal stock at least once. And it's just as simple as Easy Overnight Chicken Stock (page 38); the single difference is that instead of roasting a chicken, you roast veal. The hardest part of making veal stock is usually finding the veal itself.

The best cut to use for this is a 5-pound/2.25-kilogram bone-in veal breast. (If you want to make a smaller batch, do that. Fill up a pot with whatever meat bones, carrots, and onions you have, cover with water, and that's really all you need.) Call around to your various meat departments and see who can get you one. Ask the butcher to cut it into 3-inch/8-centimeter chunks if you don't want to do it yourself (the bones and abundant cartilage, the rich source of gelation, are so soft you can cut through them with a cleaver).

You can skip the thyme if it's too expensive where you are. I love leeks in my stock (especially the green parts—I usually cut off the white ends and save them for another use; they're delicious sautéed in butter), but you can skip the leeks and double the onion.

1 (5-pound/
   2.25-kilogram)
   bone-in veal breast
   (*or a mix of jointy, meaty
   veal bones), cut into
   3-inch/8-centimeter
   chunks (bones and all*)

1 tablespoon whole
   black peppercorns

2 leeks, *halved
   lengthwise and cleaned,
   then cut crosswise into
   1-inch/2.5-centimeters
   pieces (save the tender
   ends for another use if
   you like*)

1 pound/450 grams
   carrots, *cut into
   1-inch/2.5-centimeter
   pieces*

1 pound/450 grams
   onion, *cut into large
   dice*

2 tablespoons tomato
   paste

5 to 10 thyme sprigs

3 bay leaves

4 quarts/4 liters
   water, *or as needed*

Preheat your oven to 425°F/218°C.

Spread out the veal chunks on a rimmed baking sheet and roast until they're dark golden brown and smell good enough to eat, 45 to 60 minutes. Remove from the oven and reduce the temperature to 200°F/93°C.

Meanwhile, put the peppercorns in a large skillet (cast iron is best) over high heat. Swirl them around to heat them. When you can smell them, after about a minute, transfer them to a mortar and grind them with the pestle until they're coarse. (Or put them on a cutting board, crack them with a heavy sauté pan, and chop them with a knife until they're coarse.)

Combine the roasted veal, leeks, carrots, onion, tomato paste, thyme, bay leaves, and toasted cracked pepper in a large pot. Pour in the water; add more if it's not enough to cover everything—better to err on the side of a little too much water as it can always be reduced. Bring the water to a simmer, then put the pot, uncovered, in the oven and cook for 8 to 10 hours.

Strain the stock through a fine-mesh strainer or cheesecloth. Consider reserving the bones for use a second time (see the sidebar on Remouillage). You may want to reduce your stock by a quarter or a third to make it more flavorful and easier to store. Store it in plastic containers or ice cube trays in the freezer for up to 3 months. Frozen cubes of veal stock are incredibly convenient to have on hand for adding to sauces and braises.

*Sauces,
Stocks, and
Broths*

REMOUILLAGE:
Do You Want Even More Veal Stock
Without Buying More Bones?

Because veal stock was so valuable in the classical French kitchen, chefs got as much out of bones as possible by creating what was called a *remouillage*, literally a "rewetting" of the bones. They basically made a second, weaker stock using the cooked veal bones and combined it with the first stock. When I have the time, I do it because it works. After you've made veal stock, cover the reserved bones with fresh cold water, bring to a simmer, and put it in a 200°F/93°C oven for another 8 to 10 hours. Strain, add it to your first veal stock and reduce by about a third or to your taste or needs.

BONE BROTH

For years now, "bone broth" has been a thing. Previously, "bone broth" was called "stock." Presumably some enterprising chef decided to call a rich stock "bone broth" and sell it as a protein-rich, steaming hot drink on a cold fall afternoon. In fact, stock made only from bones tastes boney—and that's not good. Bones give a stock body; meat and vegetables give it flavor. Happily, bone broth is delicious and nutritious (there's a great company called Brodo, started by chef Marco Canora, of Hearth in Manhattan, that makes it in bulk and sells it retail, which I highly recommend).

THE BULLSHOT SERVES 1

This old-school cocktail was a favorite of my mom's when she worked in Manhattan's garment district. It originated as a substitute for a Bloody Mary (in a Detroit hotel, if internet sources are to be believed— and as my mom is from Detroit, I'm going with it). I I'm guessing that it fell out of favor because people started making it with canned broth, which is nasty (even with vodka in it). For this muscular urban cocktail, you must make beef stock from scratch or buy good frozen bone broth if available.

I like this cocktail best served warm in a mug, but my mom would order it on the rocks—for this you basically need a double-strength consommé. To do that, you'll need to reduce the One-Hour Beef Stock (page 142) by half, then chill it.

4 ounces/120 milliliters strong beef broth	Dash Tabasco
	Ice
2 ounces/60 milliliters vodka	Celery salt
1 teaspoon lemon juice	Piment d'Espelette or cayenne
1 teaspoon Worcestershire sauce (*or to taste*)	Slim lemon wedge or celery stick, *for garnish*

To serve cold: Combine all the liquids in a mixing cup with a Hawthorne strainer. Add ice and stir till well chilled. Strain into a glass with fresh ice. Add a pinch each of celery salt and piment d'Espelette or cayenne. Taste and add more lemon, Worcestershire, or Tabasco to taste. Garnish with a lemon wedge or celery stick.

To serve warm: Combine all the liquids in a mug and heat in a microwave. Add a pinch each of celery salt and piment d'Espelette or cayenne. Taste and add more lemon, Worcestershire, or Tabasco to taste. Garnish with a lemon wedge or celery stick.

THE THAI BULLSHOT SERVES 1

Drinks

I had leftover pho when writing out the recipe for the Bullshot, so it wasn't a stretch to think to turn the leftover broth, strengthened by the beef and enhanced with sweet spices, into a warm cocktail. It's really good, especially with an extra squeeze of Sriracha.

4 ounces/120 milliliters strained broth from Pho Bo (page 144)	Sriracha
	Slim lime wedge, *for garnish*
2 ounces/60 milliliters vodka	

Combine the broth and vodka in a mug and heat in a microwave. Season with Sriracha to taste and garnish with a lime wedge.

A WAY TO THINK ABOUT SALAD

I tend to divide salads into two basic categories. There are simple salads, such as arugula with lemon juice—which is peppery and acidic and, I think, makes the perfect accompaniment to steak frites. And then there are composed salads, which include a variety of non-lettuce components. A Cobb salad is a classic composed salad, as is a salade niçoise. What follows are examples of a simple salad, a composed salad, and a classic Caesar, one of the all-time great salads.

ARUGULA SALAD
SERVES AS MANY AS YOU LIKE

If you have access to excellent arugula, that makes all the difference for this simple salad. Figure on one handful per person.

Arugula	Lemon juice
Extra-virgin olive oil	Parmigiano-Reggiano (*optional*)
Kosher salt and freshly cracked black pepper	

In a large bowl, drizzle the arugula lightly with oil, tossing it to coat. (This can be done up to a half hour before you wish to serve the salad.) Sprinkle the greens with salt. Squeeze lemon over the greens, being careful to catch any seeds. Taste the salad. Add more lemon or oil as needed. Crack fresh pepper over the greens and serve immediately, grating the cheese over each serving if you wish.

SUMMER TOMATOES

When local tomatoes are at their peak, they can serve as a dish in and of themselves (one of my favorite meals is a plate of corn on the cob with fat wedges of juicy, ripe tomatoes—the butter dripping from the cobs enriches the tomatoes and their juices). The tomato provides a great expression of salt; to see the power of salt, place two slices of tomato side by side. Give one piece a delicate sprinkle of salt and let it sit for 60 seconds. Taste the unsalted tomato, then taste the salted one, and you can appreciate the powerful effects of salt on our food. There are now many varieties of flavored and smoked salts, which are excellent on tomatoes.

Simply cut tomatoes as you wish—depending on size and shape, slices or wedges or halves. Salt them 5 to 10 minutes before serving them. Finish them with a drizzle of extra-virgin olive oil.

CLASSIC CAESAR SALAD
SERVES 4 TO 6

The best Caesar dressing I've ever had was at the Culinary Institute of America's Escoffier Room restaurant, made tableside by a young, confident woman a month from graduating. Lemon juice, minced anchovy (just enough to season the salad), minced garlic, all enriched with an egg yolk. That's the easy part. The critical point in the excellence of a Caesar salad is the quality of the romaine lettuce. Try to find the freshest, crispest romaine available. Use the hearts of romaine only, and make sure they are cold. And finally, the better the croutons, the better the Caesar. A salad with so few components requires that each of those components—greens, dressing, croutons—be excellent.

1 or 2 hearts of romaine (*you'll need about 5 medium pale green or yellowish leaves per person*)

½ teaspoon minced anchovy (*about 1 anchovy*)

1 teaspoon minced garlic

2 tablespoons lemon juice

Kosher salt and freshly cracked black pepper to taste

1 teaspoon Dijon mustard

2 large egg yolks

⅓ cup/80 milliliters vegetable oil

2 tablespoons extra-virgin olive oil

½ cup/40 grams freshly grated Parmigiano-Reggiano

2 cups/60 grams croutons, *store-bought or homemade (see sidebar)*

Wash the romaine leaves, shake off the excess water, and put them in a paper towel–lined bowl, uncovered, in the refrigerator.

In a large wooden bowl, combine the anchovy and garlic and mash it together with a fork. Pour the lemon juice over, add a pinch of salt, and let it sit for a minute or two. Add the Dijon and egg yolks and mix them in with the fork.

Combine the vegetable and olive oils in a measuring cup with a spout. Add one or two drops of oil to the bowl and mix that tiny bit in thoroughly. Then, whisking rapidly and continually with the fork, add the remaining oil in a thin, steady stream until you have a creamy dressing. Taste and adjust with more lemon or salt as you wish.

Tear the romaine leaves into large bite-size pieces and add them to the bowl. Toss to coat them with the dressing. Crack pepper generously over the salad. Sprinkle with the Parmigiano. Top with croutons and serve immediately.

HOW TO MAKE CROUTONS

Cut a loaf of French country bread into 1-inch/2.5-centimeter cubes (it's up to you if you want to remove the crust). Heat ½ cup olive oil in a large skillet over medium-high heat. Add 2 or 3 peeled, lightly smashed garlic cloves and swirl the oil around so the garlic cooks. When the garlic is bubbling, add 5 to 10 thyme sprigs, then the bread cubes. Cook the bread till all sides are golden brown, adding more olive oil if needed. Remove with a slotted spoon and drain on paper towels. The croutons can be stored in an airtight container but are best used the same day.

Salads

A COMPOSED SALAD: GREEN BEANS, POTATO, CORN, FENNEL, AND RADISH SERVES 4

Salads

This is the kind of salad that can makes a complete and satisfying meal, especially if you add a toasted baguette and butter. It's a great meal to serve on hot summer nights when you don't want to heat up the kitchen right before dinner (the beans, potatoes, and corn do need cooking, but they can be boiled, grilled, or roasted ahead of time). The potato and beans give it heft, the fennel and radish a peppery aromatic freshness, the corn sweetness. You can cut the fennel and radish by hand, but it's best to cut them uniformly on a Japanese mandoline. Leave the fennel fairly thick, about 1/4 inch/6 millimeters, so that it stays crisp and doesn't get lost among the greens.

Prepare this salad as presented once, then make any number of variations. Add sautéed mushrooms, sautéed or grilled onion, grilled radicchio, and/or hard-cooked egg; if you want to move it into Cobb salad territory, add bacon and julienned turkey breast.

8 ounces/225 grams green beans, *grilled, roasted, or blanched and shocked*

1 russet potato, *peeled if desired, diced, boiled, and cooled*

2 ears corn, *grilled or boiled and shocked*

1 cup/100 grams thinly sliced fennel

1/2 cup/50 grams thinly sliced radish

1 cup/15 grams watercress

2 cups/60 grams mixed greens

Balsamic Vinaigrette

Kosher salt and freshly ground black pepper *to taste*

Combine all the vegetables in a large bowl. Pour the vinaigrette over them and toss to coat. Season with salt. Taste and add more vinaigrette or salt as necessary. Season with freshly ground black pepper and serve.

BALSAMIC VINAIGRETTE MAKES ABOUT 1/2 CUP/120 MILLILITERS

Enhance this basic vinaigrette as you wish with fresh soft herbs (flat-leaf parsley, chive, tarragon) and/or minced shallot macerated in the red wine vinegar.

2 tablespoons red wine vinegar

1 tablespoon balsamic vinegar

1 tablespoon Dijon mustard

Kosher salt and freshly ground black pepper *to taste*

6 tablespoons/ 90 milliliters extra-virgin olive oil

Lemon juice

Combine the vinegars, mustard, salt, and pepper in a small bowl. Slowly whisk in the olive oil. Taste it and add more salt and/or pepper if needed. Whisk in a squeeze of lemon juice and serve.

CHAPTER 5

Paella

As the writer David Rosengarten put it in *Saveur* magazine, paella "exists because of rice." Other experts concur. Sarah Jay, former editor of *Fine Cooking* magazine and a self-taught paella expert who has devoted the past twenty years to selling proper pans and spreading paella gospel, says, "Paella is all about the rice." And the history of paella bears this out. Rice was brought to Spain by Arabs who had settled on the Iberian Peninsula and began to grow rice in the marshy fields on the eastern coast of Spain. This is important in terms of our agreeing on what "authentic" paella actually is, because, of course, as with cassoulet, much debate surrounds what constitutes a true paella and its exact technique.

It also gives me an opportunity to delve briefly into shellfish, as paella so often includes shellfish that we usually assume a paella will include shellfish. Yet, the very first recipes for paella did not include shellfish, but rather snails and rabbit—or, perhaps for a special occasion, chicken—as well as tomatoes and fresh pole beans. This is likely because paella (both the dish and the distinctive pan in which it's cooked) developed in inland Valencia, presumably around the rice fields there. As Jeff Koehler, a food writer and photographer expat living in eastern Spain, notes in his excellent book *La Paella*, paella "was born in the fields."

Traditionalists will insist that paella be cooked on a wood fire, a nod to its origins, when field workers cooked over olive tree branches. And the fact is, smoke adds fantastic flavor to this dish, which is why many contemporary recipes encourage cooking it over a charcoal fire, often suggesting the addition of rosemary branches to add smoke to the coals. In the absence of a cooking fire, you can simply add rosemary to the cooking liquid.

Many of the great ancient dishes that we still prepare and call classic originated as so-called "peasant" dishes, which is shorthand for dishes prepared simply, with inexpensive ingredients, and enjoyed by the majority of the people of a specific region. They are typically abundant in inexpensive starches (rice, legumes, pasta, bread), with small amounts of rarer or more expensive meats as well as the vegetables specific to that region and season. In this chapter, we focus on dishes and stews that originated because of rice, and the various offshoots that come from the idea of rice. I'm including here risotto (traveling from Spain across the Mediterranean to Italy), gumbo (from across the Atlantic in the American South), and pozole (from Mexico, which uses corn, another form of grain derived from a grass, just as rice is).

But to begin, a traditional paella.

Rice is one of the world's most important staples, and one of the great rice-based dishes is PAELLA (159), which, unlike so many dishes that use rice as an accompaniment, is _all_ about the rice. While there are meat and vegetable paellas (its likely origins were inland territories of Valencia, Spain), I love the seafood and shellfish paellas common along Valencia's coastal regions. Paella is a celebration, but if you want to enjoy rice and vegetables on a weeknight make this VEGETABLE PAELLA (163). It's all about the rice so it's worth ordering Bomba rice. A shellfish paella got me thinking about other great classic shellfish meals. MOULES FRITES (165) (mussels with fries, tying us back to steak frites thanks to the potatoes) is chief among them. If you can score great mussels, this is a simple and satisfying meal. The most time-consuming part is debearding the mussels, but after that, this dish takes minutes to finish once your fries are done. Switching bivalves and countries of origin (Brussels to New England, mussels to clams) I offer a great clam chowder — one of our country's great soups. I like to use the big quahog for the chowder, because they're inexpensive and have a great bite. I love them so much, in fact, I want to include a Rhode Island specialty called STUFFIES (169) — it's like spicy Thanksgiving dressing made with clams and served in the shell. Jumping from the rice in Spain to the rice of Italy, I offer three risottos, one for each part of the year: fall/winter, spring and summer, CLASSIC MUSHROOM RISOTTO (172), ASPARAGUS RISOTTO WITH LEMON ZEST (173) (make an asparagus puree with the bottom half of the stalks to stir into the rice), and CORN RISOTTO (175), which uses a fabulous corn stock from the cobs. I can't have a chapter on rice without including the utilitarian RICE PILAF (177), more of a method than a recipe, one that can be adapted to whatever meal it's accompanying. Then leaping down to the American southeast, I feature GUMBO (178), the multicultural stew of Louisiana. Customarily served over rice. And last, I move even farther south in the Americas to the corn of Mexico, another grass and one of the world's fundamental staples. Here as a POZOLE VERDE (180) inspired by Mexico City and Oaxaca.

CLASSIC PAELLA WITH SHELLFISH   SERVES 8 TO 10

When I used to cook for a rowdy bunch of sailors in Key West during race week there, one of them always asked me to make paella for dinner. He would bring a giant paella pan that I could use over a fire. I always had leftover lobster and all their legs and shells to make a shellfish stock with. And I'd include shrimp and mussels and chicken and sausage. This was not, of course, true paella, rather a mix of shellfish and meat with a medium-grain rice, but it was terrific, especially cooked over a smoky fire.

There's a lot of hot air blown over what a true paella is, as there always is over national dishes, this one from the Valencia region of eastern Spain. Some people insist that combining land animals (chicken) with seafood for a *paella mixta* is an abomination, maintaining that mixing the two muddies the flavor, a point I don't argue. I would have, in Key West, thrown in some chorizo for color and intensity had I thought to buy some. To that, traditionalists would reiterate what someone tweeted to me: "Don't call something with chorizo a paella." Indeed, when the British chef Jamie Oliver posted a recipe for paella with chicken and chorizo, he said he got actual death threats. "They went medieval on me," he told the *Independent*. (He didn't seem to be bothered by it—"It tastes better" seems to be his final opinion on the matter.)

And that is the bottom line: taste and the pleasure of it. Taste always wins in the end. But as someone rather fond of words and precision, I would have preferred he call it Arroz con Pollo y Chorizo. Or if he wanted to avoid the controversy, he could have called it a *cazuela*, casserole, which is actually the shape of the pan he used in the paella photograph accompanying the recipe. Because there's everything right in combining chicken and chorizo and rice.

The most sensible response to the "authentic" question comes from the aforementioned Sarah Jay, a writer, editor, and cook who fell in love with paella two decades ago. She told me, "An authentic paella is more about technique and equipment than what you put in it." She would say it must include medium-grain rice, saffron, and a sofrito, one of the key techniques in a paella, and it must be cooked in a shallow paella pan. (She is now the owner of paellapans.com.) She would also note, and I would underscore, that while other ingredients should be plentiful, rice should be the dominant ingredient. I've seen paella recipes that have so many ingredients beyond the rice that the rice is lost. Rice should be central, flavored and supported by the additional meat or seafood or vegetables.

The traditional rice for paella is the Spanish medium-grain rice bomba. It's very absorbent but retains a distinct bite. There really isn't a substitute, though I've used Arborio with acceptable results, and really, any medium-grain rice will work. But for the best paella, seek out bomba at a store or online. I like to toast the rice before adding other ingredients, for any rice-based dish. It adds flavor.

Traditional paella includes the elegant and fragrant spice saffron, lightly toasted to draw out its flavors and dry it out so that it can be pulverized. Yes, it's pricey, but a little goes a long way, and it really does add a flavor that makes it unique.

The sofrito is a great technique for any rice dish, be it a risotto or a pilaf. It is the result of cooking sweet ingredients so slowly and for so long that their flavors transform into something far deeper and richer than what they were to begin with, or even than what they would have been if cooked only briefly. Here I'll use olive oil, onion, and tomato. Traditionalists might not even use onion, but that seems foolhardy to me. Onion gives so much sweetness and depth to the finished dish that it should never be omitted from paella or risotto. I grate both onion and tomato so that I have a watery puree of each. This water needs to cook off before the vegetables can brown, so you'll need 45 minutes or so until the sofrito is deeply colored and intensely flavored.

The final critical component to a great paella is a great stock, because that's going to be the dominant flavor of the rice. If you use canned broth, your rice is going to taste like canned broth. If you intend to use store-bought broth, try to find fresh-frozen broth or, if those aren't available, organic broth in cartons.

With a seafood paella, there are two strategies you can use: Cook the shellfish ahead of time and use all that good cooking liquor for your stock, or cook the shellfish in the rice as you go, allowing them to open up in the rice and dump their juices into the rice as it cooks.

Having used both methods, I prefer the former, even though it doesn't make intuitive sense. After all, putting raw shellfish into the paella to cook is not only traditional, it saves the step of cooking them separately, and those juices are going to wind up there no matter how you cook them. There are a few problems with this thinking, though. One, you don't know how much liquid the shellfish are contributing, so you won't know how much stock to use, given that the rice typically requires 3 parts liquid to 1 part rice. There's less judging by sight in a paella than there is in a risotto, and paella should not be stirred once it gets simmering (in this way it is more like a pilaf in technique). You need to have a lot of paella experience to perfect the strategy of cooking raw shellfish in your paella and still have the bottom of the pan be dry enough to create the socarrat, the browned crust of the rice that is one of the great pleasures of a paella.

Therefore, I prefer to cook the shellfish separately while I'm cooking the sofrito, then hold them in the warm liquid, covered with plastic wrap so they don't dry out, while the rice cooks. Then I add them to the paella toward the end to reheat as I raise the temperature to create the all-important socarrat.

The following recipe will serve 8 to 10 and uses a 22-inch/55-centimeter paella pan. Paella is a celebratory meal meant to be shared, and it's visually dramatic and fun to present at a big table. But the recipe can be halved and cooked in a large skillet or a 14- to 16-inch/35- to 40-centimeter paella pan, adjusting the rice to 1¾ cups/350 grams and the liquid to 1½ cups/1.125 liters.

This recipe has a lot of details and so might seem complicated, but it's essentially just three steps: (1) Make the sofrito, (2) Cook the shellfish and create a flavorful broth, and (3) Cook the rice in that broth, adding the shellfish at the end.

⅓ cup/180 milliliters plus 1 tablespoon olive oil

1 large onion, peeled and grated (about 1 cup), plus 1 small onion, thinly sliced

1 large tomato, skinned and grated (about 1 cup)

5 garlic cloves, chopped

1 carrot, thinly sliced

8 to 10 jumbo (U12) shrimp, peeled (shells reserved) and deveined

1½ teaspoons tomato paste

1 cup/240 milliliters dry white wine

2 cups/480 milliliters water

6 thyme sprigs (optional)

4 to 6 large cherrystone clams

16 littleneck clams, soaked for 30 minutes in cold water and scrubbed

16 mussels, debearded

Fish stock, clam juice or Vegetable Stock (page 114), as needed

Large pinch saffron (½ gram, or about ½ teaspoon when toasted and crushed)

3¼ cups/625 grams bomba rice

6 rosemary sprigs

2 lemons, each cut into 8 wedges

¼ cup roughly chopped fresh flat-leaf parsley

First, make the sofrito (this can be done hours before you begin cooking the rice, if you wish): Heat ⅓ cup/80 milliliters of the olive oil in a 22-inch/ 55-centimeter paella pan or a large, shallow sauté pan over medium-high heat. When the oil is hot, add the grated onion and tomato. Bring the mixture to a simmer, then reduce the heat to medium-low and cook, stirring frequently, until the mixture is a deep reddish brown, about 45 minutes. When the sofrito is close to done, add the garlic. Be careful once the mixture begins to brown; it happens fast after most of the liquid has cooked off. If your pan has hot spots and the sofrito sticks, scrape it off with a flat-edged wooden spoon so that it doesn't burn. You can

deglaze these spots with water to help lift the stuck bits from the pan.

While the sofrito is cooking, make the shrimp stock and cook the shellfish (this, too, can be done hours ahead of time): Heat the remaining 1 tablespoon olive oil in a high-sided saucepan. When it is hot, sauté the sliced onion and carrot until they're tender. Do not add salt (the shellfish will add plenty). Add the shrimp shells and cook until they're hot and pink. Stir in the tomato paste. Add the white wine and simmer until half of the wine has cooked off. Add the water (the shells should be covered; add a little more if they're not) and the thyme (if using). Gently simmer for 30 minutes. Strain the shrimp stock into a large saucepan.

Bring the shrimp stock to a simmer and add the cherrystones. Cover the pot and cook just until they open; use tongs or a slotted spoon to transfer them to a bowl as they do, and cover the bowl. Next, add the littlenecks to the stock and do the same; transfer them to the bowl with the cherrystones and cover. Finally, add the mussels and do the same; transfer to the bowl and cover. Strain the stock through a fine-mesh strainer (if you wish, line it with a coffee filter or a double layer of cheesecloth to catch any last sand or grit). Measure the stock you now have. You will need 9½ cups/2.3 liters in all. If you don't have that much, supplement it with fish stock, clam juice, or vegetable stock (or a combination of white wine and water). Taste the mixture to determine how salty it is from the clams. If it's too salty, pour off a cup of it (save it for another use) and replace with water or unsalted stock. Return the 5¼ cups/1.25 liters of shellfish stock to the saucepan.

Put your smallest saucepan over high heat for 30 seconds or so. Remove it from the heat and add the saffron, tossing it so it toasts evenly. When the pan has cooled enough to touch, crumble the saffron between your fingers until it is all pulverized. Add the saffron to the shellfish stock. Bring the broth to a simmer, then remove it from the heat. Return the clams and mussels to the shellfish broth and cover the pan to prevent the shellfish from drying out.

When the sofrito is properly reduced and browned, add the rice and turn the heat up to medium-high. Stir the rice continually to toast it, a minute or so. Strain the shellfish stock into the paella pan, keeping the shellfish in the saucepan, covered. Add the rosemary springs to the paella pan. Stir well so that the rice and sofrito are uniformly mixed. When the liquid comes to a simmer, reduce the heat to medium-low and don't stir it again. Remove and discard the rosemary stems after they've simmered 2 to 3 minutes. Rotate the pan, or pull it over the heat to ensure even cooking over the entire bottom of the pan. You might also be able to use a combination of front and back burners depending on your stove.

After 12 minutes, press each shrimp into the cooking rice. After 3 more minutes, turn the shrimp over and arrange the clams and mussels evenly across the top of the paella. Cover the pan with aluminum foil for 2 or 3 minutes, continuing to ensure that the bottom is uniformly heated.

Taste the rice; it should be al dente. If it needs a little more cooking, cover again with foil and cook for a couple more minutes.

When the rice is just done, remove the foil and turn the heat to medium-high. Keep the pan moving over the heat to make sure the bottom is evenly heated. You should hear a gentle crackle as the socarrat forms. Push the tip of a spoon into the paella in various places; if it catches on rice stuck to the bottom, you've created a socarrat. The paella should smell browned and fragrant.

Remove the pan from the heat, cover it with a towel or tent loosely with foil, and let it sit for 5 minutes.

Remove the towel, arrange the lemon wedges around the pan, and garnish with the chopped parsley. Serve immediately.

WEEKNIGHT VEGETABLE PAELLA SERVES 4

Sometimes we don't have time to create a proper sofrito, but we still want the pleasure of paella and the prized socarrat. So instead, we can sauté diced onion and add ketchup—yes, you read that right. Ketchup works perfectly here—it's already cooked down and intensely flavored, and has both the sweetness and acidity that a sofrito takes 40 minutes to achieve.

Use chicken stock for the best flavor, or vegetable stock if you want to keep it vegetarian, or even water. If you're using water, include a sliced or diced carrot, season it aggressively with salt, and finish it with a good sherry vinegar or lemon juice.

Shellfish
Meals

¼ cup olive oil, *plus extra-virgin olive oil for drizzling*

1 medium onion, *minced*

4 garlic cloves, *roughly chopped*

1 cup/240 milliliters ketchup

Large pinch saffron (*about ½ gram, or about ½ teaspoon when toasted and crushed*)

1 red bell pepper, *seeded and cut into strips*

1 yellow bell pepper, *seeded and cut into medium dice*

1 small fennel bulb, *cut into ¼-inch/ 6-millimeter strips, fronds reserved for garnish if desired*

2 artichokes, *leaves and choke removed, cut into six wedges each, held in water with some lemon to prevent oxidation* (optional)

1¾ cups/350 grams bomba rice

12 ounces/340 grams green beans

½ cup/120 milliliters dry white wine

5¼ cups/1.25 liters Easy Overnight Chicken Stock (page 38), Vegetable Stock (page 114), store-bought broth, or water, *heated to a simmer*

Kosher salt and freshly ground black pepper *to taste*

5 to 7 thyme sprigs (*optional*)

Heat the oil in a 14-inch/35-centimeter paella pan or large skillet over medium heat. When it is hot, add the onion and garlic and sauté till they are tender, 5 to 10 minutes. Add the ketchup and continue to cook for a few more minutes.

Meanwhile, put your smallest pan over high heat for 30 seconds or so. Remove it from the heat and add the saffron, tossing it so it toasts evenly. When the pan has cooled enough to touch, crumble the saffron between your fingers until it is all pulverized. Set aside.

Add the bell peppers, fennel, and artichokes (if using) to the paella pan. Sauté to heat through, a couple of minutes.

Add the rice and turn up the heat to medium-high. Stir the rice to toast it, a minute or so. Stir in the green beans. Add the wine and stir till it comes to a simmer. Add the hot stock, a generous pinch of salt, the thyme, and the reserved saffron and stir to combine. Once the stock comes to a uniform simmer, lower the heat to maintain a gentle simmer and cook it for 15 minutes, moving and rotating the pan over the heat frequently to prevent burned spots and ensure even cooking. I also like to tilt the pan to make sure the liquid is evenly distributed throughout. Taste the rice and add more salt if it needs it. Feel free to crack pepper over it. After another 3 minutes or so, most of the liquid should have cooked off and the rice should be done. Turn the heat to medium-high and continue to cook, rotating the pan, to crisp the rice that has stuck to the bottom and create the socarrat. Remove the pan from the heat, give the paella a generous drizzle of extra-virgin olive oil, and serve directly from the pan.

SHELLFISH MEALS

If you have access to good clams and mussels, they can be the centerpiece of a great meal. That they take just minutes to cook makes them virtually a convenience food, when served simply. Most require some cleaning, but the quick cooking time cancels that out. Plus, they come with their own built-in sauce, to which you can add flavor and fat—or not. It's up to you.

Mussels are a great example of how simple a meal can be if you have good ingredients. A bowl of mussels, their sauce enriched with fresh herbs, wine, and butter or crème fraîche, plus a slice or two of grilled bread and a cold white wine, makes a heavenly meal. I like mussels garnished with parsley; I think thyme is best suited to clams and always throw a bunch of it into the pot when cooking clams.

I love steamers, tender little clams served in a bowl with their broth and some lemon, plus some butter for dipping. A pleasure in themselves. But I also like bigger clams for their fresh sea flavor and chewiness. When I moved to Rhode Island, I was amazed by how inexpensive the biggest of these clams, quahogs, were (pronounced *KO-hog,* by the way, unless you're in wacky Rhode Island, where it is pronounced *KWA-hog*). They're perfect for chowder, one of my favorite soups. They release tons of liquid on their own, as much as half a cup, which adds flavor to the milk-based soup.

I also fell in love with a Rhode Island dish called "stuffies," essentially the quahog shell filled with a stuffing of bread, sausage, sautéed aromatics, and chopped quahogs, then baked and served with hot sauce. They're addictive.

A final note about buying bivalves. Remember that all clams, mussels, and oysters degrade the longer they're out of the water, so freshness is paramount. They should smell fresh like the sea, not rank like low tide. Ask your fishmonger for their date of harvest, required information on all bags of shellfish. It's best to cook them the same day you buy them; if you need to store them overnight, refrigerate them in a bowl covered by damp paper or cloth towels (don't put them in a closed container or they'll die). Cook them within a day of buying them.

MOULES FRITES   SERVES 4

This is a perfect dish to make if you have already parcooked and frozen your own fries (see page 137) and can take the time to whip up a quick aioli. But it's even great with well-prepared store-bought frozen fries and a dish of Hellmann's mayo on the side. Of course, the more you make from scratch, the greater the flavor and pleasure of this classic dish.

The timing is easy, because the mussels and fries both take only a few minutes to finish, and the mussels, once opened, can remain in the covered pot until you're ready to serve them.

You'll usually have to remove the mussels' "beard," protein threads secreted by the mussels to attach themselves to a surface, commonly a pole (they don't typically grow in sand as clams do).

This is a good all-purpose way to cook clams and mussels: Steam them with wine and aromatics just until they open and you're good to go. This recipe can easily be adjusted up or down depending how many people you're serving—figure on 1 pound of mussels per person.

For the aioli:

1 garlic clove, *smashed and chopped or ground to a paste*

Generous pinch kosher salt

2 teaspoons lemon juice

1 teaspoon water

1 large egg yolk *(save or freeze the white for a Whiskey Sour, page 120)*

1 cup/240 milliliters extra-virgin olive oil

For the fries:

3 russet potatoes

2 to 3 quarts/2 to 3 liters vegetable oil

Kosher salt *to taste*

For the mussels:

4 tablespoons/ 60 grams unsalted butter

1 shallot, *sliced*

1 leek, *halved lengthwise and cleaned, sliced crosswise* (*optional*)

1 cup/240 milliliters dry white wine

1 bunch thyme

4 pounds/1.8 kilograms mussels, *cleaned and debearded*

Roughly chopped fresh flat-leaf parsley, *for garnish*

Optional: extra butter or crème fraîche (*see Note for mustard-saffron variation*)

Make the aioli first: Combine the garlic, salt, and lemon juice in a medium bowl and let sit for 10 minutes. Add the water and egg yolk and whisk to combine. Whisk continuously as you pour in the oil in a hair-thin stream. Once the emulsion is established, you can add the oil a little faster. You should have a thick sauce that clings to your whisk (you can also use an immersion blender; see page 23). Cover and refrigerate until ready to serve.

Start the fries: Cut your potatoes as desired, ideally into 1/4-inch/6-millimeter matchsticks (see page 136). Fill a large Dutch oven halfway with vegetable oil. Add the fries and put the pot over high heat. Stir the fries regularly as the oil heats to keep them from sticking to the bottom. Once it's hot and bubbling, let the fries cook until they're golden brown, stirring frequently so they don't stick to the bottom. It will take about 40 minutes total, from the time you put them in the oil until they're nice and crisp.

When the fries are nearly done, cook the mussels: Melt the butter in a large pot over medium-high heat. When the oil is hot, add the shallot and leek (if using) and cook, stirring until softened, a minute or so. Add the wine and several thyme sprigs. Then add the mussels. Turn the heat to high and bring to a simmer, then cover the pot and reduce the heat to medium-high. When the mussels are hot and have opened, about 3 minutes unless you're cooking a real lot of them, remove the pan from the heat. Discard any mussels that did not open.

Use a skimmer to transfer the fries to a wide bowl lined with paper towels. Shake them in the bowl while seasoning them with kosher salt.

Sprinkle the parsley over the mussels and divide them among serving bowls. If you wish, reheat the cooking liquid and whisk in additional butter or crème fraîche. Ladle the sauce or liquid over the mussels. Serve with the fries in a separate bowl, with aioli for dipping on the side.

Note: Here is a great sauce variation I first had while working with Thomas Keller and Jeffrey Cerciello on the *Bouchon* cookbook. After removing the mussels, add about 1 teaspoon crushed saffron to the hot broth in the pan. Whisk ½ cup/120 milliliters crème fraîche and ¼ cup Dijon mustard into the broth, and ladle this sauce over the mussels.

NEW ENGLAND CLAM CHOWDER   SERVES 8

If there's a better soup to serve on a cold November night, I don't know what it is. This centuries-old dish was born on the New England coast, where clams are abundant. Like many traditional dishes, it's named for the vessel it was cooked in, a *chaudière*, a cauldron-shaped pot that could be suspended above a fire. Its ingredients are, also, true to traditional regional dishes, simple, abundant, and inexpensive: salt pork, potatoes, clams, and milk. I like to serve it with oyster crackers.

Use quahogs for this if they're available; if not use the biggest clams available. Use 1 to 1½ big clams per person (use your common sense—generally, the more clams, the better).

Contemporary chowders usually contain bacon, but salt pork is what would have been used in colonial days. When Tim Ryan, now president of the Culinary Institute of America, commented on my book *The Making of a Chef*, he sounded incredulous that one of the instructors had told my class to use bacon in the chowder. "He should know better than that," Ryan said, incredulous. "Salt pork is what is used in chowder."

Salt pork is essentially salted fatback, with very little meat. I recommend that you make your own salt pork, using uncured, unsmoked salted pork belly (page 200)—and then you'll really have a taste of ye olde chowder.

---

12 quahogs or other large clams

1 bunch thyme

½ cup/120 milliliters water

8 ounces/240 grams salt pork, salted pork belly, or bacon, *diced small or pureed in a food processor, or ground*

1 Spanish onion, *cut into medium dice*

½ cup/60 grams all-purpose flour

1 to 1½ quarts/1 to 1.5 liters cold milk, *or as needed*

4 medium russet potatoes, *peeled and cut into medium dice*

1 cup/240 milliliters heavy cream

Freshly ground black pepper to taste (*optional*)

Put the quahogs, thyme, and ¼ cup of the water in a large pot and bring to a boil over medium-high heat. Cover the pot, reduce the heat to medium, and cook until the clams open, 5 to 10 minutes, depending on their size. Transfer them to a bowl as they open. Strain the cooking liquid through cheesecloth or, better, through a coffee filter. Measure the amount and make a note of it. You should have 3 to 4 cups/710 to 950 milliliters.

In the pot you will cook the chowder in, combine the pork and the remaining ¼ cup water. Bring to a boil over medium-high heat. When the water cooks off, lower the heat and cook until the pork is cooked and the fat has completely rendered out. Add the onion and cook it in the fat till tender.

While the pork is cooking, remove the clams from their shells and chop them coarsely; if you wish, remove any of the brown stuff in the clam's stomach, mainly plankton and other digested food (some people like the flavor it adds and include it, but I usually discard any that is easily scraped away).

Add the flour to the pork fat to make a roux and cook until it smells like cooked pie crust and is evenly coated with fat.

recipe continues

Whisk 1 quart/1 liter of the cold milk into the roux and onion. Bring the mixture to a simmer, dragging a flat-edged spoon across the bottom to prevent the flour from sticking. When the milk is simmering and thickened, stir in 2 cups/480 milliliters of the quahog liquid and taste. If you fear the mixture will be too salty, hold back on adding more. Add another 2 cups/480 milliliters of quahog liquid and/or milk to taste, for a total of 2 quarts/ 2 liters. The idea is to add as much quahog liquid as possible without making the chowder too salty (it's a forgiving dish, so don't be obsessive about the exact quantity of liquid; evaluate and adjust according to the taste and texture that pleases you).

Add the potatoes and quahogs and simmer gently until the potatoes are tender, 10 minutes or so. Add the cream and continue to cook until it's simmering again. Taste the potatoes and continue cooking until they're tender. If the chowder becomes too thick, add more milk or quahog liquid. Add plenty of cracked black pepper if you like. Serve.

STUFFIES MAKES 16 STUFFIES, OR 8 PORTIONS, THOUGH YOU'LL WANT MORE

This is an economical and tasty side dish or starter course that uses big clams called quahogs. You can also use large cherrystone clams if quahogs are not available. This is an unbeatable combination of sausage, clam, and aromatics bound with bread. If you like stuffing, this is one of the most sublime versions I know—spicy, chewy, crispy, and satisfying.

Shellfish Meals

12 quahogs

1 ½ cups/ 360 milliliters water

6 tablespoons/ 90 grams unsalted butter

1 medium onion, *cut into small dice (about 1 cup)*

3 garlic cloves, *roughly chopped*

1 red bell pepper, *seeded and cut into small dice (about ½ cup)*

2 celery ribs, *cut into small dice (about ½ cup)*

¼ to ½ teaspoon red pepper flakes *(optional)*

Kosher salt *to taste*

8 ounces/225 grams Portuguese or Spanish chorizo (or other spicy cured sausage), *cut into small dice*

1 ½ cups/100 grams seasoned bread crumbs

½ cup/30 grams pulverized Ritz crackers *(10 or so)*

¼ cup grated Parmigiano-Reggiano

1 lemon, *cut into wedges, for serving*

Hot sauce, *for serving (I'm old-fashioned and prefer tangy Tabasco, but any hot sauce will do.)*

Preheat your oven to 350°F/175°C.

Put the quahogs and water in a large pot and bring to a boil over medium-high heat. Cover the pot, reduce the heat to medium, and cook till the clams open, 5 to 10 minutes, depending on their size. Transfer them to a bowl as they open. Strain the cooking liquid through a double layer of cheesecloth or a coffee filter.

When the clams are cool enough to handle, remove the meat and roughly chop it (it should be well chopped but with plenty of chewy chunks). Break apart the clamshell halves and set aside.

In a sauté pan, melt the butter over medium-high heat, then add the onion, garlic, bell pepper, celery, and red pepper flakes (if using). Season it with a four-finger hit of salt. When the vegetables have softened, add the chorizo and chopped clams and stir to heat through, another minute or so.

Stir in two-thirds of the bread crumbs and the Ritz crackers. Stir in ½ cup/120 milliliters of the clam cooking liquid. Continue to add liquid until the mixture is moist and can be packed into the clamshells. If you add too much liquid, add some of the remaining bread crumbs.

Stuff 16 of the clamshell halves with the mixture, sprinkle with the Parmigiano, and place on a rimmed baking sheet. Bake until piping hot and browned, about 20 minutes. If they aren't sufficiently browned on top, broil them until they have an appealing crust.

Serve with lemon wedges and hot sauce.

RISOTTO

Jumping across the Mediterranean, from Spanish paella to Italian risotto, we have a medium-grain rice that's different from the bomba variety grown in the Valencia region of Spain. Risotto rices—Arborio, carnaroli, vialone nano, to name a few of the most common ones—are a little less absorbent than bomba. This is important because risotto, unlike paella, is stirred throughout the cooking, a process that encourages the rice to shed its abundant starch, which helps create the luxurious, creamy texture risottos are known for.

Risotto is one of those preparations that can be a simple weekday dinner or an elegant side for a more elaborate meal. If you know the basics, any number of risotto dishes are a snap—seafood risotto, chicken and sausage risotto, zucchini and pea risotto—or you can turn to classic pairings for ideas. You could make risotto with lardons, finish it with lots of Parmigiano-Reggiano, and top each portion with an egg yolk for a risotto carbonara. While I was at the French Laundry, chef Keller made a risotto soup by cooking a normal risotto till it was very soft and liquidy, then pureeing it and passing it through a sieve. Served over sautéed wild mushrooms, it was delicious.

Risotto is a blank canvas. Remember that, as with paella, its deliciousness is in direct proportion to the flavor of the liquids it soaks up. I almost always begin with minced or diced onion (though you can add other aromatic vegetables if you wish). Then I add the rice—a big handful per person (I rarely measure anymore, but ¼ cup per serving is a good rule). I add the rice to a dry pan to toast it (as with a paella), giving it a little extra flavor before adding the first liquid, usually white wine. (You can use a red wine if you wish, though it will darken the rice to an unappealing reddish brown—which is fine if you're doing, say, a mushroom risotto finished at the end with diced tender beef and garnished with chopped fresh herbs.) When the wine has completely cooked off, I add the stock in increments of ½ to 1 cup/120 to 240 milliliters and bring it to a fairly vigorous simmer. As it cooks off and is absorbed by the rice, there is plenty of friction to knock starch granules off the rice as you stir. You'll need as much as 1½ quarts/1.5 liters of liquid in all for every cup of rice; always have plenty on hand as you could need more than this depending on how quickly it cooks off and is absorbed. As with so many preparations, it's best to cook risotto according to taste and texture rather than by strict adherence to a recipe; while truly spectacular risotto may require experience, risotto is pretty hard to mess up.

And risotto is always finished with fat, usually Parmigiano and butter, but you can also finish it with cream (preferably whipped before being folded in).

Purists will say that a proper risotto must be made start to finish without stopping. And restaurants that make a big deal of their risotto will often have one cook who makes the risotto all night long. But more often than not, restaurants don't want to commit so much labor and time to the dish; they know that risotto will turn out perfectly delicious when cooked halfway, spread out on a cool baking sheet, and then finished hours later as needed. This makes it a great dish to serve at dinner parties, because it can be partially prepared well ahead of time and finished at the last minute.

Risotto is more obviously "all about the rice" than paella, and is much moister and creamier than paella. The following are three of my favorite risottos. The first is a basic mushroom risotto. This is the template recipe, the most classic of the risottos. The next two, asparagus risotto and corn risotto, both use the featured vegetable not only as a garnish but also as a flavoring device for the stock.

CLASSIC MUSHROOM RISOTTO (FALL/WINTER) SERVES 4

Risotto

Needless to say, the quality of the mushrooms has a major impact on this dish—but you can use white button or diced portobello mushrooms (gills scraped away and discarded) to good effect if you get a good sear on them (see page 77). A variety of wild mushrooms or a combination of button and wild, if they're available, is very nice. Here I recommend sautéing diced buttons or portobellos and then adding them to the cooking risotto, where they will continue to release their own liquids. Another option is to use dried mushrooms, rehydrated in hot water that you then strain through a coffee filter and use as the cooking liquid. If you can't get your hands on good wild mushrooms, use 1 pound/ 450 grams total of the white buttons and portobellos and reserve half of them after the initial sauté to garnish the finished risotto.

6 tablespoons/ 90 milliliters vegetable or olive oil

8 ounces/225 grams white button or cremini mushrooms, *sliced or diced*

1 shallot, *minced*

Kosher salt and freshly ground black pepper *to taste*

1¼ cups/300 milliliters dry white wine

8 ounces/225 grams assorted wild mushrooms (*such as chanterelle, oyster, morel*)

1 medium onion, *cut into small dice*

1 cup/200 grams Arborio or other risotto rice

3 to 5 cups/ 710 milliliters to 1.2 liters Vegetable Stock (page 114), mushroom stock, Easy Overnight Chicken Stock (page 38), *or store-bought broth, warm*

4 tablespoons/ 60 grams unsalted butter

½ cup/40 grams grated Parmigiano-Reggiano

Heat 2 tablespoons of the oil in a large, heavy sauté pan over high heat. When it's smoking-hot, add the sliced mushrooms and three-quarters of the minced shallot. Try to get a good sear on the mushrooms by pressing down on them. Give them a pinch of salt and several grinds of black pepper. When they're completely tender, deglaze the pan with 1 cup/240 milliliters of the white wine. Bring the wine to a simmer, then transfer the wine and mushrooms to a bowl.

Wipe out the sauté pan and repeat the searing with another 2 tablespoons oil and the wild mushrooms, adding the remaining shallot and deglazing with the remaining ¼ cup white wine, and cook until all the liquid has cooked off. Transfer these to a separate bowl.

Wipe out the pan again and heat the remaining 2 tablespoons oil over medium-high heat. When it is hot, add the onion and another pinch of salt. Cook until the onion is tender, a few minutes. Add the rice and stir to coat the rice in oil and lightly toast it.

Add the sliced mushroom and wine mixture and bring to a fairly aggressive simmer over medium to medium-high heat. When the wine is almost all absorbed, begin adding the warm stock in ½-cup increments, stirring continually. As the stock is absorbed and cooks off, the rice should look increasingly creamy. Continue to add more stock. Taste the rice. It should still be a little crunchy but getting close to being cooked after 3 to 5 cups of stock have been added. Taste the risotto and add more salt if it needs it. If it's still not cooked to your liking and you've run out of stock, add water until it is.

Meanwhile, reheat the wild mushrooms in a microwave or a separate sauté pan.

When your rice is al dente and you don't need to add more liquid, lower the heat to medium and stir in the butter, continuing to stir until the butter has been completely incorporated. Stir in the cheese, top with the wild mushrooms, and serve immediately.

ASPARAGUS RISOTTO WITH ASPARAGUS RIBBONS AND LEMON ZEST (SPRING) SERVES 4

Risotto

This is another example of using a main ingredient in creative ways to add powerful flavor to your risotto. Here we use an asparagus-vegetable stock, as well as—if you want to go the extra mile—an asparagus broth from the pureed stalks, to enrich your risotto. (The broth technique is worth doing on its own as an asparagus sauce or soup.) Asparagus is an elegantly flavored vegetable, but you lose a lot of that flavor if you discard their woody stalks. This dish tries to wring all possible flavor out of the asparagus. I also like to finish this dish with raw ribbons of asparagus and lemon zest. This is the risotto to make at the height of spring, when fat but tender asparagus is plentiful.

Note that the following stock is very simple; feel free to include additional ingredients—fresh herbs, cracked black peppercorns, bay leaf, garlic—as you wish.

For the asparagus-vegetable stock, asparagus ribbons, and asparagus puree:

1½ quarts/1.5 liters water

1 onion, *thinly sliced*

3 carrots, *thinly sliced*

2 teaspoons kosher salt

1½ to 2 pounds/ 680 to 1000 grams asparagus, *very woody pale ends removed*

For the risotto:

6 tablespoons/ 90 grams unsalted butter

1 medium onion, *cut into small dice*

Kosher salt and freshly ground black pepper *to taste*

1 cup/200 grams Arborio *or other risotto rice*

1 cup/240 milliliters white wine

3 to 5 cups/ 710 milliliters to 1.2 liters Vegetable Stock (page 114), Easy Overnight Chicken Stock (page 38), *or store-bought broth (optional; if not making vegetable-asparagus stock)*, warm

1 cup/80 grams freshly grated Parmigiano-Reggiano, *plus more for serving*

1 lemon

MAKE THE STOCK:

Combine the water, onion, carrot, and salt in a pot large enough to hold the asparagus. Bring the water to a simmer over medium-high heat, then lower the heat and gently simmer for 30 to 40 minutes. Strain into another large pot that can accommodate the asparagus and bring to a boil over medium-high heat. Reserve 8 to 12 asparagus stalks; add the rest to the boiling stock. Cook the asparagus till tender, then use tongs or a skimmer to transfer them to an ice bath and thoroughly chill.

Cut off the tips from the reserved raw asparagus stalks. Using a vegetable peeler, cut enough ribbons from the stalks to garnish each serving. Cut the ribbons in halves or thirds if they are long; they should be bite-sized. Set them aside on a plate, covered with a damp paper towel. Reserve the raw tips and remaining raw stalks.

When the cooked asparagus are thoroughly chilled, drain them. Cut off all the tips, leaving about ½ inch/1 centimeter of stalk still attached, and set aside. Cut the stalks into ½-inch/1-centimeter pieces. Put these pieces in a blender, along with 1 cup/240 milliliters of the vegetable-asparagus stock, and puree. The finer you puree them, and the better your blender, the better the finished broth will be taste. Strain the puree through a fine-mesh strainer, pressing out as much liquid as possible. You should have about 2 cups/480 milliliters asparagus puree.

recipe continues

Risotto

MAKE THE RISOTTO:

Melt 2 tablespoons/30 grams of the butter in a large sauté pan over medium-high heat. When it is hot, add the onion and hit it with a good pinch of salt. Cook till the onion is tender, a few minutes. Add the rice and stir to coat the rice in butter and lightly toast it.

Turn the heat to high and add the wine, stirring and scraping the bottom of the pan with a flat-edged spoon or spatula. When the wine comes to a boil, reduce the heat to medium-high to maintain a fairly aggressive simmer. When the wine is almost all absorbed, begin adding the warm asparagus stock in ½-cup/120-milliliter increments, stirring continually. As the stock is absorbed and cooks off, the rice should look increasingly creamy. Continue to add more stock. Taste the rice. It should still be a little crunchy but getting close to being cooked after 3 to 5 cups/710 milliliters to 1.2 liters of the stock have been added. At this point, add half of the asparagus puree. Taste the rice and add more salt if it needs it. When the puree has cooked off, add the rest of the puree and continue to stir. Taste the rice. If it's not quite done, add more stock or water and continue to cook until it's al dente and creamy.

When you've added all the liquid you want, reduce the heat to medium and add half of the cooked asparagus tips, reserving the other half to reheat as garnish (or you can add all of them now if you don't want to bother with the garnish), along with the reserved raw tips and any reserved raw stalks from making the asparagus ribbons. Then add the remaining 4 tablespoons/60 grams butter and stir until it's completely incorporated into the risotto. Finally, add the cheese and continue to stir until it is melted into the risotto.

Top each serving with more Parmigiano if you wish, then the asparagus ribbons. Grate lemon zest over each, add a few grinds of black pepper, and serve.

CORN RISOTTO (SUMMER) SERVES 4

Corn stock is optional in the way that everything is pretty much optional (see page 53), but part of the pleasure of this dish is the stock and what it brings to the dish, and also, if you haven't made corn stock before, I hope it brings a small revelation to you. When I first realized how packed with flavor all those discarded cobs still were, I marveled at the possibilities. Make corn stock for a corn chowder (follow the New England Clam Chowder recipe on page 167, replacing the clams with corn kernels and corn stock, and using bacon for your salty pork). Or make it the base for a fresh corn soup, which you can serve hot or cold. Corn stock with fresh corn and thyme, finished with a little cream, is delicious.

Here the corn stock suffuses the rice with fresh corn flavor. But if you find yourself scrambling and still want corn in your risotto, use chicken or vegetable stock and skip the stock-making process here.

I've always loved how corn on the cob that is cooked and then shocked until it's thoroughly chilled can be cut from that cob and retain its cohesiveness—it comes off the cob in planks that are the perfect way to finish the risotto. This is a fabulous way to use corn in a composed salad as well.

For the stock:

- 1½ quarts/1.5 liters water
- 2 ears corn, *shucked*
- 1 onion, *sliced*
- 3 carrots, *sliced*
- 1 bunch thyme
- 1 bay leaf
- 2 teaspoons kosher salt

For the risotto:

- 6 tablespoons/90 grams unsalted butter
- 1 medium onion, *cut into small dice*
- Kosher salt *to taste*
- 1 cup/200 grams Arborio or other risotto rice
- 1 cup/240 milliliters dry white wine
- 3 to 5 cups/480 to 1200 milliliters Vegetable Stock (page 114), Easy Overnight Chicken Stock (page 38), *or store-bought broth (optional; if not making corn stock)*, warm
- ½ cup/40 grams grated Parmigiano-Reggiano
- 2 scallions, *thinly sliced on the bias, for garnish*

MAKE THE STOCK:

In a large pot, bring the water to a boil over high heat. Add the corn and cook for 2 minutes, then use tongs to transfer the corn to an ice bath; reserve the cooking water. Agitate the corn for a minute or so to get them chilled through as efficiently as possible. When they are cold, drain them.

Using a sharp chef's knife, cut the kernels off the cobs in long planks. (I stand the cobs, fatter end down, in a large wooden salad bowl to catch the kernels.) Slice as smoothly as possible, then carefully remove 8 to 12 of the corn planks and set aside separately from the rest of the corn.

Cut the cobs into three or four pieces each and return them to the corn water, along with the onion, carrots, thyme, bay leaf, and salt. Bring the water to a simmer, then reduce it to the gentlest of simmers and cook for 45 minutes or so. Strain through a fine-mesh sieve and set aside.

recipe continues

MAKE THE RISOTTO:

Melt 2 tablespoons/30 grams of the butter in a large sauté pan over medium-high heat. When it is hot, add the onion and hit it with a good pinch of salt. Cook until the onion is tender, a few minutes. Add the rice and stir to coat the rice in butter and lightly toast it.

Risotto

Add the wine and bring to a fairly aggressive simmer over medium to medium-high heat.

When the wine is almost all absorbed, begin adding the warm corn stock in $\frac{1}{2}$-cup increments, stirring continually. As the stock is absorbed and cooks off, the rice should look increasingly creamy. Continue to add more stock. Taste the rice. It should still be a little crunchy but getting close to being cooked after 3 to 5 cups of stock have been added. Add all the corn that was not set aside as planks and stir it in. If the rice is not yet al dente, add the remaining stock as needed and cook this down. Taste the risotto for seasoning and add more salt if it needs it.

When your rice is al dente and you don't need to add more liquid, lower the heat to medium and stir in the remaining 4 tablespoons/60 grams butter, continuing to stir until the butter has been completely incorporated. Stir in the cheese and serve immediately, garnishing each portion with 2 or 4 of the reserved corn planks and the scallions.

RICE PILAF SERVES 4

This great, easy side dish was one of the first my class learned in the first kitchen at the Culinary Institute of America. It's that basic, and yet I don't know many people who use it anymore. Maybe we stopped when companies started making it for us, sold in boxes with packets of seasonings.

It's an infinitely variable and foolproof method. Cook aromatics in a flavorful fat, add rice and flavorful liquid, bring to a simmer, cover, and put in a hot oven for 20 minutes. Perfect every time. (You can put the burner on low and finish it on the stovetop, but the oven method obviates having to worry about overcooking or hot spots in your pot.) Keep it simple and use just some minced onion and stock. Or use sautéed mushrooms (see page 77) as your pilaf starter, or sauté diced red and green bell peppers for a more colorful version. Add saffron or curry powder for additional flavor.

Historically, some form of pilaf was made wherever rice grew, and it could contain anything edible—all manner of meat, vegetables, dried fruits, and seasonings. Here, as we move along the rice continuum, I offer the most basic of rice pilafs. If you use your own stock, it will be heavenly. If you use store-bought broth, I recommend cutting it with 40 to 50 percent water. And always be careful when seasoning a dish that includes store-bought broth, which often contain high levels of salt.

2 tablespoons/
30 grams unsalted
butter or olive oil,
plus more to taste

1 medium onion, *cut
into small dice*

Kosher salt *to taste*

1 cup/180 grams
long-grain rice

2 cups/480 milliliters
Easy Overnight
Chicken Stock
(page 38), Vegetable
Stock (page 114), *or
store-bought broth*

1 bay leaf

Preheat your oven to 300°F/150°C.

Heat 1 tablespoon of the butter or oil in a high-sided pot over medium-high heat. When it is hot, add the onion and a pinch of salt and cook, stirring, until the onion is tender, a few minutes. (The more you cook it, the more flavorful it will become—you can even caramelize it if you wish.) Add the rice and stir to coat it with the fat. Add the stock and bay leaf. As it's coming to a simmer, taste the stock. However heavily seasoned that stock is, that's how seasoned your rice will be, so if you think the stock could use a little salt, add it now. Add the remaining 1 tablespoon butter or oil, give it another stir, cover, and put it in the oven for 20 minutes.

The rice will stay warm for a while after being removed from the oven. Remove the bay leaf and fluff the rice with a fork before serving. Taste it and add more butter if you feel like it.

TURKEY AND ANDOUILLE GUMBO   SERVES 8

Rice Dishes

Gumbo is one of the great American dishes, a reflection of our melting-pot culture. It's a hearty, satisfying stew that causes arguments, even fists on occasion, to fly. It's the kind of dish that has so many potential variations, it's impossible to say when a pot of roux-thickened broth stops being a gumbo and starts being something else (as when a paella stops being a paella and becomes stuff mixed with rice).

Because rice—and a specific rice, American long-grain rice—is a fundamental component of gumbo, I had to include a recipe here. Being a boy from Cleveland, America's heartland and a thousand miles from gumbo's birthplace, I have to be careful about cultural appropriation. So I decided to lean on a longtime New Orleans resident (but not native), the writer and photographer and gastronome Pableaux Johnson, for my lessons in gumbo. He's a student of the great cultural dishes like gumbo, like red beans and rice, like cassoulet. On a recent trip to NOLA, I stood beside him in his kitchen as he prepared a vat of it for a party on a cold January evening.

There are four main branches of the gumbo tree. There is gumbo thickened with roux and gumbo thickened with file powder (or okra, or a combination). Branching from either of those are the other two: seafood gumbo (containing shellfish native to the gulf—shrimp, small hard-shelled crab, oysters) and poultry and andouille gumbo. That last one is on offer here, with turkey instead of the typical chicken.

The main maxim is to make your own stock using smoked turkey wings, or other smoked turkey parts, available at most grocery stores these days. Turkey stock should be a part of your culinary repertoire. It has a deeper, richer flavor than chicken stock. Turkey, likewise, is a more flavorful bird than chicken. That our national bird is relegated to being eaten just once a year is a shame. Yes, we buy it sliced at the deli counter for sandwiches, but it's a great meat that we should take advantage of all year round. Try making consommé (page 41) with turkey and you'll never go back.

In the following recipe, the stock is from scratch, but if you want a partial shortcut, simmer a couple of smoked turkey wings in 2 quarts/2 liters of store-bought chicken broth for an hour or two for a similar effect. (If you have an onion lying around, quarter it and throw that in with the turkey. Same with some carrots. But be careful, pretty soon you're just making your own stock.)

A rich turkey stock thickened with a roux is the backbone of this gumbo, a recipe developed by Pableaux. And he doesn't use just any roux, but a brown roux, a roux in which the flour is cooked to a deep, nutty mahogany, thickening the stock as it imparts a nutty roasted aroma to it. I include the drumstick bones, reserving the roasted meat for the gumbo.

Here, you can go all-out if you have the equipment—a smoker and a sausage stuffer—and make your own andouille and your own tasso ham, even smoke your own turkey. But a fabulous gumbo is yours easily if you can get your hands on some good andouille (D'Artagnan makes an excellent version) and a really good stock.

For the turkey stock:

2 turkey drumsticks

2 pounds/900 grams smoked turkey wings *or other parts*

4 carrots, *halved*

4 celery ribs, *halved*

1 large Spanish onion, *skin on, quartered*

2 tablespoons tomato paste

3 bay leaves

1 tablespoon whole black peppercorns, cracked

1 teaspoon kosher salt

4 quarts/4 liters water

For the gumbo:

4 tablespoons/60 grams unsalted butter

½ cup/60 grams all-purpose flour

1 Spanish onion, *diced*

3 celery ribs, *diced*

2 quarts/2 liters Easy Overnight Chicken Stock (page 38) or store-bought chicken broth (*optional; if not making smoked turkey stock*)

4 bay leaves

2 teaspoons freshly ground black pepper

2 pounds/900 grams smoked andouille, *cut into ¼-inch/ 6-millimeter pieces*

8 ounces/225 grams tasso ham (*optional*)

2 cups/400 grams cooked long-grain rice

MAKE THE STOCK:
Preheat your oven to 425°F/218°C.

Roast the turkey drumsticks in a roasting pan for 40 to 45 minutes. Set aside to cool a bit, and turn the oven down to 180°F/82°C (or the lowest setting).

When the drumsticks are cool enough to handle, remove and set aside the meat, and put the skin and bones in a large stockpot. Add the smoked turkey wings, carrots, celery, onion, tomato paste, bay leaves, peppercorns, and salt to the pot, then pour in the water. When the oven temperature has come down, put the pot in the oven, uncovered, and cook for 8 to 10 hours. (Alternatively, you can bring the water to a simmer on the stovetop, reduce the heat to its lowest setting, and cook it on the stovetop for 4 hours.) Strain.

MAKE THE GUMBO:
Melt the butter in a large pot or Dutch oven over medium heat. When it's bubbling, add the flour and stir to cook the flour and butter, or roux, until it is dark brown and nutty. This takes some time—perhaps 20 to 30 minutes. Take care not to burn the roux.

Add the onion and celery and cook them till tender, 5 minutes or so. Add 2 quarts/2 liters of the smoked turkey stock, the bay leaves, and the pepper. Simmer for 30 minutes, then add the reserved turkey drumstick meat, andouille, and tasso ham (if using). Simmer for another 15 minutes. Serve in bowls over the cooked rice.

(There's usually plenty of salt in the turkey and other meats to season the gumbo, but add salt if you think it needs it.)

POZOLE VERDE SERVES 8

Rice Dishes

Pozole is made from field or dent corn that's been treated with calcium hydroxide, aka slake lime or pickling lime, which softens the skin and makes this corn cookable (a process called nixtamalization). It also results in a unique flavor, the flavor of genuine corn tortillas. This corn also has a wonderfully dense bite and is especially nutritious, as the process releases the corn's niacin, a B vitamin. This corn, here called hominy, can be found canned in Mexican markets and most large grocery stores. Dried hominy is harder to find. I recommend the online source Rancho Gordo, a Napa-based company selling organic heirloom beans and other Mexican products; they also sell to various markets throughout the country.

But clearly this corn is making inroads into our culture. In need of dried hominy and caught short at the last minute in Providence, Rhode Island, where I live part-time, a friend connected me with Jake Rojas, a chef who runs a popular taco joint here, Tallulah's Taqueria. He did indeed have some dried corn, which his restaurant cooks and grinds into masa. In fact, he had four varieties, one of which came from a local farmer who grew it from seed for Rojas, who had brought it back from Oaxaca, Mexico.

Not only did he have dried corn, but he also had the pickling lime with which to nixtamalize it. And so came another lesson for me by a chance encounter. (See the instructions following the pozole if you want to try it yourself—highly recommended.)

I include a version of pozole here because it's one of my favorite dishes but also because it seems a fitting end to a chapter that begins with Valencian rice, another cereal from the same plant family, *poaceae*, the grasses.

I confirmed this fact with my dear friend Andrew Swanson, a biologist who works for the New Jersey–based vertical farming company AeroFarms. Noting that these two grasses diverged 50 to 70 million years ago and that one was domesticated in Central America and the other in East Asia, the other side of the world, just ten thousand years ago, he added: "Culinary fusions are fun, aren't they? I always get a kick out of fact that pasta from Asia and tomatoes from South America combined into *Now, that's Italian!*"

And so it goes in our constantly growing and blending culinary world. But without further ado, I present a green pozole using tomatillos and green chili powder from the American southwest. I like this as a vegetarian dish, but feel free to use chicken stock if you wish (and for a red pozole that uses pork, see page 217). And if you can't find green chili powder, feel free to use a red one (the tomatillos are what makes the sauce green). Or a mix of toasted ground Mexican chiles, such as ancho and guajillo.

recipe continues

1 cup/200 grams
dried hominy, *soaked in abundant water for at least 6 hours and drained*

2 large Spanish
onions, *1 unpeeled and quartered, 1 peeled and diced*

2 or 3 large carrots

2 bay leaves

Kosher salt *to taste*

4 tablespoons/
60 milliliters
vegetable oil

2 tablespoons green
chili powder
(*or good-quality red chili powder*)

6 garlic cloves,
peeled

20 tomatillos, *paper skins removed*

2 jalapeño peppers

1 poblano chile

1 serrano chile

1 tablespoon dried
oregano

1 teaspoon freshly
ground black
pepper

Chopped fresh
cilantro, *for garnish*

Fried corn tortillas
or tortilla chips,
for serving

Combine the soaked hominy, quartered onion, carrots, bay leaves, and 1 teaspoon salt in a pot and cover with about 3 inches/8 centimeters of water. Simmer till the corn is tender, 1 to 2 hours. Toward the end of the cooking, taste and add more salt till the water tastes pleasantly seasoned. Remove and discard the vegetables and bay leaves. You should have just enough cooking broth to come up to the level of the corn. If you're not planning to use it right away, allow the hominy to come to room temperature. Refrigerate it in its cooking liquid, covered, until ready to make the pozole.

PREHEAT YOUR BROILER.
In a large pot, heat 2 tablespoons of the oil over medium-high heat. When it is hot, add the diced onion and 1 teaspoon salt, then reduce the heat to medium-low.

Meanwhile, toss the garlic cloves, tomatillos, and all the chiles on a rimmed baking sheet with the remaining 2 tablespoons oil. Put them under the broiler, close to the heat, and broil until they are charred, about 10 minutes, depending on your broiler. Remove from the oven. Cut the stems from the poblano and serrano chiles and remove their seeds. Remove the stems from the jalapeños but leave the seeds for some heat. Put all the charred vegetables in a blender and puree. Taste the puree. Depending on the chiles you've used, it might be mild or spicy. If it is very spicy, then use it to taste; you can add tomato or more tomatillos if you want to make it milder.

Add the hominy and enough of the cooking liquid to make a thick soup-like composition, or all of it if you wish. Add the onion and tomatillo puree and bring to a simmer. Add the oregano and black pepper. Cook for about 20 minutes, adding water if the level of liquid goes below the hominy.

Garnish with plenty of cilantro and serve with crispy tortillas.

TO NIXTAMALIZE DRIED CORN:

These instructions come from Jake Rojas, a chef who has gotten a New England farmer to grow a Oaxacan breed of dried corn for his restaurant, Tallulah's Taqueria in Providence, Rhode Island. It requires a scale and using metric measurements, but it's very easy and works beautifully. The resulting corn will need to be simmered for about 4 hours to be fully tender, but even then it will retain its distinctive al dente bite.

1 kilogram dried corn

2 liters water

100 grams slake lime or pickling lime (*Rojas uses the Mrs. Wages brand of pickling lime*)

Combine all the ingredients in a large pot and bring the mixture to a boil over high heat. Reduce the heat and simmer for 1 hour, adding more water if it goes below the level of the corn. The water will turn thick and milky. Turn off the heat off and allow the corn to sit for 12 to 24 hours.

Drain the corn, then return it to the pot and rinse it in cold running water; repeat several times until the kernels are clean.

CHAPTER 6

Cassoulet

As a paella is all about the rice, a cassoulet is all about the beans. Like paella, cassoulet is named for what it is cooked in, a *cassole*, or casserole dish—specifically, one that's narrow at the base but broad at the top, allowing for a large surface area, relative to its volume, for maximum surface browning. And like paella, cassoulet spawns heated debate over what is *vrai* and what is *faux*. Much wind has been blown with regard to whether or not to top the dish with bread crumbs. And how many times should that crust be broken during its cooking—seven? Or is it eight? Early writers about the dish advocate including mutton. Others would sooner put chorizo in their paella than they would mutton in a cassoulet. I have been unable to find a brotherhood of the paella that is similar to the Grande Confrérie du Cassoulet; their members place the birth of cassoulet somewhere around the time of the Hundred Years' War in the town of Castelnaudary in southern France. But even if you go back that far, to the fourteenth century, it's hard to imagine that no one had previously combined beans and meat, which is what a cassoulet is at its core.

Having conferred with both bean and cassoulet experts, I am prepared to argue that a proper cassoulet *should*—not *must*, mind you—have salted pork, duck confit, and a plain Toulouse-style sausage. And that sausage, according to one of my experts, Kate Hill, should contain nothing but a mix of pork shoulder and belly, seasoned with salt and pepper and stuffed into a natural casing. Hill is an expat living in Gascony, the spiritual home of the cassoulet and the confit, and I defer to her. As she writes in *Cassoulet: A French Obsession*, her slender, excellent volume: "No wine. No garlic. No sugar. No spices. Get it?"

Got it.

Place matters. Place arguably created these and other great dishes. They were made with what was grown in the area—in the case of paella, the medium-grain rice of Valencia; for cassoulet, the Tarbais beans of southern France. And the dictates of place are what I use in re-creating a so-called authentic dish. You don't have to use Tarbais beans for a true cassoulet, but I would argue that you should use a bean like it, a medium-size, white, creamy bean.

Gascony is also the home of preserved duck legs, or duck confit, also a cassoulet component. And some form of pork belly should be included—traditionally ventrèche—that is salted, rolled, and allowed to cure.

In centuries past, meat would have been a highly prized commodity and therefore used sparingly, for its flavor and fat and in support of the beans, not as the feature. Again, cassoulet is about the beans. So, this chapter is not solely about cassoulet; rather it is about beans generally, as well as the many great preparations that are included in this classic beans-and-meat casserole.

How to Cook Beans

Beans are an extraordinary food—nutrient-dense and delicious, rich in both fiber and protein. Much has been written about the do's and don'ts of bean cookery—to soak or not to soak, changing the soaking water to decrease potential GI discomfort, when to salt—most recently correctives to a lot of folk "wisdom" and misinformation.

For a definitive discussion of the issues, you can't do better than to listen to Steve Sando, who founded Rancho Gordo, a purveyor of heirloom legumes in Napa, California. Steve has not only sourced some of the greatest beans grown and written about them in several excellent books, he's been cooking them for years, all kinds of them and, as an engaged and engaging cook, his observations and experience are comprehensive. One of the things I love that Steve stresses is how delicious the unadulterated bean broth is. If you've got great beans, you really don't need anything more for flavor. An onion and a carrot, maybe a bay leaf, add to it, but really the broth gets most of its flavor from the beans. Get some really good beans and just cook them in about four times the amount of water. Add a couple pinches of salt, and they're terrific—no other seasonings required. And the smaller beans can go from the bag into your belly in an hour and a half.

Beans

Russ Parsons is another writer who, in his book *How to Read a French Fry*, addresses issues of bean cookery, and he and Steve have had their own bean debates. And one new voice has entered the discussion with an important experiment, about which more in a moment.

Herewith, then, a concise account of the current state of bean wisdom distilled from some of the leading voices in beanery:

On soaking: Some people say that beans are best if they're soaked for 6 hours or more, but many others don't believe in soaking, such as "the entire country of Mexico," Steve Sando says. And still others advocate a "quick" soak, bringing beans and water to a boil, then covering the pot, letting them sit for an hour, and draining. This, of course, cooks them, so you needn't think of it as an extra step; it only delays the rest of the cooking process. The bigger (and older) the bean, the more advisable it is to soak, but it's hardly required. And it seems especially irrelevant if you're using very fresh dried beans, such as those recommended for Magic Beans (page 191).

On salt: It has long been believed, without verification, that salting the bean cooking water would inhibit the beans' hydration and, further, that salting the water too early would result in tough beans. This led Sando to the practice of salting the beans two-thirds of the way through the cooking ("once I know they're my bitch," as he puts it).

But what about that new voice I mentioned? Kenji López-Alt, mentioned earlier, author of *The Food Lab*, did a great experiment: He put salt in the bean soaking water and discovered that the salt softened the skin of the beans, allowing a smoother absorption of water and fewer blown-out beans. Beans cooked in salted water also absorbed less water, resulting in more flavorful beans. This is now standard practice for me—salting the soaking water when I do soak (usually I don't) and then adding salt right away when cooking the beans. Start with a small amount of salt and season as necessary toward the end. (Generally, anything you're simply hydrating—think rice or pasta—will be seasoned to the level of its cooking liquid, so season the water and then, after the salt has dissolved and dispersed, taste the water. That will be your seasoning level. This is not the case with beans, though, as so much water cooks off. So finish seasoning toward the end of cooking.)

On acid: Adding an acidic element, some say, can cause the beans to seize somewhat and slow the cooking, though Russ Parsons argues that you'd have to add a lot of acid to make a noticeable difference in their cooking. Still, it may not be a bad idea to add acidic ingredients at the end.

On the "musical fruit": For years people have been trying to reduce the toots that beans tend to cause after we eat them. Not possible, says Russ, who explains that dried beans have complex sugars that we can't digest, which, along with the high fiber, results in flatulence. (The product Beano, created to minimize gas, contains an enzyme that does digest these sugars.) Part of the problem may be that we don't eat enough fiber generally, so when we do eat high-fiber foods, it results in gas. Sando maintains that if you eat beans on a regular basis, your body will adjust.

And that's really all there is to cooking great beans. But I can't stress enough how big a difference buying quality beans makes.

Cassoulet
FROM SCRATCH

1. MAKE SOME **MAGIC BEANS** (191)

while we're talking about

NEXT → YOU'LL WANT TO MAKE SOME **DUCK CONFIT*** (199)

* *although if you're smart you will have made them weeks ago & can now just pull them from the fridge!*

TOULOUSE-STYLE **SAUSAGE** (200) AND SOME → **VENTRECHE** (200)

A FRENCH preparation for PORK Belly that gives this dish its unique Gascon panache

PASTE (chapter 3, 115) e **CECI**

which uses the equally magic chick pea

↓ OR

BEAN DIP (191)

OR ↓

NOW *you're ready to* MAKE

classic **cassoulet** (195) ------→ *leftovers?*

you should TRY

DUCK confit WITH Roasted **POTATOES** (202)

OR CONSIDER MAKING → **DUCK RILLETTES** (202)

A N D

Falafel (chapter 9, 300) with TAHINI

the same technique used with the DUCK can be applied to →

CHICKEN CONFIT (204)

OR →

PORK Belly CONFIT (205)

MAGIC BEANS SERVES 2 AS AN ENTRÉE OR 4 AS A SIDE DISH

Before I get to the great cassoulet, here is a delicious bean recipe. This can't be made with commodity beans from the grocery store, so either order beans online from Rancho Gordo or check the company's website for a listing of stores that carry them. The following recipe takes about 90 minutes, but only a minute of actual work.

Beans

To make a great meal of this, serve it with rice, or sprinkle it with panko bread crumbs toasted with butter to give the beans some crunch, and serve with a salad. Add a link or two of sausage for some heft. Or simply serve it as a side dish; you could garnish with thinly sliced scallion or chives, but that's gilding the lily as far as I'm concerned.

1 cup/200 grams Rancho Gordo Vaquero or Domingo Rojo beans

1 quart/1 liter water

1 teaspoon kosher salt

In a heavy, high-sided pan (it should be deeper than it is wide), combine the beans, water, and salt. Bring the water to a boil over high heat, then reduce it to the gentlest of simmers. Cook until the beans are tender, 75 to 90 minutes. There should be a thin layer of water just covering the beans when they are done. Add more water if the level goes below that of the beans before they are cooked. Serve the beans with their broth.

KATE HILL'S VARIATION ON MAGIC BEANS
Use only ¼ teaspoon salt (until seasoning at the end, if necessary) and add 2 ounces/60 grams finely chopped prosciutto to the pot along with the beans. This adds depth and richness to the beans.

BEAN DIP

It should be noted that any beans can be cooked and pureed in a food processor to make a bean dip. Making a dip is a great way to use leftover beans. If they're good beans, you can simply puree them with a bit of good olive oil. But you can also flavor them with sautéed garlic, cumin, coriander, roasted peppers, or chili powder. It's all up to your imagination and taste.

CASSOULET
from Scratch

If you want to make a great, hearty meal for plenty of people (or even just a few), cassoulet is one of those big preparations that's worth the effort. It takes time, but nothing is particularly difficult—you just have to plan ahead. Of course, you can buy the duck confit and sausages, and use fresh pork belly or slab bacon—and, frankly, this is what I typically do. But if you've got the time, there's something uncommonly satisfying and delicious when you make all the components—duck, cured pork, sausage—yourself.

And these are all preparations that can be made weeks in advance. If you are the kind of cook who likes to make your own sausages, you'll want to make a big batch and eat some of them right away (sautéed sausages and Magic Beans, page 191, make a great meal), then freeze the rest to have on hand for other uses. If you make a big batch of duck confit—and why not, as it keeps all winter—you can likewise pull these from their fat when you need them. And the ventrèche, the French version of pancetta, can be cured in advance and used (as you would pancetta or bacon) as needed for up to a month, or it can be cut into portions and frozen.

So, if you have a little inkling, like an itch in your cooking brain, that you'd like to make a cassoulet one day in the coming winter, make one component every couple of weeks or as your schedule allows. Maybe you won't even make that cassoulet—who knows? The weeks can get away from us. But that's no matter—even if you don't, you've got great sausage and duck and salt-cured pork belly on hand for any number of meals.

What follows first is a recipe for the cassoulet itself, followed by recipes for all the components should you want to make them yourself—whether for a cassoulet, or just to have on hand. These are preparations that are meant to last you a while. If you're going to go to the effort of stuffing sausage, you'll want to make plenty, since it takes about the same time to make a pound as it does to make five pounds. Same with duck confit—it takes just as long to make a dozen legs as two. And I've never known a household to complain about having too much bacon on hand.

CLASSIC CASSOULET SERVES 8

The best cassoulet I've ever had was the one Anthony Bourdain prepared for the Cleveland episode of his show *No Reservations*, in my old kitchen. He was still on good terms with Les Halles, the Manhattan restaurant where he'd been working when he published *Kitchen Confidential*, and he had brought some great sausages that kitchen made. He also came with a huge sheet of pig skin with which to line the cooking vessel (a great luxury). I don't remember specifically how the cassoulet tasted, only that it was extraordinary—because it was about more than the taste. It was the whole experience of making it and sharing it, an example of the true power of food. It's not only about pleasing our palate and sating our hunger; it's about bringing people together. Which was Tony's gift to the world up until his death in 2018.

A cassoulet is traditionally cooked in an earthenware bowl that is narrow at the bottom and wide at the top, which is important, as this creates more surface area relative to the total quantity of stew. The surface area browns during the cooking—and this kind of browning of proteins, of course, is flavor. Continuously pressing the dried, browned crust that forms on the surface into the stew gives that flavor to the cooking broth. The crust is "broken" or pressed down seven or eight times depending on your source. But this number is about right—it amounts to roughly once every 15 minutes after it has developed a crust. So that magic number seven may have developed as a way to keep track of the time more than some sort of cassoulet divination.

There are those who like to cover the cassoulet with bread crumbs. If you start with bread crumbs, then you won't be able to get the extra flavors of the gratin protein noted above back into the stew, which is the main reason I don't favor bread crumbs. Kate Hill believes that bread crumbs are for doctoring up canned cassoulet (which I didn't know existed and don't know why anyone would bother). But another estimable cook, writer, and expat in France, David Lebovitz, says that bread crumbs "are for those of us who don't have a wood oven and/or who like crunchy toppings." And who doesn't like a crunchy topping? So, if that is your preference, I'd recommend adding them toward the end of the cooking, allowing just long enough for them to soak up the broth and brown. But for this version, I'm sticking with Kate: no bread crumbs.

Once you have all your components, there are three main steps to the cassoulet: cooking the beans, browning the meat, and then cooking the cassoulet. I recommend cooking the beans a day or two ahead as it makes cassoulet day more convenient and enjoyable.

Remember that this dish is about the beans and that beans are half about the broth. The broth is fantastic plain (see Magic Beans, page 191), but here we load up the cooking water with lots of aromatics and one smoky hock. It's a good idea to reserve 1 to 1½ cups/240 to 360 milliliters of the broth to bring hot to the table to ensure that the cassoulet is moist and juicy; I find that when you reach for the inevitable seconds, the beans have absorbed most of the juices as the pot has rested. The following recipe is for eight people, but to decrease or increase that number, plan on ½ cup/ 100 grams dried beans per person.

For the beans:

- 1 pound/450 grams salted pork belly, Ventrèche (page 200), or pancetta

- 1 smoked or fresh ham hock

- Fresh pork rind (about a 6-inch/ 15-centimeter piece if available; *it's loaded with gelatin),* rolled and tied

- 1 pound/450 grams Tarbais-style beans (or other medium-size white bean), *ideally soaked for 6 hours or overnight, then drained*

- 2 large carrots

- 1 Spanish onion, *peeled, halved through the root, and studded with 5 cloves*

- 3 bay leaves

- Small bundle of fresh thyme, *tied with string for easy removal*

- ¼ teaspoon kosher salt

- ½ teaspoon freshly ground black pepper

For the cassoulet:

- 4 legs Duck Confit (page 199), plus 2 tablespoons duck confit fat

- 8 links (about 2 pounds/900 grams) Toulouse-Style Sausages (page 200) *or other plain pork sausage or garlic sausage*

- Freshly ground black pepper *to taste*

For the beans, cut off a quarter of the salted pork and reserve the rest for the cassoulet. Combine the quarter with the remaining ingredients in a large pot and cover them with about 2 inches/5 centimeters water. Bring the water to a simmer over high heat, then reduce the heat to the gentlest of simmers. Cook until the beans are just barely tender—start checking them after 1 hour. Add more water, if necessary, to keep them comfortably covered. They can take between 1 and 2 hours, depending on the beans.

Remove and discard the pork belly, hock, carrots, onion, bay leaves, and thyme. Remove and reserve the pork rind (if using). Reserve 1 cup/240 milliliters or more of the bean broth.

To make the cassoulet, preheat your broiler to high. Put the duck legs on a rimmed baking sheet and broil until the skin is golden brown and crisp (you can also do this on the stovetop in a skillet, preferably nonstick as the skin tends to stick). Set the duck aside and preheat your oven to 300°F/150°C.

Heat the duck confit fat in a large skillet over medium-high heat, then add the sausage. Cook until they're nicely browned on all sides.

Ladle enough beans to cover the bottom of your cassoulet pot (any large, deep Dutch oven or casserole dish will do). Nestle the duck confit into these beans. Add another layer of beans to cover the duck. Add the rind (if using) and the sausages. Cover them with the remaining beans. Cut the reserved salted pork belly into 12 to 15 lardons and press these into the surface. If there is not enough broth, add water to cover by about ½ inch/1 centimeter. Give the whole thing a few generous grindings of black pepper.

Put the pot in the oven, uncovered. After 1½ hours, press down on the surface with a flat-edged wooden spoon or spatula to submerge the top layer of beans. Repeat every 20 minutes or so (whenever the top looks nicely browned). The cassoulet should cook for about 3 hours total. If the top is not sufficiently browned after that time, feel free to put it under the broiler briefly just before you bring it to the table and serve. Reheat the reserved bean broth and use it to moisten the cassoulet if it's too thick.

DUCK CONFIT MAKES 12 LEGS

Duck confit is a traditional component of cassoulet, but it's also the perfect convenience food. Make a dozen legs in the fall and pull from the batch as needed all winter long. Had a late day at work and don't have time to cook? Duck confit can be a centerpiece to a great weeknight meal. Or turn it into rillettes (see page 202). You can mail-order duck confit, but if you have a farmers' market near you, check if there are any farmers in your area who raise ducks and see how easy and satisfying it is to make confit on your own.

This recipe is for 12 duck legs because that's a manageable size, but you can do more or less as you wish, adjusting the other ingredients as needed. If you have access to rendered duck fat or wish to order it, this is the best fat to use. But you can also confit just as well in olive oil. (I've tried various vegetable oils, but you really lose flavor this way.)

Coarse kosher salt
to taste

12 duck legs

4 garlic cloves,
smashed with the flat side of a knife

12 thyme sprigs

2 teaspoons whole black peppercorns,
cracked in a mortar or beneath a sauté pan

2 quarts/2 liters warm melted duck fat or olive oil, *or as needed*

Salt each duck leg so that it's nicely coated with salt (you'll probably need a teaspoon each) and put them in several large zip-top plastic bags or other containers. Divide the garlic, thyme, and peppercorns evenly over the legs. Seal the bags or cover the containers and refrigerate overnight or for 24 hours.

Preheat your oven to 200°F/93°C. Rinse the duck legs under cold water and pat dry. Arrange the legs in a few overlapping layers in a large pot or Dutch oven; keep in mind that pots that are taller than they are wide will require the least amount of fat. Pour the warm melted duck fat or olive oil over the duck legs to submerge them completely. Put the pot in the oven, uncovered, for 6 hours, until the duck is completely tender. You can tell that the legs are done when they've sunk to the bottom and the fat has changed from cloudy to clear.

The duck legs can be used right away, but they are best left to chill in their fat completely. They can be kept in the refrigerator for up to 6 months if stored properly. Transfer the duck legs to a large glass or plastic container, then pour the cooking fat over them until they are completely submerged in fat. (Reserve the gelatinous confit liquid at the bottom of the pot; this salty, intensely flavored duck stock can be used to make a sauce or to flavor a vinaigrette.) Cover and refrigerate until needed. As you remove duck legs to use, add more olive oil as necessary to make sure the remaining duck legs are covered in fat. Air is their enemy, and exposed duck will eventually mold and spoil.

To cook the duck confit, in a large skillet (preferably nonstick), heat a little confit fat over medium-high heat, then lay a few duck legs, skin-side down, in the hot fat. Work in batches if necessary so that the legs are in a single layer. Cook until the skin is lightly browned and crisp. Turn the legs and continue cooking until they're heated through. For more uniform crisping of the skin, finish the legs under a broiler.

TOULOUSE-STYLE SAUSAGE
MAKES 16 (6-INCH/15-CENTIMETER) LINKS

Here's a formula for the perfect sausage to include in a stew: 3 parts pork shoulder and fat to 1 part fatty pork belly, 1.5 percent salt, 1 percent black pepper. It's a great ratio. If your quantity of meat varies, calculate the amount of salt and pepper by multiplying those percentages by the meat's total weight. While it's not strictly necessary, the sausage will be better seasoned if you toss the meat with the salt and pepper and refrigerate it the day before you want to grind and stuff the sausages.

Remember when making sausage to keep all your ingredients very, very cold throughout the process, otherwise the fat may separate out and your sausage will have a mealy texture. It's prudent to put the diced meat in the freezer until it is stiff with cold before grinding and mixing.

3 pounds/1,360 grams fatty pork shoulder, *cut into 1½-inch/ 4-centimeter dice*	½ ounce/14 grams (about 2 tablespoons) freshly ground pepper
1 pound/450 grams pork belly, *skin off, cut into 1½-inch/4-centimeter dice*	¼ cup ice water
Scant 1 ounce/ 28 grams (about 5 teaspoons) kosher salt	8 feet/2.5 meters hog casing, *soaked in tepid water for at least 30 minutes*

Combine the diced pork, salt, and pepper in the bowl of a standing mixer and toss to distribute the seasonings. Refrigerate until you're ready to grind it.

Put all the meat in your grinding tray and grind through a small (⅛-inch/3-millimeter) die back into the cold bowl of your standing mixer. Add the ice water and paddle the meat on medium-high until it's well mixed and takes on a sticky or furry appearance, 30 to 60 seconds or so.

Open the end of your casing and run water through it. Fit the casing onto your stuffer and stuff the sausage. Twist into 6-inch/15-centimeter links. Wrap well and store for about a week in the refrigerator or for a month or longer in the freezer.

VENTRÈCHE
MAKES 2 TO 3 POUNDS/1 TO 1.4 KILOGRAMS

Ventrèche is the French version of bacon, either lightly smoked or not smoked at all. When not smoked, it's exactly like pancetta. It's delicious in any stew, and it can be cut smaller and sautéed, then used for pasta, a lardon salad, or New England Clam Chowder (page 167). You could even use it in a BLT (page 277).

It's always best to use skin-on pork belly if that's available to you, because the skin is so rich in collagen, but skinless will work as well. It should be well salted, so much so that it should look as if it were dredged in salt, with excess shaken off. The salt deepens the pork flavor and the drying concentrates it. Traditionally, like pancetta, the belly is rolled, tied, and hung to dry, though it's fine to dry it flat.

1 (2- to 3-pound/ 900- to 1,360-gram) piece skin-on pork belly	Kosher salt and freshly ground black pepper *to taste*

Rinse the belly. Salt the skin side of the belly till it is uniformly coated—shake it straight from the box. Turn the belly over and coat the flesh side till it has a uniform layer of salt covering it. Put the belly in a large zip-top bag and refrigerate it for 24 hours.

Wash all the salt off the belly under cold running water. Pat the belly dry. Give the flesh side a uniform dusting of black pepper. Put the belly on a rack on a rimmed baking sheet, flesh side up. Put the sheet in a cool place and allow to dry-cure for 7 days. You can also do this in your refrigerator, but you don't need to.

Alternatively, you can punch a hole in one corner of the pork belly, thread butcher's string through the hole, and hang it to dry-cure. Or, as they do in France, you can roll it (so that the skin is on the outside) and tie it tightly with butcher's string and hang it to cure.

When it has finished curing, wrap the ventrèche in plastic and refrigerate for up to 8 weeks. Or cut it into portions, wrap it in plastic, and store in a zip-top plastic bag in the freezer.

DUCK CONFIT WITH ROASTED POTATOES
MAKES AS MUCH OR AS LITTLE AS YOU LIKE

Confits

Potatoes cooked in duck fat have an otherworldly quality to them. But even if you've used olive oil to confit the duck, that fat is still delicious to cook your duck in. They wouldn't necessarily do this in Gascony, but it's a good idea to serve a spicy-greens salad on the side with some lemon and the confit liquid if you've saved it.

1 duck leg confit per person, *plus confit fat as needed*

½ russet potato per person, *cut into small dice*

Kosher salt
to taste

Preheat your oven to 300°F/150°C.

Pour confit fat into a nonstick skillet to a depth of about ¼ inch/6 millimeters and heat it over medium heat. Lay the duck in the pan, skin side down. Cook until the skin is browned and crispy, a few minutes. Transfer the duck to an oven-safe pan or rimmed baking sheet and put it in the oven to keep warm while you make the potatoes.

Turn the heat under the skillet to high and add the potatoes to the fat remaining in the pan. Cook, stirring and flipping them, till they are golden-brown perfection. Transfer to a wide bowl lined with paper towels and add salt, shaking them as you do. Serve with the duck.

HOW TO MAKE DUCK RILLETTES FROM DUCK CONFIT

If you have a good supply of duck confit, you may not want to eat whole legs all the time. Or sometimes you want to be able to serve a lot of people with it. A great solution is to make duck rillettes, which, like pork rillettes (the original form of the preparation) are cooked till falling-apart tender, heavily seasoned, and served as a spread for croutons. Rillettes make a fabulous hors d'oeuvre.

To make them, remove one or more legs from the fat. Put them in a bowl and warm them in a microwave just until they're tender and the fat has rendered off them. Remove the skin and chop it till it's very fine. Remove the meat and discard the bones. Combine the skin and meat in the bowl of a standing mixer (or mixing bowl if you don't have a mixer). Season it as you wish (see below) and mix with the paddle attachment (or a stiff spoon), adding enough reserved fat from the bowl until it's spreadable. Transfer to ramekins or a small bowl and serve with toasted bread and whole-grain mustard and cornichons.

If the duck is nicely seasoned already from the cooking, you may not need to season the rillettes further. But the classic French combination called quatre épices works well with duck: ground black pepper, nutmeg, cinnamon, and cloves. You'll have to experiment and see what you like best, but for every cup or so of rillettes, try adding ¼ teaspoon black pepper and a pinch each of the remaining spices. Taste and add more as necessary.

In the next chapter, you'll find an all-purpose method for preparing a Slow-Roasted Pork Shoulder (page 212). Among the other things you can do with this shoulder is make pork rillettes, using this very same seasoning, along with some allspice. Make sure it's properly seasoned with salt as well.

Rillettes are traditionally preserved below a layer of fat. If you'd like to do this, render the appropriate fat, duck or pork, and pour it over the cold rillettes so that they're covered by about ¼ inch/6 millimeters of fat. They will keep like this for 3 weeks or longer in the refrigerator.

CHICKEN CONFIT   SERVES 8

Confits Sometimes we don't have access to duck, but every grocery store carries plenty of chicken. Chicken thighs make a terrific confit. It works just like duck confit—salt and season for a day, then poach in rendered fat or olive oil. You can also confit chicken wings and then deep-fry them for an unforgettable take on fried chicken. Chicken confit is a great preparation to have on hand for a last-minute delicious dinner: Serve with mashed potatoes and a green vegetable for a delightful dinner in 20 minutes. But you have to have planned ahead to make the confit in the first place! Thinking ahead is your biggest asset in the kitchen.

Here I choose sweet spices; you can use your intuition and take the flavor in any direction you wish. These are also delicious roasted or deep-fried, then tossed with a good barbecue sauce or glazed with the char siu sauce (page 218).

3 garlic cloves, *minced*

2 tablespoons brown sugar

2 teaspoons freshly ground black pepper

1 teaspoon ground allspice

¼ teaspoon ground cloves

¼ teaspoon ground cinnamon

7 to 8 sprigs thyme

8 bone-in, skin-on chicken thighs

Kosher salt *to taste*

1 quart/1 liter olive oil or rendered duck or chicken fat, *or as needed*

Combine the garlic, brown sugar, pepper, allspice, cloves, and cinnamon in a small bowl and mix to distribute the seasonings.

Coat the chicken thighs with an even layer of salt and put them in a zip-top plastic bag. Add the garlic-spice mixture, along with the thyme, and rub it around to coat the chicken as evenly as possible. Refrigerate the chicken overnight. Midway through, give them a rub and a shake to redistribute the seasonings.

Preheat your oven to 200°F/93°C.

Remove the chicken thighs from the bag and rinse off the seasonings. Pat them dry. Put them in an oven-safe pot that is taller than it is wide; it's fine to overlap and stack them. Pour in enough oil or fat to ensure that they are completely submerged.

Put the pot over high heat. When the oil reaches 200°F/93°C, put the pot, uncovered, in the oven for 4 hours, or until the chicken is fork-tender.

Remove the pot from the oven and let it come to room temperature. Transfer the chicken thighs to a container and pour the fat over the chicken until it's completely submerged (reserve the gelatinous confit liquid at the bottom of the pot for another use). Cover and refrigerate.

To finish the chicken: Preheat your oven to 350°F/175°C. Remove the chicken thighs from the fat, letting the fat fall off or brushing away excess solid fat, and put them on a rimmed baking sheet. Roast for 10 minutes, then turn on the broiler. Broil till the chicken is heated through and the skin is crisp. If you are not using all the thighs at once, be sure to add more olive oil to ensure that the remaining thighs are covered in fat.

PORK BELLY CONFIT   SERVES 8

If you really want to go over the top, confit some pork belly. The first time I had it, I nearly fell out of my chair.

Confits

3 garlic cloves, minced	¼ teaspoon ground cinnamon
2 tablespoons brown sugar	8 (2-inch/5-centimeter) chunks skinned pork belly
2 teaspoons freshly ground black pepper	Kosher salt *to taste*
1 teaspoon ground allspice	1 quart/1 liter olive oil or rendered pork fat, *or as needed*
¼ teaspoon ground cloves	

Combine the garlic, brown sugar, pepper, allspice, cloves, and cinnamon in a small bowl and mix to distribute the seasonings.

Coat the pork belly chunks with an even layer of salt and put them in a zip-top plastic bag. Add the garlic-spice mixture and rub it around to coat the pork as evenly as possible. Refrigerate the pork overnight. Midway through, give them a rub and a shake to redistribute the seasonings.

Preheat your oven to 200°F/93°C.

Remove the pork chunks from the bag and rinse off the seasonings. Pat them dry. Put them in an oven-safe pot that is taller than it is wide; it's fine to overlap and stack them. Pour in enough oil or fat to ensure that they are completely submerged.

Put the pot over high heat. When the oil reaches 200°F/93°C, put the pot, uncovered, in the oven for 6 to 8 hours, until the pork is fork-tender.

Let the pot come to room temperature, then transfer the pork to a container and pour the fat over the pork until it's completely submerged (reserve the gelatinous confit liquid at the bottom of the pot for another use). Cover and refrigerate.

To finish the pork: Go over the top and deep-fry it in vegetable oil until it's crispy on the outside and hot and tender inside.

CHAPTER 7

Slow-Roasted Pork Shoulder

I've spent a hefty chunk of my writing career devoted to the miracle that is the pig. I have signed easily a thousand copies of my book *Charcuterie* with the words "Honor the pig." The pig is indeed bounty itself, and it is incumbent upon everyone who cooks to be openly and continuously grateful wherever we encounter bounty, whether for the farmers' market at the height of summer or for fabulous and nourishing beans in the dead of winter.

Charcuterie—a term that literally translates as "cooked meat," but that is really about preservation methods—is all but synonymous with the pig. Granted, there are preparations in charcuterie that don't involve the pig: Duck Confit (page 199) is one example. But by and large, an entire culinary specialty is devoted to this single animal.

The flavors of meat from the pig have an astonishing range—broader by far than any other animal we raise for food. Beef tastes like beef—sure, it can be a rare steak or a braised short rib, different results, but both are similarly beefy. Same with lamb and chicken. But the pig has a far broader range of flavors, and many other flavors that can be brought *to* it, from salt, from smoke, from curing. A great prosciutto doesn't taste anything like a pork chop. Bacon is unto itself, period. Barbecued spare ribs aren't even in the same family of flavors as a headcheese.

That my carnivorous heart is close to the pig is in evidence in other chapters (the ventrèche in the cassoulet chapter, the cured and smoked belly in the BLT chapter). This chapter discusses the most versatile and also most economical cut of the pig, the pork shoulder. (This is often called, confusingly, the Boston butt. Butcher terminology generally is idiosyncratic and often dependent on the area a cut comes from; apparently in Boston, meatpackers would store inexpensive cuts like the shoulder in barrels called butts.) If you've got a lot of people to feed and have a tight budget, pork shoulder is the ticket. You can feed fifteen people with a fifteen-dollar pork shoulder—if you know how to handle it. And once you know how to handle it, the best chili, pozole rojo, pork rillettes, and pulled pork are mere hours away.

I say hours because the pork shoulder is a heavily worked muscle, and muscles that are heavily worked develop a lot of connective tissue to support the muscles in that part of the animal. Connective tissue is mainly very tough protein, which, when cooked in low, moist heat over time, dissolves into gelatin, that wonderful substance that gives stews and stocks great body. And so, the primary way to tenderize pork shoulder is in a moist environment—either in an enclosed pot in a low oven, or in liquid or stew. It can be mechanically tenderized—cut very thin or completely ground to drastically shorten fibrous connective tissue—but almost always, when we cook the pork shoulder, we do so low and slow.

The other great quality of the pork shoulder is that it's got a goodly amount of fat marbling the meat. Fat, of course, is flavor, but we don't want too much fat. A great sausage, for instance, is 25 to 30 percent fat, and this is pretty much exactly how the pork shoulder is composed, an ideal combination of meat and fat.

And did I mention flavor? Heavily worked muscles such as the shoulder tend to be the most flavorful cuts on an animal.

Thus, a chapter devoted to the pork shoulder is really an appreciation of what I would argue is the single most versatile cut of meat, period, from any animal. Whether as sausage, a pork and bean stew, chili, pulled pork, cured into tasso ham, turned into rillettes, or chunks of salt pork, the pork shoulder is the star all-around player in the kitchen, and knowing all you can do with it gives you not just a few recipes but dozens. It's even great cured like bacon or confited. There's almost nothing you can't do, given shoulder from a properly raised hog. The only thing you probably couldn't get away with is pork tartare, although it is popular in some countries (my stepson, Sam, recently ordered pork tartare off a menu in São Paulo, Brazil). Even I'd have a hard time enjoying that, though raw pork is likely no longer dangerous (trichinosis hasn't been a problem in pigs for many decades). Our taboo against eating rare or raw pork runs pretty deep, but if you wanted to make pork tartare, you'd certainly want to use the shoulder.

This chapter is also about technique: moist heat and its power to transform tough cuts into exquisitely tender voluptuousness. This process is also referred to as braising, but that word in a way obscures the underlying principle of the technique. Much as dry-heat cooking (sautéing and roasting) implies a heat level (high), moist heat cooking does too: low. When liquid is present, only low heat is possible. This is best illustrated by French fries started in cold oil (see page 136); the oil itself won't rise above 210°F/99°C for almost all the cooking time, but as soon as the moisture has cooked out of the potato, the oil temperature shoots way up. The presence of moisture prevents high temperatures—whether you're poaching something in water or roasting something in a covered pot.

Bottom line: The slow-roasted pork shoulder (and other similarly tough cuts of meat) leads us to a truly diverse and mouthwatering set of preparations and dishes.

SLOW-ROASTED
PORK SHOULDER (212)

from SCRATCH
IS ABSURDLY easy to make
and it has so many possible uses.

you can slather it in

LEXINGTON
BBQ SAUCE (214)

OR

EAST CAROLINA
BBQ SAUCE (214)

and serve it on a roll
for some killer barbecue;

the same method can be used for
SLOW-ROASTED
SPARE RIBS (213) too

you can take a trip to Mexico and simmer it with

hominy for a
PORK POZOLE
ROJO (217), or

venture into Chinese
cooking with

CHAR SIU
PORK IN
LETTUCE
WRAPS (218)

The SLOW-ROAST
method used in these
dishes, and the related
technique of braising
(slow cooking in liquid to
break down tough con-
nective tissue) can also
be applied to beef, as in a

TEXAS-STYLE
PORK AND
BEEF
CHILI (228)

and if it works for Beef why not for veal or chicken? A BLANQUETTE DE VEAU (230) and a CHICKEN FRICASSEE (232) show that braising is a method that works for just about any cut of meat.

and in this chapter I'll wax poetic about the importance of TOASTING SPICES (227) and about THE SMELLS OF COOKING AT HOME. (221)

a method of preserving, including HOW TO MAKE YOUR OWN PICKLING SPICE (226)

HOW to CORN YOUR OWN BEEF (224)

for the latter I will tell you

or a HUNGARIAN BEEF GOULASH (220) or a traditional CORNED BEEF WITH BRAISED CABBAGE WEDGES (223)

SLOW-ROASTED PORK SHOULDER SERVES 8

This is so simple it almost shouldn't be allowed. But it is. Put a seasoned pork shoulder in a heavy pot, cover it tightly with a lid, and put it in a low oven (it can be as low as 200°F/93°C or as high as 275°F/135°C—the lower the temperature, the longer it will take). As the pork slowly heats and the fiber tenses up, water and juices are squeezed from the meat, filling the pot with liquid and vapor. So dead simple, it almost seems like cheating—as long as you think ahead (at least 4 hours, but the initial cooking can be done a day or two in advance and finished as needed). Once the shoulder is done, it can be taken in any number of directions—here, the American South, Mexico, Eastern Europe, and Asia. (You can also use a beef shoulder cut, typically sold as a chuck roast, with the same cooking technique; see Hungarian Beef Goulash, page 220.) One of my favorite ways to finish a slow-roasted pork shoulder is with barbecue sauce, for an East Carolina or Lexington-style BBQ. But it can also be turned into a chili or a pozole.

As a rule, a bone-in pork shoulder will give you a better result, but they're often sold boneless, and these work fine as well. This technique works with any size shoulder (it may be called pork butt or Boston butt at your grocery store or butcher's). I usually plan on 8 ounces/225 grams per serving, so a 4-pound/1.8-kilogram bone-in shoulder will be enough for eight people. If you're using a boneless shoulder, count on 6 ounces/170 grams per serving. Leftovers will keep for up to 5 days in the refrigerator and also freeze well, so I find that making extra is never a bad idea. A larger shoulder will need closer to 6 hours in the oven.

1 (4-pound/
  1.8 kilogram)
  bone-in pork
  shoulder, or
1 (3-pound/
  1.36-kilogram)
  boneless pork
  shoulder

Kosher salt and
  freshly ground
  black pepper *to taste*

Preheat your oven to 275°F/135°C.

Give all surfaces of the pork a generous coating of salt. Put the pork in a Dutch oven or other large pot, cover it, and put it in the oven for 4 hours (or a little less for a boneless shoulder).

Remove the lid and check to see if it's tender by shredding it with two forks. If it doesn't pull easily, cover the pot and return it to the oven for another hour, or until it does.

If you're in a hurry, you can cook the shoulder at 300°F/150°C for about 3 hours; or cut the pork into large chunks, add ¼ cup water, and cook it at that temperature for 2 to 2½ hours. If, on the other hand, you've got plenty of time, cook the shoulder at 225°F/107°C for 6 to 8 hours, or at 200°F/93°C overnight.

PERFECT SLOW-ROASTED SPARE RIBS

If you don't have the luxury of cooking ribs over a low, smoky fire for hours and hours but still want perfect ribs (either chewy or falling off the bone), the same principles that make Slow-Roasted Pork Shoulder (opposite) so delicious and simple work for spare ribs. Spare ribs, which are lower on the hog along the tough belly, need long, slow cooking to become tender. Salt and pepper them aggressively and sprinkle them with a little water, then wrap them tightly in aluminum foil and roast them low and slow until they reach the desired tenderness—typically 2 hours at 275°F/135°C will give you chewy ribs and 4 hours will give you falling-off-the-bone ribs.

When they are cooked to your liking, slather them with your favorite homemade or store-bought sauce and grill or broil them (on both sides or just the meaty side) till the sauce has caramelized and charred.

EAST CAROLINA BBQ AND LEXINGTON BBQ SERVES 8

*Preparations
Using the
Pork
Shoulder*

I'll start with perhaps my favorite use of the slow-roasted pork shoulder technique: East Carolina BBQ, which I first encountered when I was in college down there in the 1980s and have adored ever since. The straightforward vinegar and brown sugar mix was meant for pork shoulder cooked low and slow over a smoky fire—that's true barbecue. I highly recommend cutting your raw pork shoulder into slabs and grilling them over flames or, better still, throwing a lot of soaked wood chips in your charcoal grill and getting that pork very smoky. Once grilled or smoked, the slabs of pork can be slow-cooked in a covered pot as noted above.

If you're not grilling or adding some form of smoke, then use the Lexington-style sauce, which includes, by definition, some form of tomato product, typically ketchup, as I suggest here. (Locals never include fish sauce, but I do—fish sauce ties together all the umami ingredients going on in this sauce.)

I like to serve either type on a soft bun, with bread and butter pickles and chopped pickled chiles (page 296) along with some of the pickled chile liquid. If you order this in the South, you might very well be served a couple slices of Wonder Bread on the side. In North Carolina, you'd likely get a side of hushpuppies, basically cornbread batter deep-fried in bite-sized portions, and fried okra with your pile of barbecue. But you can serve barbecue however you like—on English muffins would be excellent, and the meat would make the beginnings of a great taco.

1 recipe Slow-Roasted Pork Shoulder (page 212)

East Carolina BBQ Sauce

1 cup/240 milliliters cider vinegar

¼ cup packed brown sugar

1 teaspoon freshly ground black pepper

1 to 2 teaspoons red pepper flakes (*optional*)

1 to 2 teaspoons liquid smoke (*optional*)

Lexington BBQ Sauce

1 cup/240 milliliters cider vinegar

½ cup/120 milliliters ketchup

¼ cup packed brown sugar

1 tablespoon smoked paprika

1 teaspoon chipotle powder

1 teaspoon freshly ground black pepper

1 tablespoon Worcestershire sauce

1 tablespoon fish sauce

Mix your choice of sauce ingredients together and serve with the pulled pork.

Note: Lexington BBQ sauce is popular in western North Carolina, and East Carolina BBQ sauce is from the part of that great barbecue state noted by its name. In between the two, and in South Carolina, a yellow mustard sauce is common. To make a version of that, replace the ketchup in the Lexington recipe with French's yellow mustard and change the brown sugar to honey.

If you would like to make your own soft rolls for these sandwiches, see pages 285 and 290, and follow instructions for making individual rolls.

PORK POZOLE ROJO   SERVES 6 TO 8

I love, love this dish. You can add as much or as little of the slow-roasted pork as you wish; I like an even amount of hominy and pork. The key is using a high-quality chili powder—just make sure it's fresh. Or combine a mix of your favorite dried chiles (ancho, guajillo, árbol, chipotle), toast them in an oven or dry skillet till crisp, dump out their seeds, and pulverize them in a spice or coffee grinder. Equally important is the hominy itself. You can buy it canned, but it doesn't come close to dried corn that you soak and cook yourself. (See page 183 for information on turning dried corn into hominy.)

If you want an amazing breakfast the next day, heat up a bowl of leftover pozole, top with two poached eggs, and season with cayenne or piment d'Espelette.

1 cup/200 grams dried hominy, soaked in 6 cups/1.4 liters water for at least 6 hours, undrained, or 3 cups/500 grams canned hominy

1 tablespoon vegetable oil

1 large Spanish onion, *cut into medium dice*

1 teaspoon kosher salt

2 tablespoons chili powder

1 tablespoon ground cumin

½ teaspoon freshly ground black pepper

½ teaspoon chipotle powder (*optional*)

1 (28-ounce/794-gram) can whole peeled tomatoes

½ recipe Slow-Roasted Pork Shoulder (page 212), *shredded between two forks*

Leaves and thin stems from 1 bunch cilantro, *for garnish*

Fried corn tortillas or tortilla chips, *for serving*

If using soaked dried hominy, pour the hominy and its soaking water into a large pot and bring to a boil over high heat, then reduce the heat and simmer until the corn is tender, about 90 minutes.

In a large pot or Dutch oven, heat the oil over medium-high heat; when it's hot, add the onion and salt. Cook until the onion is tender and even beginning to brown slightly, 10 minutes or so. Push the onion to one side of the pan and add the chili powder, cumin, black pepper, and chipotle powder (if using). Stir the spices and toast them briefly, then stir them into the onion.

Add the juices from the can of tomatoes, then add the tomatoes, squeezing them to crush them and expel their inner juices. Simmer for 20 minutes. Add the cooked (or canned) hominy, reserving its cooking liquid. Bring the pot back to a simmer, then stir in the cooked shredded pork. If you prefer your pozole looser, ladle in some of the reserved hominy liquid. Garnish with the cilantro and serve with crispy tortillas.

Note: Making your own tortillas is easy and worth the extra effort, especially if you buy corn tortillas at the store. Simply cut them into six triangles and fry. Do this for guacamole; season with salt and chili powders—they're so much cleaner and more flavorful and have a thicker texture than bagged tortilla chips. If making them for a soup or pozole garnish, I cut them in strips, leaving them all connected at one end to make frying them easier. if you want to go the From Scratch route, make your own corn dough by mixing a cup of corn flour, usually labeled masa harina in grocery stores, with ¾ cup/180 milliliters water and a pinch of salt, into a dough. Make about 8 balls of the dough and flatten them between sheets of plastic wrap beneath a skillet or Dutch oven. Toast them in a hot pan till nicely browned. When they're cool, cut and fry. (Or use some slow-roasted pork shoulder to make tacos!)

CHAR SIU PORK IN LETTUCE WRAPS   SERVES 8

Char siu, the hoisin-based sauce, is one of my favorite preparations, and it goes beautifully with slow-roasted pork in lettuce leaves, along with plenty of fresh, crunchy carrot and radish. Serve it with jasmine rice and a stir-fried or pan-steamed green vegetable such as snow or snap peas.

For the sauce:

½ cup/120 milliliters soy sauce

½ cup/120 milliliters hoisin sauce

¼ cup honey

¼ cup dry white wine

3 tablespoons sugar

2 tablespoons red wine vinegar

2 tablespoons toasted sesame oil

3 garlic cloves, *minced to a paste*

2 teaspoons five-spice powder

For the pork in lettuce cups:

½ recipe Slow-Roasted Pork Shoulder (page 212), *shredded between two forks*

16 butter lettuce leaves

1 cup/75 grams julienned daikon radish

1 cup/75 grams julienned carrot

1 cup/50 grams thinly sliced scallions

Preheat your oven to 425°F/218°C.

Combine all the sauce ingredients in a bowl and stir to combine.

Put the pork in a saucepan and reheat it over medium heat if necessary. Add the char siu sauce and mix to combine. Bring the sauce to a simmer. The pork and sauce should be very juicy, with plenty of sauce but not swimming in liquid.

Transfer the pork to a serving bowl and serve with the lettuce and vegetable garnishes. Put a few tablespoons of the pork in the center of a lettuce leaf and top with a sprinkling of carrot, radish, and scallion. Fold up to eat.

HUNGARIAN BEEF GOULASH   SERVES 6

This recipe takes the slow-roasted pork shoulder technique and applies it to another tough cut, the beef chuck roast (truth be told, you can make a perfectly good, if inauthentic, goulash with pork shoulder, too). Just as with the pork shoulder, here a tough cut of meat is cooked in a moist environment, and the heat and moisture work in tandem to break down the tough connective tissue. The stew comes together just like a chili or pozole: Onion is sautéed, spices are added and toasted, liquid—here in the form of tomatoes—goes in, and the dish is simmered till it's done. What I like about this is that the meat doesn't give up all its flavor to the braising liquid as it does in a traditional braise, wherein the meat would simmer for several hours. In this dish, the sauce is enriched with sour cream and the stew is garnished with parsley.

1 (3-pound/ 1.36-kilogram) chuck roast

Kosher salt *to taste*

¼ cup water

1 tablespoon vegetable oil

1 large Spanish onion, *cut into medium dice*

2 tablespoons good-quality sweet Hungarian paprika

1 tablespoon hot smoked paprika

2 teaspoons ground cumin

½ teaspoon freshly ground black pepper

¼ teaspoon cayenne pepper (*optional*)

1 cup/240 milliliters dry red wine

1 (28-ounce/794-gram) can crushed tomatoes, or 1 recipe Winter Tomato Sauce (page 101)

½ cup/120 milliliters sour cream

¼ cup minced fresh flat-leaf parsley

Buttered egg noodles, *for serving*

Preheat your oven to 275°F/135°C. Season the roast with salt and put it in a large pot or Dutch oven. Add the water, cover the pot, and put it in the oven for 3 to 4 hours, until fork-tender. Transfer the roast to a cutting board; pour off and reserve any juices in the pot.

Wipe out the pot. Place it over medium-high heat and add the vegetable oil. When it's hot, add the onion and give it a four-finger pinch of salt. Cook the onion until it's tender and just beginning to brown, about 5 minutes. Add both paprikas, the cumin, black pepper, and cayenne (if using) and stir to cook the spices for about a minute. Add the wine and bring it to a boil, then add the tomatoes and bring the pot to a simmer. Lower the heat to maintain a gentle simmer for about 15 minutes.

Meanwhile, cut the beef into 1-inch/2.5-centimeter chunks. Add the beef to the pot, along with any reserved juices. Continue to simmer for 20 to 30 minutes. Taste the sauce. Add more salt or seasonings if you wish. When the sauce is cooked and the beef is tender, stir in the sour cream. Garnish with the parsley and serve over buttered egg noodles.

A NOTE ABOUT THE SMELLS
OF COOKING AT HOME

Much is made of the importance of cooking at home. The benefits, of course, are many—economy, nutrition, sharing food together, and the conversation that happens at a bountiful table. My list can go on and on, but one of the most valuable and less recognized benefits is the power of aroma, of smell, and the impact on our brains and bodies of the smells of home cooking.

Almost unfailingly, when people walk into a house where delicious food is cooking, someone will say, "Oh, it smells so good in here!" There's a reason for this beyond sensory enjoyment.

Our olfactory system is perhaps the most deeply connected of our senses to our limbic system, that ancient part of our brain that is the seat of memory and emotions. I know that smells, even more than music, can return me to a specific time and place. When I returned as an adult to my freshman dormitory at Duke University, the characteristic smell of the place returned me powerfully to how and who I was as a freshman, my eighteen-year-old self. When I smell Dove soap, it returns me to my grandmother's home in suburban Detroit in the 1970s.

And when I walk into a home where something delicious is simmering on the stovetop or baking in the oven, I simply feel good. This good feeling comes from the fact that smells affect our parasympathetic nervous system, part of which is responsible for involuntary responses. One of those involuntary responses is stress versus relaxation. The smells of food cooking, which are invariably associated with being nourished and taken care of, relax us. So, when we walk into a kitchen where a chicken is roasting, or a corned

continues

beef is simmering, or a loaf of bread is baking, we immediately and involuntarily lose stress and feel an immediate sense of relaxation, one that is so powerful we remark on it, by saying "It smells good in here" or "I could smell it from the hallway!"

So, when you are braising beef short ribs in the oven or simmering a vegetable curry on the stovetop, you are filling the house with smells that make people feel more relaxed—yourself included. I know from personal experience that if I have a pot of Bolognese simmering on the stove on a Sunday afternoon, it seems that the bills are easier to pay. When my son and daughter were growing up, their rooms were on the third floor of our old suburban house. And while they were two floors distant from the kitchen, the aromas of that chicken roasting, of that stir-fry raging, rose all the way up, and I knew it had a comforting impact on their mood.

Much of the impact of smell has to do with associative emotion, emotions we felt when we first smelled something. You know exactly how you feel when you enter a dentist's office. If you own pets, you know *they* know exactly where they are when you bring them to the vet.

The smells of food are linked to nourishment, which makes our bodies feel good. When we smell food cooking that we aren't preparing, we know we're going to be sharing it with people who care about us. That feels good.

The smell of good food cooking in the home is one of the most powerful impacts that cooking for our friends and family has on those friends and family.

CORNED BEEF WITH BRAISED CABBAGE WEDGES SERVES 4 TO 6

Reporting a story about a great and unexpected food mecca, Dingle, Ireland, I interviewed the father of a chef who recited his weekly menu growing up in what was then a barren and poor culinary land. Corned beef and cabbage and potatoes. Bacon, corned beef, and potatoes. Cabbage, carrots, and potatoes. Fish on Friday, of course. But corned beef was a peasant-style meal prevalent there, brought to America by the wave of Irish immigrants. It remains a stellar meal today when prepared well. While you can cook the corned beef in a 275°F/135°C oven, I prefer simmering it on the stovetop, because it makes the household smell so good. I like to cook the cabbage in bacon fat for the flavor, but you can omit the bacon and use vegetable oil if you prefer. Serve this with boiled red potatoes topped with butter and sprinkled with minced fresh parsley.

Other Slow Roasts and Braises

1 (2- to 3-pound/ 0.9- to 1.36-kilogram) corned beef, *homemade (page 224) or store-bought*

1 onion, *peeled and halved through the root (so that it stays together)*

2 carrots, *roughly chopped*

2 celery ribs, *roughly chopped*

2 tablespoons Pickling Spice (page 226)

4 ounces/110 grams bacon lardons or thickly sliced bacon, *cut into ½-inch/1-centimeter strips*

4 to 6 cabbage wedges

Put the corned beef in the smallest pot that will hold it, add the onion halves, carrots, celery, and pickling spice, and cover with water. Bring the water to a simmer over high heat, then cover the pot, reduce the heat to low, and simmer gently for 3 hours, or until the beef is tender. Strain the cooking liquid and reserve.

Put the bacon in a skillet and add ½ cup/120 milliliters water. Bring to a boil over high heat and cook until the water cooks off and the bacon fat begins to crackle, then reduce the heat to low and cook gently to brown the bacon. Transfer the bacon to a paper towel–lined plate or bowl, reserving the bacon fat in the pan.

Turn the heat to medium-high. Add the cabbage wedges to the bacon fat and sear to brown the cabbage on both sides. When they are nicely browned, add ¼ cup of the strained corned beef

cooking liquid and ¼ cup water. Bring it to a simmer, then cover and cook the cabbage just until it's tender, adding more cooking liquid if you wish.

To serve, slice the corned beef and serve it with the cabbage wedges, moistening it all with additional strained cooking liquid.

CORNED BEEF   SERVES 8

If you can brine chicken, you can corn (preserve) beef. As with everything in the kitchen, it's all a matter of planning ahead, because corning beef takes several days. You also need to have some pink curing salt on hand, which you typically need to order by mail (my go-to online source is Butcher & Packer). Strictly speaking, you don't have to use curing salt, but if you don't, the meat will look like a pot roast, not corned beef, and it won't have quite the same flavor (though it will still be delicious).

Pink salt is sold under the names DQ Cure #1, Insta Cure #1, Prague Powder #1, and TCM #1. They are all the same, a mixture of salt and sodium nitrite, tinted pink so that no one will mistake it for regular salt. Ingested in large quantities, it can be harmful. (The #1 is to distinguish it from #2 curing salt, which is used exclusively for dry-curing sausages.)

Curing salt's primary function is to prevent botulism poisoning, but it also keeps meat pink and gives it a piquant flavor. Used in very small quantities—that is, 0.25 percent of the weight of the meat—it is not harmful. It is a remarkable substance, which you will also need to make your own bacon (see page 279).

I'm using chuck roast here, rather than the traditional brisket, because briskets these days are far too lean and dry. A chuck roast has better marbling and so makes a better corned beef, in my opinion.

The steps are simple: Make a brine, let it cool, put the meat in it, and refrigerate it (or put it in a cold place) for 5 days, then cook it in heavily spiced water. That's it. (Here's another project for you: If you have a smoker or a charcoal grill, try making your own pastrami. After the beef has brined for 5 days to become corned beef, coat it in a mixture of coarsely ground coriander and black peppercorns and smoke or grill it. Any beef can be treated this way. Short ribs are especially good corned and coated with pepper and coriander.)

This recipe has the salt percentages built into it, so it's important that you use a chuck roast that is pretty close to 4 pounds/1.8 kilograms (note that this is the same amount of water called for in the recipe—that is, equal weights of water and meat). If you want to cure smaller or larger amounts of meat, do what I did for this recipe: Use the same weight of water that your chuck roast weighs. Add the two weights together for the total meat-water weight. Then calculate 2 percent of that total weight to determine how much kosher salt you will need for the brine. This is also the amount of kosher salt you will need for the cooking liquid (which should be the same amount of water as for the brine). Then calculate 0.25 percent of the total meat-water weight and that is how much pink salt you will need. The rest—sugar, aromatics, and spices—can be added at your discretion. This way you can cure any amount of meat you have.

recipe continues

*Other Slow
Roasts and
Braises*

For the brine:

Scant 2 quarts/
1.8 liters water

5 tablespoons/
72 grams kosher
salt

¼ cup brown sugar

2 tablespoons
Pickling Spice
(at right)

1½ teaspoons/
10 grams pink
curing salt

5 garlic cloves,
*smashed with the side
of a chef's knife*

1 medium onion,
thinly sliced

1 carrot, peeled and
roughly chopped

1 celery rib,
roughly chopped

For the beef:

1 (4-pound/
1.8-kilogram) beef
chuck roast

Scant 2 quarts/
1.8 liters water

5 tablespoons/
72 grams kosher
salt

2 tablespoons
Pickling Spice
(at right)

1 medium onion,
*peeled and halved
through the root
(so that it stays
together)*

1 carrot, peeled and
roughly chopped

1 celery rib,
roughly chopped

First, make the brine: In a large pot, combine the water, kosher salt, brown sugar, pickling spice, pink curing salt, garlic, onion, carrot, and celery. Bring to a simmer, stirring until the salt and sugar are dissolved. Remove the pot from the heat and let cool to room temperature, then refrigerate until chilled.

Place the beef in the brine and weight it down with a plate to keep it submerged; cover. Refrigerate for 5 days. Remove the beef from the brine and rinse thoroughly.

Put the beef in a pot just large enough to hold it and the other ingredients. Add the water, kosher salt, pickling spice, onion, carrot, and celery. Bring to a boil over high heat, reduce the heat to low, and cover. Simmer gently (or put in a 275°F/135°C oven) until the beef is fork-tender, about 3 hours, adding more water if needed to keep the beef covered.

PICKLING SPICE
MAKES ABOUT 1 CUP

You can find pickling spice at most grocery stores—McCormick and other companies offer their versions—but this pickling spice, based on a recipe from Brian Polcyn, my *Charcuterie* coauthor, is far superior. It's a similar profile but much more flavorful, like the difference between the Beatles' version of "Eight Days a Week" and a Muzak version. Store it in your refrigerator and it keeps for months.

3 tablespoons whole
black peppercorns

3 tablespoons
coriander seeds

2 tablespoons
mustard seeds

2 tablespoons
allspice berries

2 tablespoons whole
cloves

2 tablespoons red
pepper flakes

1 tablespoon ground
mace

1 tablespoon ground
ginger

2 small cinnamon
sticks, *cracked and
broken into pieces*

4 bay leaves, *crumbled*

Toast the peppercorns, coriander seeds, mustard seeds, allspice berries, and cloves in a dry pan over high heat for a minute, just till they smell fragrant (be careful not to burn them). Crack them beneath a sauté pan or chop with a knife. Transfer them to a small jar or zip-top plastic bag and add the red pepper flakes, mace, ginger, cinnamon, and bay leaves; mix well. Store in the refrigerator to use as needed.

THE IMPORTANCE OF TOASTING SPICES

You may notice that recipes often suggest toasting whole spices in a hot, dry pan for a minute or so, until they become fragrant. The oils in the seeds are released or intensified in high heat, less so when added raw to water. In fact, I know at least one chef who contends that adding whole black peppercorns to stock has absolutely no effect unless they're cracked, and I'm inclined to agree. Does this mean I always crack my peppercorns before adding them to stock? No. Reason? Lazy or pressed for time. Both of which are fine. You get what you put into it.

But it's important at least to be aware that toasting spices before they are combined with a liquid has a powerful impact on how those spices affect your dish. This is why in chilis and curries, I almost always add them to a dry pan, usually after sautéing onion but before adding any liquid ingredients (water, tomatoes, stock).

Toasting has the biggest impact on whole spices. I suspect this is in part because whole spices are fresher for not being pre-ground at a factory. But for whatever reason, I know from experience that peppercorns and whole cumin seeds and the like are twice as effective when toasted before being ground or cracked and added to the pot.

So, if you have time and want to make your spices as powerful as they can be, toast them first. If you cook them too long, they can burn, so don't leave them alone. Get your pan hot, add the spices, and swirl them around. It takes a minute or less, just till you can smell them.

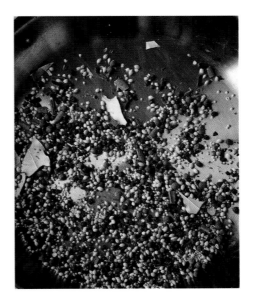

TEXAS-STYLE PORK AND BEEF CHILI SERVES 8

This recipe takes us into more straightforward braise territory, searing the same cuts we've been using, then simmering the meat in a liquid (another form of moist heat cooking), though there's no reason you couldn't use the slow-roast method. Here the meat is diced and seared, which develops flavor from the browning. Searing also sets the protein so that blood and impurities don't leach out into the stock. You can use a store-bought beef broth (see page 18 on enhancing store-bought broth), but homemade brown veal stock really puts this over the top and is highly recommended. That and using very fresh spices, and making sure they are nicely toasted before adding the liquid. An alternative to searing is to oil the diced meat, spread them out on a baking sheet (don't crowd them), and put them in a 450°F/230°C oven until they're nicely browned. You can cook the onion and toast the spices while the meat roasts. Or you can take the extra step of flouring the meat after it's been seasoned and then searing it. This adds even more flavor to the sauce and also helps thicken it a little. And if you're running short on time, you can skip the searing stage altogether (but I think it's worth the extra effort).

I call it Texas style to denote that it doesn't include beans, as many traditional American chilis do. But if you like beans in your chili, feel free to add any variety you wish, either to replace some of the meat or just to add to the dish as a whole.

2 pounds/900 grams boneless pork shoulder, *cut into 1-inch/2.5-centimeter dice*

2 pounds/900 grams boneless chuck roast, *cut into 1-inch/2.5-centimeter dice*

Kosher salt and freshly ground black pepper *to taste*

Vegetable oil *as needed*

1 large onion, *diced*

2 tablespoons high-quality chili powder

2 tablespoons ground cumin

1 tablespoon ground coriander

2 teaspoons chipotle powder

1 cup/240 milliliters dry red wine

1 quart/1 liter Classic Brown Veal Stock (page 146), or 2 cups/480 milliliters each Classic Brown Veal Stock and One-Hour Beef Stock (page 142), *or store-bought beef broth*

1 (28-ounce/794-gram) can whole peeled tomatoes

2 tablespoons honey

1 tablespoon fish sauce

To serve:

2 cups/360 grams long-grain rice, *cooked according to the package instructions*

1 cup/240 milliliters sour cream

1 cup/110 grams grated cheddar cheese

1 bunch scallions, *finely sliced*

Give the pork and beef an aggressive salting and then pepper the meat. Pour enough oil into a heavy pot or Dutch oven to cover the bottom. Heat the oil over high heat. When it is smoking-hot, add the meat in one layer, taking care not to crowd the pieces, and sear it well. You may need to sear the meat in batches depending on the size of your pot.

Transfer the meat to a paper towel–lined bowl. Pour off all but about a tablespoon of oil from the pot. Add the onion and reduce the heat to medium-high. Give it an aggressive hit of salt. Cook, stirring, until the onion is tender and just beginning to brown, 3 to 5 minutes. Push the onion to the side of the pan and add the chili powder, cumin, coriander, and chipotle powder. Stir the spices so they toast on the bottom of the pan, then stir them into the onion.

Add the red wine to deglaze the pan. When the wine has cooked off, add the stock. Add the tomatoes and their juices, squeezing to pulverize each tomato, and the honey and fish sauce. Return the meat to the pot and bring it to a simmer. Simmer over low heat loosely covered, for 2 to 3 hours (or transfer to a 300°F/150°C oven) for 3 to 4 hours, until the meat, when pierced with a fork, gives no resistance.

Serve over rice and garnish with the sour cream, cheese, and scallions, or as you wish.

Other Slow Roasts and Braises

BLANQUETTE DE VEAU   SERVES 4 TO 6

This simple beef stew was one of the most exciting dishes I learned to make in my earliest days at culinary school. Why? Because it was the simplest of stews but one that, through care, resulted in a finished dish of extraordinary elegance. It was a dish that one of the early skills classes prepared for the graduation-day banquet, to which the Culinary Institute of America's president, Ferdinand Metz, always came. And I was alerted to the fact that President Metz, a man greatly respected by the students, always looked forward to this dish in particular.

As I was a journalist just learning culinary craft, the information made a big impact. It said to me that a so-called peasant dish, a meat stew, could be four-star cooking. And, further, that four-star cooking did not mean truffles and foie gras or veal Orloff served tableside. Rather, it meant care. Care on the part of the cook (for instance, this recipe calls for blanching the veal first, so that the resulting sauce is free of impurities that meat can release when added raw to stock). That's what blanquette de veau means to me, that it is the cook who determines whether or not a dish is four-star, not the dish itself, nor the ingredients that went into it.

Blanquette de veau also means a delicious dinner. My kids loved this dish when they were younger—and it was something that I could make on a weekday night provided I had some beef stock on hand. I hadn't yet come up with the idea that you could make beef stock in an hour, but whenever I made traditional beef stock, I'd save some for this stew. I make this only if I have good stock on hand, but if you want to use store-bought broth, it will still be a good veal stew—and even better than good if you add some aromatics to the broth before or while you're cooking the veal.

An additional enhancement to the stew is a miraculous little lever of richness and texture called a liaison, which is simply a mixture of cream and egg yolk. I don't know exactly how it works, but this combination turns a regular sauce into something beguilingly smooth and delicious on the tongue. The liaison is stirred into the blanquette just before serving. (Be careful not to let the liquid boil after you've added the liaison, or the egg can cook and curdle.)

I like to serve the blanquette on buttered egg noodles, topped with a sprinkle of minced parsley to add some color. No matter how you finish it, this is a heavenly dish primarily because of the cook's care.

2 pounds/900 grams veal stew meat, *cut into large dice*

4 to 5 cups/950 to 1200 milliliters One-Hour Beef Stock (page 142) *or store-bought beef broth*

Kosher salt *to taste*

4 tablespoons/ 60 grams unsalted butter

6 tablespoons/ 45 grams all-purpose flour

12 cipollini onions, *trimmed, blanched, and peeled*

12 ounces/340 grams white button mushrooms, *brushed clean and quartered*

1 lemon wedge

2 large egg yolks

½ cup/120 milliliters heavy cream

Buttered egg noodles, *for serving*

Minced fresh flat-leaf parsley, *for garnish*

Other Slow Roasts and Braises

Bring a large pot of water to a boil over high heat. Add the veal and allow the water to return to a boil. When the water has come to a boil and the foam from the meat has risen to the top, drain the meat and rinse under cold running water.

Put the veal in a 3-quart/3-liter pot or Dutch oven and add enough stock to cover the meat by an inch or so. Bring the stock to a simmer, then lower the heat and simmer, uncovered, for about 90 minutes, until the veal is tender. Add a teaspoon of salt, or to taste, while it's simmering.

While the veal is cooking, melt the butter in a small sauté pan over medium heat to start a roux. When it has melted completely (the idea is to cook off as much water as possible before adding the flour), add the flour and cook until the flour smells like pie crust, a couple of minutes. Set the roux aside to cool.

When the meat is tender, add the onions and mushrooms and cook for about 10 minutes, until the onions are tender. Whisk in the roux in increments, allowing the sauce to thicken until it is exactly as you like it. Add a squeeze of lemon (1 or 2 teaspoons) and more salt as needed.

In a small bowl, whisk together the yolks and cream until they're uniformly combined to make the liaison. Stir the liaison into the stew, then remove the pot from the heat.

Serve on buttered egg noodles, topped with a sprinkling of parsley.

CHICKEN FRICASSEE SERVES 4 TO 6

This rustic preparation uses the same technique as in the refined Blanquette de Veau (page 230), bringing moist heat to chicken instead of veal. (Note that we've gone from pork to beef to veal to chicken, all using a similar technique employed on a tough muscle with plenty of connective tissue.) Here the chicken is floured and then seared, and vegetables are added to make it more of a stew. Fricassee can be made using bone-in, skin-on chicken parts (or even a whole chicken, cut up as for Neath Pal's Cambodian Chicken Curry, page 257), though they need to cook a little longer, an hour or so, and you'll need to add a little water. This version, using boneless, skinless thighs, can be done entirely on the stovetop.

You can use one of two strategies for the vegetables. I like to see bright vegetables and be able to taste them. If they cook for 30 to 45 minutes, they become mushy and dull in color and give up most of their flavor to the sauce, as is the case with most stews. There's really nothing wrong with this—indeed, if you're using store-bought broth, I recommend sautéing all the vegetables together before adding the liquid. But if you already have delicious stock, try adding the carrots late in the cooking and the celery just before you finish the stew. This will keep them bright and firm when you serve. If you want to add even more nutrition, add a cup or more of frozen peas, bring it back to a simmer, then add the celery and finish the stew.

I use beurre manié (see page 32) to thicken the sauce at the end (though the flour from the chicken will have already begun the process). Traditionally, a liaison, like the one used in the blanquette, is not called for, but it adds such great texture to the finished stew that I don't see any reason not to include it as an option here.

3 tablespoons all-purpose flour, plus *more for dusting the chicken*

3 tablespoons/ 45 grams unsalted butter, *at room temperature*

6 to 8 boneless, skinless chicken thighs

Kosher salt and freshly ground black pepper *to taste*

⅓ cup/80 milliliters vegetable oil, *plus more if needed*

1 Spanish onion, *cut into medium dice*

5 garlic cloves, *coarsely chopped*

1 leek, *halved lengthwise, white and pale green parts thinly sliced, dark green parts tied with kitchen string*

1 cup/240 milliliters dry white wine

1 quart/1 liter Easy Overnight Chicken Stock (page 38) or store-bought chicken broth

2 bay leaves

1 small bunch thyme, *tied with kitchen string*

2 carrots, *peeled and cut into medium dice*

2 celery ribs, *cut into ½-inch/1-centimeter slices*

2 large egg yolks *(optional)*

½ cup/120 milliliters heavy cream *(optional)*

1 large wedge of lemon

Make a beurre manié by mixing the flour and butter with a fork or your fingers until it is a uniform paste. Refrigerate until ready to use.

Season the chicken with a generous amount of salt and let it sit for 10 minutes (or refrigerate it until you're ready to cook it), then give it an aggressive dusting of pepper. Put enough flour in a zip-top plastic bag to coat the chicken. Put the chicken in the bag and shake. Remove the chicken, gently shaking off the excess flour, and place on a wire rack to allow more excess flour to fall off.

In a Dutch oven or large, heavy skillet, heat the vegetable oil over high heat. When it's hot and rippling, add the chicken and cook till it's nicely browned on both sides, lowering the heat as necessary to avoid burning the flour. Depending on the size of your pot, you may need to do this in two batches. Transfer the chicken to a paper towel–lined plate.

If the excess flour in the pan is burned, wipe out the pan completely and add a tablespoon or two of vegetable oil. If the flour is merely browned, leave it in the pan and pour off all but a tablespoon or two of oil. Return the pan to medium high-heat and add the onion. Give the onion a four-finger pinch of salt and cook, stirring, for a minute or two to get them browning. Add the garlic and thinly sliced leek. (If you're using store-bought broth or simply want to cook everything at once, you may want to add the carrot and celery here as well.) Turn the heat to high and add the white wine. Simmer, stirring frequently.

When the wine has cooked off, add the stock, leek greens, bay leaves, and thyme and simmer for 30 to 45 minutes. If the level of the stock goes below the chicken and vegetables, add water as necessary. Add the carrots; when they are al dente (after a few minutes), add the celery. Remove and discard the leek greens, bay leaves, and thyme. Stir in the beurre manié in increments till it's the consistency you like. If using the liaison, whisk together the egg yolks and cream in a small bowl, then stir the mixture into the pot. Season with fresh lemon juice and serve immediately.

Other Slow Roasts and Braises

CHAPTER 8

Curry

In India, *curry* means "sauce," and typically it refers to the sauce used in a dish. By the time you reach Southeast Asia, *curry* comes to mean "stew," typically an aromatic and spicy stew that extends across a broad expanse of the world. (The etymology of the word is somewhat obscure. Some sources suggest it comes from a Tamil word meaning "sauce," others from the word meaning "to prepare"— that's how general it is.) For those of us who did not grow up in Asia, curries are not household staples or the stuff of daily meals but are an occasional foray away from our Western staple meals. These are good and necessary diversions. They keep things lively and prevent us from getting into cooking ruts. I also suspect that part of their appeal, for those who don't make a stir-fry or a curry or two every week, is that these meals add to a nutritional diversity that our bodies respond to and crave. I believe that when we crave Chinese or Thai food or a spicy Indian curry, it's more than just our mood; it's possible that our bodies are calling out for the differing nutritional offerings from, say, the galangal and rich coconut milk in a Thai dish, the heavy clove and cardamom in an Indian curry.

Of course, maybe we like to cook and eat this way simply because it's fun and delicious. The flavors from the East are truly dynamic. Compare an American beef stew or Yankee pot roast with a Thai beef curry that uses green chile paste, cumin, coriander, lime leaves, lemongrass, lime juice, and cilantro. They are a world apart.

The New York chef Jean-Georges Vongerichten might have been a classical French chef (he's from eastern France) had he not traveled to Thailand in 1980 to open a restaurant in Bangkok for his mentor, Louis Outhier. I've tried to imagine what it must have been like for Vongerichten. Forty years ago, he'd never heard of lemongrass or galangal, let alone seen them fresh. They didn't produce dairy in Thailand at that time, but they used coconut milk. He was twenty-four and he'd never had a mango. Soon he was pairing this exotic fruit with foie gras. And when he came to the United States five years later to open more restaurants for Outhier in Boston and New York, he made an extraordinary splash by using the dramatic flavors of Asia in contemporary French cuisine.

I wonder if this could even be done today, so changed is our food world. We grow up with mangos now, and kiwi and jackfruit are in grocery stores throughout the country. Asian markets are common in smaller cities as well as in New York and San Francisco and LA. And even if we don't cook with ingredients grown on the other side of the planet, we go to restaurants where they are routinely cooked for us.

This is a good thing, of course. Happily, we can buy all manner of spices and aromatic rhizomes without traveling the world. And we should.

I grew up in Cleveland, where there were a few Asian markets where I could buy the various ingredients listed in Craig Claiborne and Virginia Lee's *Chinese Cookbook*. And that was how, using my parents' electric wok, I began cooking Chinese-style food. When I went to the Culinary Institute of America to write about becoming a chef, I was excited to be in Shirley Cheng's introduction to Asian cuisine class, where, as in all the early kitchens in that school's curriculum, we focused on the basics. When you have solid basics, you can extend them as far as you want.

The intent of this chapter is to focus on three key areas of Asian cuisine— Indian curry, Southeast Asian curry, and Chinese stir-fry—and to explore the basics of each so that you can apply those basics in any number of similar preparations and have a solid footing in each to comfortably throw together an Indian or Thai curry or a Chinese stir-fry.

As a native Midwesterner who has scarcely traveled in Asia, I felt it was incumbent on me to put some of my reportorial skills to work here, as well, to ensure my own accuracy and to include some authentic voices in this chapter. Chef Suvir

Saran, born in India, critiqued the Indian curries and offered a recipe for one of his own favorite dishes from his youth. So did Cambodian chef Neath Pal, and writer, cookbook author, and photographer, Diane Cu, born in Vietnam.

I love a roast chicken maybe more than any single home-cooked meal, but sometimes—often, in fact—I want a chicken curry. And when I crave a curry, nothing else will do.

A CURRY is one thing in India and another in Thailand or Vietnam. And yet in their wonderful diversity these dishes share common ingredients, flavor profiles, and techniques, and they do, also, with the Chinese stir-fry. Here I will explore an intensely flavorful North Indian Curry (241) and a spicy LAMB VINDALOO (242) to begin a journey into Asian seasoning.

I will talk about cooking with GHEE (244), and share THE EXTRAORDINARY SPICED BROWN BUTTER TECHNIQUE (244). Multipurpose spice mixes like GARAM MASALA (249) and VINDALOO CURRY POWDER (242) and PANCH PHORAN (249) help bring complex flavors to many wonderful meals.

Vegetarian dishes and accompaniments like SUVIR SARAN'S KITCHEREE (246), TAHIREE RICE CASSEROLE (248), DAL (245), RAITA (252), and a simple VEGETABLE CURRY with ROASTED CAULIFLOWER (251) make an appearance, and I devote a good deal of attention to THE AMAZING CHICKPEA (256) with recipes for CHANA MASALA (253), HUMMUS (253), and SPICED FRIED CHICKPEAS (254).

→ Venturing southeast,

To the flavors of China, admittedly by way of Chinese cooking as it is practiced in the U.S. I cover Stir-Fry Basics (266) and provide recipes for beloved dishes including KUNG PAO STYLE Chicken (268), Perfect JASMINE or BASMATI RICE (270), STIR-FRIED BEEF with Broccoli (269), and HOT, SWEET, CRISPY Stir-Fried CHICKEN (271), using a great technique for beef as well.

you will be rewarded with a THAI GREEN CURRY (264), including a method for THAI GREEN CURRY paste (265) as well as Neath Pals CAMBODIAN CHICKEN CURRY (257) and a recipe for YELLOW CURRY PASTE (258). Rounding out the curries is DIANE CU's VIETNAMESE CURRY (262), a simple and satisfying adaptation of an old family recipe. This culinary journey moves northward.

Toasting spices helps bring out the best flavor. You can toast them on their own or, as I advise in this recipe, clear a space in the pan to toast them alongside other ingredients.

NORTH INDIAN CURRY   SERVES 4 TO 6

Here is an intensely seasoned basic curry in the style of northern India. You can put the whole spices, the clove and cardamom, in cheesecloth if you wish, in order to remove them easily after the stew is cooked, something we almost always do in Western cooking (called a *sachet d'épices*). But chef Suvir Saran makes a good argument for the Indian tradition of leaving them to travel independently throughout the stew (see page 246). Shah jeera, also known as black cumin, is worth seeking out and getting to know. It is cumin-like but has a mild smoky flavor. This recipe presents general principles and ingredients that are found in many curries.

Indian-Style Curries

1 to 2 tablespoons vegetable oil

1 onion, *cut into medium dice*

Kosher salt *to taste*

6 to 8 boneless, skinless chicken thighs, *cut into thin strips*

2 teaspoons ground cumin

2 teaspoons ground coriander

2 teaspoons ground turmeric

1 teaspoon shah jeera (*black cumin; optional*)

¼ teaspoon Indian chili powder or red pepper flakes

1 (½-inch/1-centimeter) piece ginger, *grated*

1 green bell pepper, *seeded and cut into medium dice*

1 red bell pepper, *seeded and cut into medium dice*

2 cups/480 milliliters Easy Overnight Chicken Stock (page 38) or store-bought chicken broth

1 (14.5-ounce/ 411-gram) can whole peeled or diced tomatoes

6 green cardamom seeds

6 whole cloves

1 short cinnamon stick, *halved*

2 bay leaves

½ cup/120 milliliters heavy cream

Steamed basmati rice (see page 270), papadums, and Raita (page 252), *for serving*

In a Dutch oven, heat 1 tablespoon oil over medium to medium-high heat. When the oil is hot, add the onion and hit it with a four-finger pinch of salt. Cook until the onion is translucent, then push it to the side of the pan and add the chicken. Brown the chicken on all sides, adding another tablespoon of oil if necessary. When the chicken has gotten good color, push it into the onion to clear a spot to cook your spices. Add the cumin, coriander, turmeric, shah jeera (if using), chili powder, and ginger. Stir these around to toast them. Add the bell peppers, then stir everything together. Add 1 cup/240 milliliters of the stock and scrape up any fond (browned matter) stuck to the pan. Add the tomatoes and their juices; if using whole, crush each in your hand as you add it. Add the cardamom, cloves, cinnamon, and bay leaves and simmer on low for 45 to 60 minutes.

Stir in the cream and serve immediately with the rice, papadums, and raita.

LAMB VINDALOO SERVES 4 TO 6

Indian-Style
Curries

This is a famously spicy dish from southern India, most associated with the city of Goa. It apparently began as a pork curry, and I encourage you to make it this way, simply adding Slow-Roasted Pork Shoulder (page 212) after the sauce has cooked properly. But I wanted to use lamb here because I love the way the sweetness of the meat goes with the dramatic seasoning.

2 pounds/900 grams boneless lamb shoulder, *cut into large dice*

Kosher salt *to taste*

3 tablespoons vegetable oil

1 medium onion, *diced*

1 (1-inch/½-centimeter) piece ginger, *grated*

4 garlic cloves, *minced*

2 to 3 tablespoons Vindaloo Curry Powder (*at right*)

2 cups/480 milliliters Vegetable Stock (page 114), Easy Overnight Chicken Stock (*page 38*), or store-bought broth

1 (14.5-ounce/ 411-gram) can whole peeled tomatoes

Leaves and thin stems from 1 bunch cilantro, *for garnish*

Season the lamb aggressively with salt. In a Dutch oven, heat the oil over high heat; when it's hot, add the lamb. Sear the lamb on all sides, then transfer it to a plate. Add the onion to the pot and season with salt. Cook the onion till it's tender, adding the ginger and garlic as you do.

Push the aromatics to the side of the pan and add the vindaloo curry powder. Stir it to cook the spices, 30 seconds or so. Return the meat to the pan and stir to incorporate it all.

Add the stock and tomatoes with their juices (squeezing the tomatoes to mush as you add each one). Simmer on low for 45 to 60 minutes. Taste and adjust the seasonings as necessary, then serve, garnished with the cilantro.

VINDALOO CURRY POWDER

MAKES ¼ CUP/25 GRAMS

1 tablespoon coriander seeds

2 teaspoons black peppercorns

1 teaspoon cumin seeds

12 green cardamom pods

12 whole cloves

1½ teaspoons ground turmeric

2 to 4 teaspoons Indian chili powder (*2 is considered spicy by many, but if you like it hot, use 4*)

¼ teaspoon ground cinnamon

Toast the coriander, peppercorns, cumin, cardamom, and cloves in a hot, dry skillet over medium-high heat. Grind these toasted spices in a mortar, discarding the cardamom husks as they separate from the powder. Combine with the turmeric, chili powder, and cinnamon. Alternatively, you can put it all in a spice grinder and pulverize it. Store in an airtight container for up to 4 months.

CLARIFIED BUTTER, GHEE, AND AN EXTRAORDINARY SPICED BROWN BUTTER

To make a quick clarified butter, an extremely tasty fat to cook with, simply melt 8 tablespoons/115 grams unsalted butter in a measuring glass in the microwave (or melt it in a pot on the stovetop and then pour it into a measuring glass). Allow the solids and water to sink to the bottom. Skim any protein from the top, then very carefully strain into another measuring glass, just until the milky stuff is about to start coming with it. Use this clarified butter in Suvir Saran's Birbal Kee Khitcheree (page 246) instead of vegetable oil, or for Fried Chickpeas (page 254). Or as the fat in any of the curries.

Ghee, browned clarified butter, is another of the primary fats used in Indian cooking. It's worth making because it tastes so good: Simply melt unsalted butter in a saucepan, skimming the surface solids as they form (these are proteins). The water and milk solids will sink to the bottom. As the water cooks off, the solids get hot enough to brown. Allow them to brown, then strain the butter through a fine-mesh strainer or coffee filter.

In India, most curries would use ghee as the main cooking fat, but I prefer to use a spiced brown butter because it includes the tasty butter solids. The culinary term for the method is tempering, which denotes the blooming of spices in fat. This method can be put to use in any curry or bean dish (I use it in my Dal, page 245). Here's how it works:

In a small sauté pan, melt 2 to 3 tablespoons/30 to 45 grams unsalted butter. Continue to cook it till it stops foaming, which means the water is almost cooked off and the butter will begin to brown. When the butter is beautifully browned, add all your spices and aromatics. These will cool the pan so the butter doesn't burn. When they're all cooked and the butter is heating up and turning golden brown again, stop the cooking with a big squeeze of lemon and remove the pan from the heat. Add this to your cooked legumes and behold the amazing transformation.

DAL SERVES 4

Dal is one of my favorite things to eat. Long ago, when I worked for a magazine in my hometown of Cleveland, I profiled an Indian chef/restaurateur named Sheela Sogal. She taught me her dal, a fascinating combination of mung beans and earthy black-eyed peas, cooked in water for 45 minutes or so. But what I found remarkable was the way she finished it. It would be years before I heard a technical term for what she did, which was tempering. But it makes so much sense, and even mimics the ghee that would have been used in her native land, though it includes the tasty browned butter solids.

It works with all sorts of beans—red, yellow, or green lentils or Sheela's mung beans. As Suvir Saran describes it, the seasonings bloom in the hot fat. Do they ever.

Indian-Style Curries

- 1 cup/200 grams lentils
- 3 cups/710 milliliters water
- 2 teaspoons ground cumin
- 1 teaspoon ground turmeric
- ½ teaspoon shah jeera (black cumin seeds)
- ½ teaspoon kosher salt
- ¼ teaspoon chili powder
- 1 (1-inch/ 2.5-centimeter) piece ginger, *grated*
- 1 garlic clove, *minced*
- 4 tablespoons/ 60 grams unsalted butter
- 1 tablespoon lemon juice (*or a generous squeeze*)

Combine the lentils and water in a saucepan and bring to a simmer over high heat. Cover, reduce the heat to low, and cook until tender, about 45 minutes. Combine the cumin, turmeric, shah jeera, salt, chili powder, ginger, and garlic in a ramekin.

In a small sauté pan over high heat, melt the butter. When it is quiet and expands in froth, add the spices and aromatics. Cook until the clear part of the butter is a deep brown, then remove the pan from the heat and add the lemon juice. Stir, then stir this mixture into the lentils. Simmer for 5 or so more minutes, then remove from the heat. This can sit and be reheated or served immediately.

SUVIR SARAN'S BIRBAL KEE KHITCHEREE   SERVES 6 TO 8

Indian-Style Curries

Years ago, I met a wonderful chef born in New Delhi named Suvir Saran. He was such a gentle and friendly soul that I attached myself to him immediately and was soon eating regularly at his restaurant Dévi on East Eighteenth Street in New York City. Several years later he competed on *Top Chef Masters* and was sent packing for making a veggie burger instead of the requested bacon cheeseburger, describing to the judges the ill effects of eating too much red meat. Here he is most welcome to introduce his khitcheree, an Indian bean-rice-vegetable stew, a one-pot meal that in India may be eaten for breakfast, lunch, or dinner. He also offers several of his standard spice mixtures. (If you're interested to dive deeper into Indian curries, I highly recommend his books, *American Masala* and *Indian Home Cooking*.)

When I asked Suvir for his favorite dish, this is the one he sent, explaining that it was one of the most popular dishes at another restaurant he ran in New York City, Tapestry.

"This is the chicken soup of India," he told me by phone from New Delhi. "But people treat it like that, quickly and without care. They make it bland food, punishment food. I wanted this dish to be a celebration. So, I do it the way few other people do it, with many layerings of texture, flavor, and contrast.

"The concept is simple, a lentil and rice porridge. When you are sick, you make it without any spices, the way Americans eat toast and applesauce. Here I make two differently spiced oils and a flavorful topping."

This dish is indeed elaborate, and worth every moment of the effort. Go all out and make the spice mixtures as well (or you can order them online or find then in Indian markets). Asafetida, a powder derived from various rhizomes, is very strong (according to Wikipedia it's sometimes called devil's dung!) and is used like garlic or onion powder in very small amounts. If you don't have it, feel free to omit it, Suvir says.

For the toppings:

- 1½ to 2 quarts/1.5 to 2 liters peanut oil
- 1 large red onion, halved *and thinly sliced*
- ¼ cup finely chopped fresh cilantro
- ¼ cup finely chopped fresh mint leaves
- 1 (4-inch/10-centimeter) piece ginger, *peeled and sliced into very thin matchsticks*
- 1 jalapeño, seeded if desired *and finely minced*
- 2 tablespoons lime juice
- 2 teaspoons honey
- ½ teaspoon Garam Masala (page 249)

For the khitcheree:

- 1 cup/200 grams dal (split and hulled yellow lentils)
- 2 tablespoons ghee or clarified butter (see page 244)
- 10 green cardamom pods
- 8 whole cloves
- 3 bay leaves
- 1 (2-inch/5-centimeter) cinnamon stick
- 1 teaspoon Panch Phoran (page 249)
- ¾ teaspoon ground turmeric
- ⅛ teaspoon asafetida (*optional*)
- 1 cup/180 grams basmati rice

1 small cauliflower,
*divided into very small
florets*

1 medium red potato,
*cut into ½-inch/
1-centimeter pieces*

4 medium carrots,
peeled *and finely
chopped*

10 cups/2.3 liters
water

For the first tempering:

2 tablespoons ghee
or clarified butter
(see page 244)

½ teaspoon Panch
Phoran (page 249)

½ large red onion,
halved and thinly sliced

1 ½ tablespoons
kosher salt

2 teaspoons ground
coriander

2 large tomatoes,
finely diced

⅛ teaspoon cayenne
pepper

For the second tempering:

2 tablespoons ghee
or clarified butter
(see page 244)

½ teaspoon cumin
seeds

¼ teaspoon cayenne
pepper

Pinch asafetida
(*optional*)

MAKE THE TOPPINGS:
Pour 2 inches/5 centimeters oil into a large
Dutch oven and heat it over medium-high heat
until it reaches 350°F/175°C on an instant-read
thermometer. Add the onion slices and fry until
crisp and browned, about 2 minutes, turning them
occasionally. Use a slotted spoon or spider to
transfer the onions to a paper towel–lined plate and
set aside.

In a small bowl stir together the cilantro, mint,
ginger, jalapeño, lime juice, and honey and set aside.

MAKE THE KHITCHEREE:
In a large skillet, toast the dal over medium heat
until fragrant and lightly golden, 3 to 5 minutes.
Transfer the dal to a large plate and set aside.

Add the ghee, cardamom, cloves, bay leaves,
cinnamon, panch phoran, turmeric, and asafetida (if
using) to the pan and toast over medium heat until
the spices are fragrant, about 2 minutes.

Add the rice, toasted dal, cauliflower, potato,
and carrots and cook, stirring often, until the rice

becomes translucent and the cauliflower sweats,
3 to 5 minutes. Pour in 7 cups/1.6 liters of the
water, increase the heat to high, and bring to a boil.
Partially cover the pan and reduce the heat to a
simmer for 20 minutes.

**WHILE THE RICE AND DAL MIXTURE
COOKS, MAKE THE FIRST TEMPERING
OIL:**
Heat the ghee and panch phoran in a large skillet
over medium heat until the cumin in the panch
phoran begins to brown, 2 to 3 minutes. Stir in the
onion and salt and cook until the onion is browned
around the edges and soft, about 10 minutes. If the
onion begins to get too dark or stick to the bottom
of the pan, splash the pan with a few tablespoons
of water and scrape up the browned bits. Stir in the
coriander and cook, stirring, for 2 minutes, then
stir in the tomatoes and cayenne and cook, stirring
occasionally, until the tomatoes are jammy, 6 to 8
minutes. Remove the skillet from the heat and set
aside.

Once the rice and dal are cooked, remove the
lid and use a potato masher to smash the mixture
until only about half of the vegetables are still whole
and the stew is pleasantly thickened (remove the
whole or large spices while mashing if you like). Stir
in the first tempering oil, along with the remaining 3
cups/710 milliliters water. Return to a boil and cook
for 2 minutes. Turn off the heat.

MAKE THE SECOND TEMPERING OIL:
Wipe out the skillet from the first tempering oil
and heat the ghee for the second tempering oil over
medium heat. Add the cumin, cayenne, and asafetida
(if using) and cook, stirring often, until the cumin
begins to brown, about 2 minutes. Immediately stir
it into the rice and dal mixture.

Divide the khitcheree between serving bowls
and top each with some of the ginger mixture, a
pinch of garam masala, and some fried onions and
serve.

TAHIREE RICE CASSEROLE   SERVES 8

Indian-Style
Curries

This is Suvir's go-to dish when he needs comfort food and needs it fast. An intertwining of a khitcheree and a biriyani, it's a kind of layered casserole, but it packs a great spice punch. You can leave the vegetables whole or mash them slightly with a potato masher as with the khitcheree for a smoother texture.

Note that Suvir leaves the heavy spices of clove and cardamom whole. When I asked if he wasn't concerned about people biting into a whole clove and getting walloped with spice, he explained, "I leave them in. It's a reminder that we should eat slowly and thoughtfully and know what we are putting in our mouths. We should be aware. If you don't want to eat it, put it to the side."

A lesson for us all: whole spices as a way of eating mindfully.

¼ cup vegetable oil or clarified butter (see page 244)

9 green cardamom pods

6 whole cloves

3 bay leaves

3 dried red chiles

1 ½ teaspoons cumin seeds, plus 1 teaspoon toasted cumin seeds

½ teaspoon whole black peppercorns

½ teaspoon cracked black pepper

½ teaspoon coriander seeds

1 large red onion, *halved and sliced*

1 tablespoons kosher salt, *plus more to taste as needed*

1 ¼ pounds/560 grams cauliflower florets (*from about ½ large head cauliflower*)

2 medium red potatoes, *peeled and cut into large chunks*

1 teaspoon ground turmeric

2 cups/360 grams basmati rice

1 ½ cups/200 grams frozen peas

1 quart/1 liter water

½ teaspoon Garam Masala (*opposite*)

Heat the oil in a large pot over medium-high heat. Add the cardamom, cloves, bay leaves, chiles, raw cumin seeds, peppercorns, cracked pepper, and coriander. Cook, stirring often, until the cumin browns, about 2½ minutes. Add the onion and 1 tablespoon of the salt and cook, stirring occasionally, until the onion just starts to soften, about 2 minutes. Stir in the cauliflower, potatoes, and turmeric, reduce the heat to medium, and cook for 1 minute. Add the rice and cook, stirring occasionally, for 1 minute, then add the peas and water. Bring to a boil, then reduce the heat to low. Stir in the garam masala, toasted cumin seeds, and salt to taste and cover. Cook for 20 minutes, then turn off the heat and let the tahiree rest for 5 minutes. Fluff with a fork and serve.

GARAM MASALA
MAKES ABOUT ¾ CUP

Garam masala, from northern India, is the most common Indian spice blend. It's widely available in Indian markets but, as always, the vitality and brightness of whole spices you toast and grind yourself cannot be bought. This is Suvir Saran's blend.

1 (1-inch/ 2.5-centimeter) piece cinnamon stick, *broken into pieces*

4 bay leaves

⅓ cup coriander seeds

¼ cup cumin seeds

6 green cardamom pods

2 brown cardamom pods

1 tablespoon whole black peppercorns

1 tablespoon whole cloves

1 dried red chile

¼ teaspoon freshly grated nutmeg

⅛ teaspoon ground mace

Heat the cinnamon, bay leaves, coriander seeds, cumin seeds, cardamom pods, peppercorns, cloves, and chile in a medium skillet over medium-high heat, stirring often, until the cumin becomes brown, 2½ to 3 minutes.

Transfer the spices to a rimmed baking sheet to cool. Once cooled, transfer the spices to a spice grinder, coffee mill, or small food processor, add the nutmeg and mace, and grind into a fine powder. Store in an airtight container for up to 4 months.

PANCH PHORAN
MAKES 5 TABLESPOONS

Indian-Style Curries

Panch phoran is available from specialty retailers, but Suvir Saran shared his recipe. It is typically used as a whole spice, adding texture as well as flavor, but Suvir says you can also pulverize it if you wish.

1 tablespoon cumin seeds

1 tablespoon fennel seeds

1 tablespoon brown mustard seeds

1 tablespoon nigella seeds

1 tablespoon fenugreek seeds

Mix together and store in an airtight container for up to 1 year.

SIMPLE VEGETABLE CURRY WITH ROASTED CAULIFLOWER SERVES 4

This is an excellent curry enhanced with whole toasted spices. All the vegetables except for the butternut squash are added toward the end so they don't overcook. I like zucchini and summer squash, along with cauliflower that's roasted ahead of time and used more as a garnish on top (though you could cook it in the curry as well). You could also add green beans, 10 minutes before the curry is done, for more color and a different texture. Of course, you could also add some Slow-Roasted Pork Shoulder (page 212) to make a pork curry or sliced boneless chicken thighs for a chicken curry (I'd sauté the chicken with the spices or roast it separately to brown it). The zucchini is more flavorful if you quarter it and sear the quarters till they are browned, if you want to take this extra step.

Indian-Style Curries

20 or so cauliflower florets

1 teaspoon coriander seeds

1 teaspoon cumin seeds

1 teaspoon yellow mustard seed

2 teaspoons black mustard seed or more yellow mustard seed

6 whole cloves

2 teaspoons ground turmeric

1 teaspoon ground cardamom

7 tablespoons/ 105 grams unsalted butter

2 garlic cloves, *roughly chopped*

1 (1-inch/ 2.5-centimeter) piece ginger, *grated*

1 small butternut squash, *peeled, seeded, and cut into ½-inch/1-centimeter dice*

16 cremini mushrooms, *quartered*

1 yellow bell pepper, *seeded and sliced*

1 red bell pepper, *seeded and sliced*

2 cups/480 milliliters Vegetable Stock (page 114) *or store-bought broth, or more as needed*

1 zucchini, *quartered, browned in hot oil (optional), and cut into 2-inch/5-centimeter pieces*

½ cup/120 milliliters sour cream

2 tablespoons all-purpose flour

Steamed basmati or jasmine rice (see page 270), *for serving*

¾ cup/120 grams cashews, *toasted and roughly chopped*

Leaves and thin stems from 1 bunch cilantro, *for garnish*

Preheat your oven to 425°F/218°C.

Put the cauliflower in an oven-safe skillet and put in the oven to roast for about 30 minutes.

Meanwhile, toast the coriander, cumin, mustard seed, and cloves in a dry skillet over high heat for about 1 minute, till the mustard begins to pop and the spices smell fragrant. Transfer them to a mortar or spice grinder and pulverize. Add the turmeric and cardamom.

In a soup pot large enough to contain the stock and vegetables, melt 3 tablespoons/45 grams of the butter over high heat. As it's frothing and about to turn brown, add the spices, garlic, and ginger and stir to cook them for 30 seconds. Add the squash, mushrooms, and bell peppers and stir to cook. Add the stock and stir. Simmer gently for 30 minutes.

When the cauliflower florets are nice and brown, turn off the oven and pull them from the oven (leave the door open to let out some of the heat). Add 2 tablespoons/30 grams of the butter. Swirl the florets around in the butter until it's all melted and the cauliflower is lightly coated. Return the skillet to the oven until ready to serve.

Add the zucchini to the soup pot and continue to simmer for 5 minutes. Stir in the sour cream. Knead together the flour and the remaining 2 tablespoons/30 grams butter to make a beurre manié (see page 32). When the curry comes back to a simmer, stir in the beurre manié. When the curry is thickened to your liking, serve over rice and top with the roasted cauliflower. Garnish with the cashews and plenty of cilantro.

RAITA SERVES 4

I love the cooling, satisfying effects of yogurt-cucumber raita—a kind of cross between a condiment and a salad. I like it cuke-heavy, though some people prefer more yogurt. You can add a bit of minced or chiffonaded fresh mint if you like.

1 cucumber	½ to 1 cup/120 to 240 milliliters full-fat plain yogurt
1 garlic clove, *minced to a paste*	
	Kosher salt *to taste*
2 pinches ground cumin	Lemon juice *to taste*
Pinch Indian chili powder (*optional*)	1 teaspoon chiffonade fresh mint leaves (*optional*)

Peel the cucumber (or half-peel it to make stripes), then cut it in half lengthwise. Use a spoon to scoop out the seeds, and discard. Cut the cucumber into medium dice.

Combine the garlic, cumin, and chili power (if using) in a bowl. Add ½ cup/120 milliliters yogurt and stir to mix thoroughly. Season with salt. Add the cucumber and stir, then add more yogurt till you have a consistency you like. Taste and adjust the salt if necessary. Stir in the mint (if using) and serve.

CHANA MASALA   SERVES 4

Chana masala, or chole masala, is one of the most popular Indian dishes in the United States. It's easy to prepare, delicious, vegetarian, and nutritious, and I find it as satisfying as any meat dish.

The idea is simple: Make a curried tomato sauce and add chickpeas. For the best flavor and texture, it's always preferable to start with dried chickpeas, but sometimes we don't have time. I welcome the convenience of canned for this recipe.

1 teaspoon grated fresh ginger

1 tablespoon Garam Masala (page 249)

1 teaspoon kala jeera (*black cumin seeds; optional*)

½ teaspoon ground coriander

½ teaspoon ground cumin

¼ teaspoon Indian chili powder

¼ teaspoon ground cinnamon

2 tablespoons/ 30 grams unsalted butter

1 (28-ounce/ 794-gram) can whole peeled tomatoes

2 (15.5-ounce/ 439-gram) cans chickpeas, *rinsed and drained*

Chopped fresh cilantro, *for garnish*

Combine the ginger, garam masala, kala jeera (if using), coriander, cumin, chili powder, and cinnamon in a ramekin.

In a saucepan that will comfortably contain all the ingredients, melt the butter over medium-high heat. When the butter begins to froth (meaning the water is nearly cooked off), add the spices, stirring to mix, and cook for 30 to 60 seconds.

Add the juice from the can of tomatoes and reduce the heat to medium. Squeeze the tomatoes into the pan, turning them to pulp in your hand. Stir and gently simmer the tomatoes for 30 minutes or so. Add the chickpeas and cook, stirring occasionally, for another 10 to 15 minutes.

Garnish with cilantro and serve.

HUMMUS   SERVES 15

This makes a big bowl of hummus, which is great for a party—easy, inexpensive, nutritious, delicious. But it's also a slightly unconventional recipe, as I use not only tahini, the sesame seed paste, but also peanut butter for extra nuttiness. (It's fine to leave out the peanut butter if peanut allergies are an issue in your house.) And I also throw in a little cream to help smooth it out. The best hummus I've had in this country is served at Shaya, in New Orleans. We were told that one of their "secrets" was that they remove the skins from the cooked chickpeas before pureeing them and passing them through a sieve.

2 cups/100 grams dried chickpeas

1 cup tahini

½ cup/120 milliliters creamy peanut butter

5 garlic cloves, *peeled*

Juice of 1 to 2 lemons

2 teaspoons kosher salt, *plus more to taste*

½ cup heavy cream

Extra-virgin olive oil, *for serving*

Soak the chickpeas in abundant water, refrigerated, for at least 8 hours or as long as 3 days. Drain the chickpeas and dump them into a saucepan. Add enough water to cover them by a few inches and bring to a boil over medium-high heat. Reduce the heat, cover, and simmer for 1 hour. Drain and pat dry with paper towels.

Combine the chickpeas, tahini, peanut butter, garlic, the juice of 1 lemon, and the salt in a food processor and puree until very smooth. Taste it. Add more lemon juice if needed, or more peanut butter or tahini if you wish. If it needs more salt, add it now. With the processor running, add the cream through the feed tube.

To serve, transfer the hummus to a bowl and smooth the surface with a spatula. Using a large spoon, swirl some indentations into the surface of the hummus and fill the indentations with olive oil.

The Amazing Chickpea

FRIED CHICKPEAS   SERVES 8

Fried chickpeas are an easy and delicious snack or offering at a party. They're simply fried for 5 minutes in oil, then generously spiced however you wish. The spices given here are one of the directions I like to take them. But you could also use salt and pepper, lemon zest, garlic salt, and Parmesan cheese. It's up to your imagination and taste.

It's important to note that while you can use canned chickpeas for this recipe, I find them to be too mushy, so I highly recommend using dried chickpeas soaked overnight. Frying dried chickpeas that have been soaked results in a cooked pea that is delicately crunchy on the outside and tender inside. Canned chickpeas are already cooked, so you're effectively cooking them twice, but if you have the hunger and only have canned—feel free to rinse, dry, and fry!

1 cup dried
   chickpeas

1½ to 2 cups/
   360 to 480
   milliliters vegetable
   oil, *for frying*

Kosher salt *to taste*

Garam Masala
   (*page 249*) *to taste*

Ground cumin *to taste*

Indian chili powder
   to taste (*optional*)

Soak the chickpeas in abundant water, refrigerated, for at least 8 hours or as long as 3 days. Drain them and put them in a bowl lined with paper towels. Dry them as best as you can.

In a large saucepan, bring the oil to 350°F to 375°F/175°C to 190°C over high heat. Make sure the oil doesn't come up beyond the pot's halfway point, as the moisture in the chickpeas will turn to vapor and cause the oil to bubble up. Working in batches if necessary, add the chickpeas and fry until they are browned and crunchy, about 5 minutes. They'll float to the surface of the oil when they're done. Remove with a slotted spoon or spider to a bowl lined with paper towels.

Sprinkle the chickpeas liberally with salt. Sprinkle with the other spices one at a time, shaking the bowl to distribute the seasoning. Use a little more than you think you need, then taste and adjust. Serve warm.

THE AMAZING CHICKPEA

Chickpeas are a staple of Mediterranean cuisine, and no wonder: They are loaded with nutrients, inexpensive, and endlessly versatile—they can be put to more uses than just about any legume I know. Well beyond Indian stews, such as Chana Masala (page 253), they can be pureed, fried, and even featured in a classic Italian dish, Pasta e Ceci (page 115). Canned chickpeas are fine to use for most preparations, but dried chickpeas are so much more flavorful that it's worth it to buy them dried and soak them. It's not difficult, of course; the key is to plan ahead so that they're hydrated when you need them.

NEATH PAL'S CAMBODIAN CHICKEN CURRY SERVES 6 TO 8

Venturing into Cambodia, we come to this yellow curry—yellow from the use of fresh turmeric. Neath Pal's family moved from Cambodia as Pol Pot rose to power. His father was a military attaché and so was able take the family to South Korea. From there a family in Providence sponsored a teenaged Neath to come to Rhode Island, where he would grow up. He has stayed in Providence, raising his family, running a Cambodian restaurant for many years, and now teaching cooking at Johnson & Wales University.

Southeast Asian–Style Curries

Over lunch Neath said that the differences among curries in Cambodia, Thailand, and Vietnam are nuanced. All rely on the trinity—lemongrass, Thai lime, and galangal—as well as shallots and chiles. And the sugar used is typically palm sugar, which he says is less sweet, more like maple sugar than regular white sugar.

The grinding of the curry paste, traditionally done start to finish in a big, heavy mortar, is taken seriously in Cambodia. When Neath traveled there recently with a group of students, one of their hosts explained that the parents of a future groom don't even need to meet his future bride. They only need to hear the way the bride-to-be handles the mortar and pestle. Not overly fast, rhythmical, strong, but in no hurry. You should be able to hear the sound of the individual leaves being smashed. In that way, they could determine if she would be right for their son.

Neath advocates first pounding the woody rhizomes, followed by the softer ingredients, then pureeing them in a food processor (with a little water if you need to get them moving), and finishing them in the mortar. The ingredients can all be ground in a blender or food processor and then finished in a mortar, but the mortar-processor-mortar method really does bring out more flavor, he says.

Other differences between the various Southeast Asian curries have to do with the two important umami ingredients—fish sauce and shrimp paste—which vary from region to region. He favors a dry shrimp paste to the very wet paste. The fish sauce in Vietnam is particularly strong and salty. Cambodian fish sauce is gentler, he explains. In Cambodia, his family used the leaves of the lemongrass as well, which are incredibly fragrant. But the flavor is volatile, and they would be dried out and useless after shipping stateside, so you can really only get them where they grow.

Cambodians also use the roots of the coriander plant, which can be found in some Asian markets, and are likewise very fragrant. Neath believes that the best pepper in the world grows in Cambodia, both black and a green version, called kampot pepper. It's these things that are the real difference in the cuisines.

This is a wonderful yellow curry; the star anise sets it apart from other countries' curries. You can make a curry, or sauce, and then cook your protein in it, as is customary, but Neath loves to rub the chili paste directly on chicken, or on pork ribs, and grill it. He urges cooks learning this style of cooking not to hew too closely to the recipe. "We don't measure. We taste, we smell—that's how you learn to cook."

I couldn't have said it better.

Southeast Asian–Style Curries

¼ cup vegetable oil

3 tablespoons Cambodian Yellow Curry Paste (at right) or store-bought yellow curry paste

1 (3-pound/ 1.5-kilogram) chicken, *cut into 2-inch/5-centimeter pieces (see Note)*

1 pound/450 grams sweet potatoes, *cut into 1½-inch/ 4-centimeter cubes*

8 ounces/225 grams carrots, *peeled and cut into 1-inch/ 2.5-centimeter pieces*

2 yellow onions, *cut in a thick julienne*

Kosher salt *to taste*

1 (14-ounce/ 400-milliliter) can coconut milk

3 cups/710 milliliters Easy Overnight Chicken Stock (page 38) *or store-bought chicken broth*

3 whole star anise

3 tablespoons fish sauce

2 tablespoons palm sugar or maple sugar, or 1 tablespoon white sugar

Lime juice *as needed*

1 (8-ounce/225-gram) can sliced bamboo shoots, drained, or one fresh whole bamboo shoot, *sliced*

8 scallions, thinly sliced, *for garnish*

½ cup/30 grams chopped Thai chiles, *for garnish (optional)*

Heat the oil in a Dutch oven, and sear the chicken until it's nicely browned. Push the pieces to the side and add the curry paste, stirring to cook it for thirty seconds or so, then stir the chicken so that it is coated with the curry paste. Add the sweet potatoes, carrots, onions, and 1 teaspoon salt and stir for 1 minute. Add the coconut milk, chicken stock, and star anise and bring to just below a boil.

Add the fish sauce and palm sugar and simmer for 25 minutes, or until the chicken is thoroughly cooked. Add a squeeze of lime juice. Taste as you go. Add more fish sauce, curry paste or seasonings, salt, sugar, or lime juice as needed.

Add the bamboo shoots, bring back to a simmer, and serve, garnished with scallions and Thai chiles if you want it very spicy.

Note: If you have a cleaver, cut the chicken into its larger pieces (1 whole breast, drumsticks, thighs, wings) and then, with the cleaver, halve the leg pieces. Cut the tip of the triangle of the breast off 2 inches/5 centimeters up the keel bone. Then cut the breast in half along the keel bone, and cut those pieces in half. Or ask the butcher to do exactly this (reserve the backbone and wing tips for stock). This recipe can be amended to use beef short ribs or beef chuck in place of the chicken; replace the bamboo shoots with peanuts. In Cambodia, beef curry is often served with a baguette.

CAMBODIAN YELLOW CURRY PASTE MAKES ABOUT ¼ CUP/ 60 GRAMS

4 to 5 dried dried red chiles

1 tablespoon coriander seeds

1 teaspoon cumin seeds

1 lemongrass stalk, white parts only *(root end, dry green tops, and any bruised exterior leaves discarded), minced*

1 (1-inch/ 2.5-centimeter) piece galangal, *thinly sliced*

1 (2-inch/5-centimeter) piece turmeric root, *thinly sliced*

5 Thai lime leaves, *cut into chiffonade*

1½ tablespoons coarsely chopped garlic

1½ tablespoons coarsely chopped shallot

1 tablespoon chopped fresh cilantro

1½ teaspoons dried shrimp paste

1 teaspoon kosher salt, *or to taste*

Put the chiles in a bowl and pour boiling water over them. Let soak for 1 hour. Drain. Remove and discard the stems and seeds.

In a dry, hot skillet, toast the coriander and cumin seeds until aromatic and beginning to change color. Transfer to a mortar and grind with the pestle. Be sure to cup your hand over the mortar so the seeds don't fly out.

In small batches, add the lemongrass, galangal, turmeric, lime leaves, garlic, shallot, and cilantro to the mortar and use the pestle to pound and grind the mixture until the paste is fairly smooth. You can also use a blender to complete this task, but I recommend that you finish by placing the mixture in a mortar and pounding it into a paste texture.

Mix in the shrimp paste. Season with salt as desired. Store in an airtight container in the refrigerator for up to 3 days or in the freezer for up to 2 months.

SHALLOTS WITH OTHER AROMATICS

FRESH BAMBOO SHOOT

THAI LIME

UNPEELED GALANGAL

LEMONGRASS, SLICED AND CHOPPED

PEELED TURMERIC

LEMONGRASS STALKS, PROPERLY THWACKED WITH BACK OF KNIFE

PEELED AND SLICED GALANGAL AND TURMERIC

DIANE CU'S VIETNAMESE CURRY SERVES 4

Diane Cu's family fled Saigon in 1975 when she was a child, and the family was raised in the Los Angeles area. Diane went on to become one half of the White on Rice Couple, with her husband, Todd Porter. Together they travel the world, teach photography and videography, blog about it, and write and photograph beautiful cookbooks. I really like and admire their work.

I asked if Diane could create a recipe that represented her Vietnamese childhood, and she sent this adaptation of her family's curry. It's fabulous and clean, heavy on the lemongrass. I love it for its simplicity—it calls for water only, no coconut milk (as is often the case in the North, she said), and chicken drumsticks, their knob ends cut off for easy eating. (See the Note below for using a whole chicken instead of drumsticks.) It's dead easy to prepare.

"Mom loves using drumsticks because they're quick cooking and because she loves brown meat," Diane wrote to me when she sent me this recipe. "Our family hails from Northern and Central Vietnam. Grandma never used coconut milk in her chicken curry, and this method has been passed down to Mom. She always cuts her drumsticks in half, crosswise, for easier handling with chopsticks. Chicken thighs are a great option, too, but expect more fat from the skin if you're using skin-on. Mom knows how much I love lemongrass, so she never fails to remind me that she added extra fresh lemongrass from her garden when she brings Todd and me a batch."

2 pounds/900 grams bone-in, skin-on chicken drumsticks or thighs

3 tablespoons vegetable oil (*if using skin-on chicken thighs, use 1 tablespoon oil*)

3 medium shallots, *roughly chopped*

4 garlic cloves, minced

1 tablespoon minced fresh ginger

2 tablespoons curry powder

3 large lemongrass stalks, *white parts only (root ends, dry green tops, and any bruised exterior leaves discarded), cut into 2-inch/ 5-centimeter pieces and smashed with the back of a chef's knife*

1 quart/1 liter water

2 tablespoons fish sauce

1 teaspoon sugar

Kosher salt *to taste*

3 medium potatoes, *cut into 1-inch/ 2.5-centimeter pieces*

2 large carrots, peeled, *cut into 1-inch/2.5-centimeter pieces*

Freshly cracked black pepper *to taste*

2 tablespoons cornstarch whisked into 2 tablespoons water (*optional*)

2 scallions, *thinly sliced*

¼ cup chopped fresh cilantro

Chopped fresh Thai bird chiles (*optional*)

Warm baguettes, rice noodles, or steamed jasmine rice (see page 270), *for serving*

Using a cleaver or heavy knife, chop the drumsticks in half to separate the knob end from the meat end. You will use both parts—the knob ends will give the sauce flavor and body, and the meat will bunch up at the top of the drumstick when cooked.

Heat the oil in a large pot over medium-high heat. When the oil is hot, sear all sides of the chicken until the skin is crisp and brown. Transfer the chicken to a plate.

Add the shallots, garlic, and ginger to the same pan and cook the aromatics until they're fragrant and translucent. The moisture they release should be enough to deglaze the pan. Scrape up any browned bits. Add the curry powder and lemongrass and cook for about 30 seconds.

Add the water, fish sauce, sugar, ½ teaspoon salt, chicken, potatoes, and carrots. Bring the pot to a boil. Reduce the heat to low and cook for 25 to 30 minutes, until the chicken and vegetables are super tender. Stir the pot occasionally, making sure the chicken is fully submerged in the delicious broth. Add more water if you think it needs it.

Taste for seasonings and add salt and pepper if needed. If you want to thicken the sauce—it's fine if you're happy to leave the sauces thin—rewhisk the cornstarch and water to remove all lumps. Add this slurry to the pot and quickly stir. Allow the curry to cook for another minute for the sauce to thicken.

Top with the scallions, cilantro, and fresh chiles (if using). Serve with baguette, rice noodles, or rice.

Note: When I first made this recipe, I had a whole chicken on hand because I knew that some of the people I'd be serving might want white meat. I also knew that the trim from breaking down the chicken would add more flavor to the sauce. It's a great way to use every bit of the bird and all its flavor.

You'll need a cleaver or heavy knife, or you can have your butcher do this for you: First cut off the legs. Separate the drumstick and thigh (when you place the whole leg skin side down, you should see a line of fat between the drumstick and thigh—draw your knife down through that line to separate the joint). Using a cleaver, chop off the knob end of the drumsticks and reserve them. Put the meaty drumsticks on a separate plate. Chop the thighs in half and reserve with the drumsticks. Cut the wings from the breast, leaving plenty of meat on the drumettes. Cut off the wing tips and put them with the drumstick knobs. Remove the backbone of the chicken and reserve. Cut the breast into four to six pieces, depending on how big it is, and put them with the legs and wings. Reserve all the fat and any skin that comes easily off the meat.

Combine the reserved skin, fat, backbone, drumstick knobs, and wing tips in a Dutch oven or large pot. Add ½ cup/120 milliliters water and heat over high heat. When the water has cooked off, turn the burner to medium-low and brown all the skin and bones and render as much fat as possible.

Remove the skin and bones. Deglaze the pan with 1 cup/240 milliliters dry white wine or water. When this has cooked off, brown the meaty chicken pieces in the fat. When they're browned, remove them from the pan and carry on with the recipe at the point when you add the shallots, garlic, and ginger.

Southeast Asian–Style Curries

THAI GREEN CURRY   SERVES 4

For this basic Thai-style green curry, you can use any meat you wish—thinly sliced flank steak or pork shoulder—or a mix of vegetables (if using vegetables only, cook the sauce first and add them at the end so that they don't overcook). Using your own curry paste creates a much more elegant stew, but canned is fine if you don't have the time. If you do use canned paste, keep in mind that it tends to be hotter than the one given here, which is heavier in aromatics than chiles.

1 tablespoon vegetable oil, *or more as needed*

1 medium onion, *cut into medium dice*

Kosher salt *to taste*

1 to 4 tablespoons Green Curry Paste (page 265)

6 to 8 boneless, skinless chicken thighs, *cut into strips or chunks*

¾ cup/180 milliliters Easy Overnight Chicken Stock (page 38) or store-bought chicken broth

1 (14-ounce/ 400-milliliter) can coconut milk

5 Thai lime leaves

1 lemongrass stalk, *white parts only (root end, dry green tops, and any bruised exterior leaves discarded), halved and thwacked many times with the back of a chef's knife to release its flavors*

1 tablespoon brown sugar

1 tablespoon fish sauce, *plus more for serving*

2 limes, 1 juiced and 1 quartered, *for serving*

8 ounces/225 grams snap peas, *trimmed*

1 red bell or red serrano pepper, *seeded and sliced*

Leaves and thin stems from 1 bunch cilantro, picked as needed, *for garnish*

Steamed jasmine rice (see page 270), *for serving*

In a medium saucepan, heat the oil over medium-high heat; when it's hot, add the onion. Hit the onion with a four-finger pinch of salt and cook until it's translucent and beginning to brown, a few minutes. Add the curry paste and sauté for a minute or two, until it's hot and fragrant. Push the onion and curry to the side of the pan and add the chicken (you may want to add a little more oil to the pan to cook the chicken). Stir to cook the chicken. Once it has lost its pinkness, stir it to combine with the onion and curry paste and cook for another minute.

Add the chicken stock, coconut milk, lime leaves, lemongrass, sugar, fish sauce, and 1 tablespoon lime juice. Simmer gently for 30 minutes. Add the peas and red pepper and cook until the vegetables are tender, 5 to 10 minutes. Taste and add more lime juice if desired. Garnish with the cilantro and serve with jasmine rice and the lime wedges, plus more fish sauce on the side.

GREEN CURRY PASTE MAKES ABOUT 1 CUP

It's hard to describe in words the difference between using homemade curry paste versus using canned paste. There's a kind of naturalness to it, an elegance that paste from a can just can't give you. If I were to tell you that you had to pound these ingredients together in a mortar and pestle for 20 minutes, Thai old-style, I might say it's worth it. Lemongrass and galangal are extremely fibrous (galangal, a rhizome like ginger, is practically like wood), and it takes some serious pounding. Happily, most of us who cook have a food processor. Combine all the ingredients and pulse until it's a paste, scraping the sides of the processor as you do. Given the ease of the processor, the most time-consuming part of making curry paste is seeding the small peppers.

Please wear rubber or latex gloves when doing this. If you have the right kind of chiles, they are *seriously* hot, and their oils will coat your fingers; rubbing your eyes after can cause considerable distress. I find that I can take out most of the seeds and ribs, where the capsaicin is concentrated, then wash them well and drain them in a colander. Most of the seeds should be gone. The heat level is something you have to gauge as you go. Peppers vary in intensity, though Thai peppers are pretty uniformly hot. I don't like my paste super hot, but if you do, simply use more peppers.

This makes more than you'll need for a single batch of curry. Freeze what you don't use for another time. Try rubbing some on ribs or chicken and then grilling them.

2 teaspoons cumin seeds or 1 teaspoon ground cumin

2 teaspoons coriander seeds or 1 teaspoon ground coriander

¼ teaspoon kosher salt

30 to 60 Thai chiles or bird's eye chiles (1½ to 2 ounces/40 to 60 grams), *stemmed, halved, and seeded*

1 (2-inch/5-centimeter) piece galangal, *coarsely grated or chopped*

1 lemongrass stalk, *white parts only (root end, dry green tops, and any bruised exterior leaves discarded), thinly sliced*

10 Thai lime leaves

2 shallots, *quartered or roughly chopped*

5 garlic cloves, *peeled*

2 teaspoons palm sugar or granulated sugar

2 teaspoons shrimp paste or 1 tablespoon fish sauce

1 to 2 tablespoons vegetable oil

If you're using whole cumin and coriander seeds, toast them in a dry pan over medium-high heat until they're fragrant, then pulverize them in a mortar or spice grinder.

Combine all the ingredients in a food processor and pulse until you have a paste, scraping down the sides as necessary. If you need more moisture to create a paste, add a tablespoon or two of warm water.

Empty the processor bowl into a big, sturdy mortar if you have one. Use the pestle to pound and grind the paste well, a minute or two, to release all the aromatic goodness and connect with the countless other cooks who have ground their curry pastes by hand.

STIR-FRY BASICS

When I rotated through cuisines of Asia at the Culinary Institute of America (it was long enough ago to be called Oriental Cuisine), the class was taught by a wonderful chef named Shirley Cheng, who had risen to high levels of the craft in her native China. It was rumored that she could take a chicken from live to cooked in under 3 minutes.

She showed us how we should wash our rice, swirling our hand around the rice in the pot, dumping out the starchy, opaque water, and running more cold water over it. A classmate of mine asked, "Is that to get rid of excess starch?" She gave him a look like he was an idiot. "No. It's because it's dirty."

Among the first things we learned was the Chinese trinity. We have the Western trinity (onion, carrot, celery), the Cajun trinity (onion, bell pepper, celery), and the Southeast Asian trinity (lemongrass, Thai lime, and galangal). For basic Chinese cookery, it's ginger, garlic, and scallion. I begin almost every stir-fry with these three ingredients. They give a dish its distinctive piquant, aromatic sweetness.

The most important other fundamental in a stir-fry is high heat. At the CIA we cooked in woks and they got crazy hot. You had to be careful. In home kitchens, it's almost impossible to get your pan too hot. Use a heavy-gauge pan, the thicker the better (a large cast-iron skillet works well, too). Let it sit over the flame till it's as hot as you can get it. When you add the oil, it should become very fluid instantly and begin to smoke. You must have all your ingredients ready to go—this is especially important when cooking beef or chicken or anything moist, as water cools a pan down faster than anything.

Other than that, it's a matter of becoming familiar with a small range of sauces: hoisin, oyster, black bean, chili sauce with garlic, black soy, and a few others. Most sauces benefit from being thickened with a slurry, which is nothing more than cornstarch mixed with water till it has the consistency of heavy cream. This thickens a loose sauce right up.

The recipes here are Americanized versions of Chinese food, the kind of food that evolved here as Chinese cooks tried to please American palates. If you want authentic Chinese from an expert, I recommend the work of Grace Young. For me, though, I like things simple and quick and delicious. Just follow the basics: very hot pan, Chinese trinity, an uncomplicated combination of sauces, thickened with a slurry.

KUNG PAO CHICKEN   SERVES 4

A staple of my teenage and college years was kung pao chicken from what was, at the time, one of the authoritative books on Chinese cookery, *The Chinese Cookbook*, by Craig Claiborne and Virginia Lee. The base combination of bean sauce, hoisin sauce, and chili sauce with garlic has been a stalwart mainstay ever since, with countless variations, and with any kind of meat or vegetable. Over the years it continues to evolve. The recipe I present here is fiery hot and pungent, crunchy and nutty. As with all stir-fries, be sure to have all your ingredients prepped and at hand before you start cooking.

If you like, you can cook your peanuts from raw. Start them in a cup of cold vegetable oil over high heat and watch them carefully till they're golden brown, tasting along the way and remembering that they'll keep cooking for several minutes once out of the oil. Reserve the oil for future cooking!

2 tablespoons black bean sauce

1 tablespoon hoisin sauce

1 tablespoon chili sauce with garlic

1 tablespoon soy sauce

1 tablespoon dry sherry or Shaoxing wine

2 teaspoons red wine vinegar

1 teaspoon sugar

2 tablespoons vegetable oil

4 to 5 scallions, *thinly sliced*

1 (1-inch/ 2.5-centimeter) ginger, *grated or roughly chopped*

4 garlic cloves, *roughly chopped*

4 to 6 whole dried chiles (*optional*)

1 pound/450 grams boneless, skinless chicken thighs or breasts, *cut into strips*

2 celery ribs, *cut on the bias into ½-inch/ 1-centimeter slices*

1 (8-ounce/225-gram) can water chestnuts, *drained and cut into medium dice*

8 to 10 shiitake mushrooms, *stemmed and thinly sliced*

2 teaspoons cornstarch whisked into 2 teaspoons water (*optional*)

¾ cup/150 grams unsalted peanuts

Steamed jasmine rice (see page 270), *for serving*

Combine the black bean sauce, hoisin sauce, chili sauce with garlic, soy sauce, sherry, red wine vinegar, and sugar in a bowl and stir to combine.

Set a wok or large, heavy sauté pan over high heat. When the pan is hot, add the oil. When the oil is hot, add the scallions, ginger, garlic, and chiles (if using). Stir-fry until fragrant and the chiles are dark, about a minute.

Add the chicken and stir-fry until the chicken is cooked through, 2 minutes or so. Add the celery, water chestnuts, and shiitakes and stir-fry for a minute longer. Add the sauce mixture and stir to combine until the sauce is simmering. If you would like the sauce to be thicker, slowly add the cornstarch slurry till you achieve the desired consistency. Add the peanuts, stir to combine, and remove from the heat. Serve immediately with rice.

STIR-FRIED BEEF WITH BROCCOLI   SERVES 4

Chinese-Style Stir-Fries

This is an easy and satisfying staple to have in your repertoire, and it's better than any takeout you can order. It begins with beef cooked in a super-hot pan to sear it and give it an almost smoky flavor. The beef is removed from the pan and the Chinese trinity is added, followed by the broccoli and sauce, and then the meat is returned. It's a simple, nutritious dish, a perfect weeknight meal. If you have the time, cut everything up long before you cook it, even the evening before—makes the meal prep go lickety-split, no longer than the rice takes to cook.

 I became somewhat obsessed with this recipe after a lovely article in the *New York Times* by Sam Sifton, who asked Jonathan Wu, a chef in Brooklyn, for his take on beef with broccoli. The revelation for me had nothing to do with the beef or broccoli, but rather with the butter. Butter? Yes, this chef finishes Chinese dishes with butter. Brilliant, of course. But then I got an idea from chef Dale Talde: Why not use beurre manié, the classic French thickener? I tried it and it worked like a charm, thickening the sauce while also enriching it and making it voluptuously glossy.

 Flank steak and skirt steak are the best cuts of beef to use for this dish, or any beef stir-fry, but most cuts that aren't too tough will work.

2 tablespoons dry sherry, Shaoxing wine, or dry white wine

2 tablespoons soy sauce, *plus more to taste*

2 tablespoons cornstarch

1 pound/450 grams flank steak, *thinly sliced against the grain*

¼ cup oyster sauce

1 tablespoon chili sauce with garlic

1 to 2 cups/240 to 480 milliliters water, Vegetable Stock (page 114), One-Hour Beef Stock (page 142), store-bought broth, *or a combination*

5 tablespoons/ 75 milliliters vegetable oil

4 scallions, *thinly sliced*

1 (1-inch/ 2.5-centimeter) piece ginger, *grated*

5 garlic cloves, *minced*

8 ounces/225 grams broccoli florets, *trimmed and halved*

2 tablespoons all-purpose flour kneaded into 2 tablespoons/ 30 grams room-temperature unsalted butter (beurre manié, page 32)

1 tablespoon toasted sesame oil

recipe continues

Combine the sherry, soy sauce, and cornstarch in a large bowl and mix well. Add the beef and toss well; allow to marinate for 30 minutes at room temperature or overnight, covered, in the refrigerator, tossing it every now and then.

In a small bowl, combine the oyster sauce, chili sauce, and ½ cup/120 milliliters of the water or stock and stir till they're well mixed.

Get a large sauté pan or wok very hot over high heat and add 2 tablespoons of the oil. When it's hot, add the beef and stir-fry till it's cooked through and the liquid has cooked off, 3 to 5 minutes. Transfer the beef to a plate. Add another ½ cup/ 120 milliliters water or stock to the pan and deglaze it. Pour the deglazing liquid and fond into the oyster sauce mixture.

Wipe out the pan and return it to high heat. When it is hot, add another 2 tablespoons oil; when the oil is smoking, add the scallions, ginger, and garlic and stir-fry till tender, about a minute. Add the broccoli and stir-fry until the broccoli becomes bright green and starts to get tender, a few minutes (if your broccoli pieces are large, add a few tablespoons of water to speed the cooking). Add the oyster sauce mixture and simmer over high heat till the broccoli is al dente, a few more minutes. Return the beef to the pan and cook for another minute or so. If you feel the dish needs more liquid, add more water or stock.

To finish, add half of the beurre manié to the pan and stir to thicken the sauce. If it is too thick, add a little more water or stock. If it's too thin, add the remaining beurre manié. Drizzle with the sesame oil and serve immediately.

PERFECT JASMINE OR BASMATI RICE

Choose a pan with a narrow base and tall sides. Pour in 1 to 2 cups/180 to 360 grams rice (figure on ¼ to ½ cup/45 to 90 grams per person). Fill the pot with cold water, stirring the rice with your hand. When the pot is full, dump out most of the water and repeat.

Fill the pot with water to roughly 1½ inches/ 4 centimeters above the rice line. Put the pan over high heat. Stir the rice well, then bring it to a boil and continue to boil till the water is at the rice's level and holes ("fish eyes") appear in the rice. Turn the heat to low and cover the pan. After 10 minutes, turn off the heat completely.

Serve when you wish, fluffing the rice with a fork before serving.

HOT, SWEET, CRISPY STIR-FRIED CHICKEN SERVES 4

Of all the styles of Chinese food, this crispy sweet-sour-spicy version is my favorite. The best-known dish in this style is General Tso's chicken, but it's also used for sweet and sour pork and crispy orange beef. This recipe is my combination of all three. Chicken is marinated, then deep-fried so that the cornstarch-flour coating forms a delicate but hard crust. Once you get the crispy crust right, you can vary it any way you wish. For extra-extra crispy chicken, dredge the chicken in the cornstarch-flour mixture, allow the coating to become damp, then dredge a second time before frying.

Chinese-Style Stir-Fries

For the chicken:

2 large egg whites

2 tablespoons water

½ teaspoon kosher salt or 1 tablespoon soy sauce

2 tablespoons plus ½ cup/60 grams cornstarch

1 tablespoon plus ½ cup/60 grams all-purpose flour

6 boneless, skinless chicken thighs, *cut into bite-size strips*

1½ cups/360 milliliters vegetable oil

For the sauce:

¼ cup hoisin sauce

2 tablespoons soy sauce

2 tablespoons red wine vinegar

2 tablespoons chili sauce with garlic

2 tablespoons sugar

1 tablespoon tomato paste

1 tablespoon fish sauce

To finish the dish:

8 to 10 dried red chiles

4 garlic cloves, coarsely *chopped*

1 (1-inch/ 2.5-centimeter) piece ginger, *grated*

6 scallions, *white and light green parts thinly sliced on the bias, plus some dark green leaves*

2 yellow bell peppers, *seeded and cut into large dice*

Grated zest of 1 orange

Grated zest of 1 lemon

To prepare the chicken, in a large bowl, whisk together the egg whites, water, and salt or soy until lightly frothy. Add 2 tablespoons cornstarch and 1 tablespoon flour and gently stir to combine. Stir in the chicken and set it aside.

In a small bowl, whisk together the remaining ½ cup/60 grams cornstarch and ½ cup/60 grams flour.

In another small bowl, combine all the sauce ingredients and mix until they are uniformly combined.

Remove the chicken strips from the egg whites and dredge each piece in the cornstarch-flour mixture. Transfer to a plate. (Wait 10 minutes and repeat for extra-crispy chicken.)

Heat the vegetable oil in a wok. When it reaches 375°F/190°C (or when chopsticks inserted into the oil bubble instantly), add the chicken, several pieces at a time, making sure to keep them separate. When they are beautifully golden brown and crisp, transfer them to a paper towel–lined bowl or plate.

Pour out all but a few tablespoons oil from the wok.

Heat that oil over high heat. Add the chiles and cook till they turn black, 30 to 60 seconds (if you have an exhaust hood, you'll want it on). Add the garlic and ginger and stir, then add the scallions and bell peppers and stir-fry until softened. Add the sauce and bring it to a simmer. Add the chicken and stir until it's coated with sauce. Add the zest and stir to combine, then serve.

CHAPTER 9

The Bacon, Lettuce, and Tomato Sandwich

As I said in my Introduction, a BLT began this book. That's how powerful a sandwich can be.

Also, it's one of my favorite sandwiches. I generally don't like to go out for lunch, but when I do, I know that a BLT will give me just the right amount of nutrition—carbohydrates and fats and protein—without leaving me feeling heavy and sleepy, and it will hold me well until dinner.

I love a BLT using the simplest grocery-store items—Oscar Mayer bacon, toasted Wonder Bread, Hellmann's mayo, lettuce, and tomato. The tomato has to be at least halfway decent (meaning if you salt a slice and eat it plain, it tastes good). But when prepared with great ingredients—flavorful bread, big slices of juicy summer tomatoes, and thick-cut applewood-smoked bacon—the BLT rises to another level of delicious.

And if you choose, like many people who read my blog and took the BLT Challenge, to cure your own bacon, grow your tomatoes, make your own bread, and so on, this sandwich becomes a kind of life event, filled with all kinds of meaning rarely accompanying a sandwich.

The sandwich as a category must be addressed. It is, after all, among the most common, if not *the* most common meal in America, according to market research. An excellent sandwich often has all the components of a traditional meal: a starch, vegetable, protein, and sauce. And this is how we need to think about the sandwich: not as just a sandwich but rather as a meal, one that we plan based on what we want. What kind of protein? What kind of bread? And what kind of seasoning do we want to bring to it—simple savory (like a BLT), or spicy and dramatic, with sliced jalapeños? What kind of sauce? Should it be tart, like a vinaigrette, or creamy and rich?

This is how anyone can invent a sandwich. Say you have some sausages, but you don't want to simply fry them and put them on a plate and maybe throw some sautéed peppers and onions on the plate with them. Using the device of a soft French roll, you could turn this sausage into a much more interesting meal. Add the sautéed peppers and onions and spread the roll with a good mustard. Or, since the onions and peppers are sweet, perhaps add sauerkraut, and then use mayonnaise as the finishing sauce rather than tart mustard, since you have acidity from the sauerkraut.

Avocado is so rich it can function like a protein in a sandwich, and it goes with almost anything. Eggs are great with avocado, so make that a component, maybe a warm cooked egg with a runny yolk, some arugula for its peppery bite, and some sunflower seeds for salty crunch. Serve it on a toasted English muffin, a great choice of bread for a sandwich. Or add crispy bacon. Or take inspiration from guacamole and add lime-macerated minced shallot, jalapeño, and diced tomato (lightly salted), and roll it in a corn tortilla.

The sandwich is a device, a vehicle, a way of approaching a meal.

The recipes in this chapter are for some of the classic sandwiches I love. Classics are classics for a reason. But because sandwiches have become so ubiquitous, we tend to think of them as simple or boring—and so do restaurants. I've had miserable, uncared-for sandwiches even at high-end restaurants because of this. All of the following sandwiches were chosen because they are classics to elevate and reiterate, to acknowledge what makes them great in the first place.

Let's take some time to respect America's most common meal.

So, you know how to make a BASIC BLT (277), right? A simple sandwich. BUT what if you decided to make a BLT from scratch (279) and I mean seriously FROM SCRATCH? You'll need to plan ahead to GROW your own LETTUCE and TOMATO (279) some months in advance. →

Then, you'd want to CURE your own BACON (279), make a dough and bake a fresh loaf of Basic SANDWICH BREAD (285). or possibly

take advantage of my SOURDOUGH HACK (283), and whip up some HOMEMADE MAYONNAISE (286)

At that point, you'd be ready to ASSEMBLE your BLT FROM SCRATCH (289), as a number of people did when I posted a BLT challenge on my blog some years back.

Once you've mastered the BLT, you're ready to make a TURKEY CLUB (293), which is basically a BLT with another sandwich layer that includes fresh roast turkey breast. BUT make sure you have some frilly toothpicks on hand and that you know how to slice it. Another classic sandwich to try from scratch is →

Earlier I discussed THE AMAZING CHICKPEA (256). Here I describe the ultimate FALAFEL SANDWICH with Tahini Sauce (300) and even tell you HOW TO MAKE PITA (299). Last, but definitely not least, is THE EGG SALAD SANDWICH (299), which also takes advantage of my homemade MAYO (286), and, if you liked my BASIC BREAD recipe (284) as well. Its an old-school classic that is often overlooked these days, but like the BLT, it's a fabulous, nutritious lunch if made with care.

The traditional BĂHN MÌ (298) calls for pork belly or pâté, but I've developed a version that uses left over MEAT LOAF (85) and is pretty much irresistable, packed with pickled vegetables (206). Some MAYO (286) for creaminess, and lots of fresh cilantro

THE REUBEN (294), which will involve learning to make corned beef (perhaps you have some left over from the recipe on page 223), as well as RYE BREAD (295) RUSSIAN DRESSING (295), and SAUERKRAUT (296), all good skills to master

OR, you could try your hand at THE FRENCH DIP (298), a mouth-watering roast beef sandwich that takes advantage of the ONE-HOUR BEEF STOCK (142) that you learned back in chapter 4

THE BASIC BLT   SERVES 2

Let's start with the simplest version of the second simplest sandwich (first: PB&J, natch). But make it good. Buy good, thick-cut bacon. So many varieties are available at grocery stores and online. I like a moderately thick cut, but you've got to cook it right for this kind of sandwich—which means so that it's crisp enough to crack when you bite through it; if it's too chewy, the sandwich becomes difficult to eat and you can pull out a whole slice of bacon without meaning to. I find white grocery store sandwich bread perfectly fine for a BLT, but if you use a flavorful bread, your sandwich will be that much better. Just be sure it's easy to eat. If the bread is a rustic country loaf cut too thick, it can be difficult to eat without tearing apart the sandwich. It shouldn't be too thick, or the other ingredients can get lost. Proportions are critical to an excellent sandwich.

But in the end, it comes down to common sense and what you like.

6 to 8 thick slices good bacon

4 (½-inch/ 1-centimeter-thick) slices white, whole wheat, or multigrain bread

Mayonnaise *as needed*

2 to 4 crisp iceberg lettuce leaves

Kosher salt *to taste*

2 to 4 (½-inch/ 1-centimeter-thick) slices ripe tomato

Sauté the bacon until it's crispy. You should be able to break it with a gentle snap. Let it drain on paper towels.

Toast the bread until it's very toasted but not burnt. Spread a goodly amount of mayonnaise across one side of each piece of toast.

Lay the lettuce on two of the toast slices so that it covers the bread and mayonnaise.

Salt the tomatoes aggressively. Put them on the lettuce. Top the tomatoes with the bacon. Put the remaining mayo-spread toast slices on the bacon. Cut the sandwiches in half diagonally and serve.

THE BLT
from Scratch

On Growing Your Own Lettuce and Tomato

You'll need to start your lettuce and tomatoes a few months before you plan to serve your BLT. Plant them at the appropriate time of year for your location. Start tomatoes indoors from seed or buy them already started by a nursery. Choose beefsteak or another delicious juicy tomato (my favorite is Green Zebra). While I prefer a crunchy lettuce, something like romaine takes a little more growing than a soft, flat-leafed lettuce (see page 67). Both are acceptable in a from-scratch BLT.

On Curing Bacon

For properly cured bacon, you need pink curing salt, which is a mixture of salt and sodium nitrite. Nitrites and nitrates are naturally occurring chemical compounds abundant in the soil (and therefore in the plants we eat) and in our body. Once thought to be bad for us, recent evidence suggests that they improve vascular health (many people are prescribed nitrates for heart issues). So, don't think of them as chemical additives. For more information on pink salt, see the recipe for Corned Beef (page 224).

Bacon is, by definition, pork belly that has been cured with pink salt and hot-smoked until it's fully cooked. But it doesn't need to be smoked. You can simply cook it in a low oven until it reaches an interior temperature of 150°F/65°C. You don't even need to cure it with pink salt—you can just salt it (see Ventrèche, page 200). It will taste much porkier and won't be pink like cured bacon, but it will still be delicious. But if you have a charcoal grill or a smoker, it's seriously worth the effort of putting some smoke on that slab.

However you want to cure the pork belly is fine, because cured pork belly is one of the most compelling, if not *the* most compelling, food preparations known. I don't know why this is, but more people seem to like bacon, and like it powerfully, than any other single food.

Always buy skin-on pork belly if you can, because the skin is so valuable for its gelatin, its protein. Boiled, this protein gives stocks and stews body. Fried, it turns delectably crispy. For bacon, it's usually removed after smoking so that the bacon is easier to cut and eat. The smoked skin, or rind, is great to add to soups and stews. But if only skinned pork belly is available, that will make delicious bacon as well.

I offer two ways to cure bacon: one using a dry-cure mixture and what's called the salt box method, and the other using precise percentages. Ideally, bacon has a 2 percent salt content and a 0.25 percent pink salt content. I like the precision of percentages, but I also like to have a store of the dry-cure mix so it's handy whenever I need it.

You can cure bacon on a baking sheet or in a large container, but I find the most convenient vessel to use is a large zip-top plastic bag. This makes it easier to "overhaul" the bacon (redistribute the salt and seasonings), and there's no cleanup.

BASIC DRY CURE
MAKES 1½ POUNDS/680 GRAMS BASIC CURE

This is enough to cure about 30 pounds/13.5 kilograms of bacon. It's a good mix to put together if you regularly cure bacon. It keeps indefinitely.

- 1 pound/450 grams kosher salt (*a scant 2 cups Morton's kosher salt, for example*)
- 8 ounces/225 grams (*1 scant cup*) sugar
- 2 ounces/56 grams pink curing salt (*10 teaspoons*)

Mix all the ingredients and store in a zip-top plastic bag or airtight nonreactive container in a cool, dry place.

DRY-CURED BACON
MAKES 3 TO 5 POUNDS/1.36 TO 2.27 KILOGRAMS

This is also known as the salt box method. It is not as accurate as using percentages, but I've used it for years with great results.

- 1 (3- to 5-pound/1.36- to 2.27-kilogram) slab pork belly, *preferably skin-on*
- ¼ cup Basic Dry Cure (at left), *or more as needed, or 2 teaspoons pink salt mixed with ¼ cup kosher salt*
- 3 to 5 garlic cloves, *smashed with the side of a chef's knife*
- 3 bay leaves, *crumbled*
- 5 to 10 thyme sprigs
- 2 tablespoons brown sugar
- 1 tablespoon whole black peppercorns, *cracked beneath a saucepan*

Liberally sprinkle or even dredge the pork belly in the dry-cure mix until it is uniformly coated. Put it in a 2-gallon/7.5-liter zip-top plastic bag and add the remaining ingredients. Rub the ingredients around to distribute them. (If you don't have a large enough bag, wrap the belly well in plastic wrap and put it on a rimmed baking sheet that will fit in your refrigerator.) Refrigerate the belly for 7 days, redistributing the seasoning two or three times during the week.

Remove the belly from the bag or plastic wrap. Rinse it thoroughly and pat it dry. Put it on a rack set in a rimmed baking sheet. Place the sheet in your oven and turn the oven to 200°F/93°C. Remove the sheet when the meat reaches 150°F/65°C, 2 to 2½ hours.

Alternatively, you can hot-smoke the meat in a smoker. If you're using a grill, set it up to smoke using wood chips and smoke on indirect heat for 1 hour, then finish it in a 200°F/93°C oven to 150°F/65°C.

If you have used skin-on belly, cut off the skin while it's still warm and reserve it to use in soups, stews, and stocks. Allow the bacon to cool and then refrigerate, cutting slices or lardons as you need them. If you intend to freeze some or all of the bacon, slice or cut it into lardons before you do.

BACON CURED USING PERCENTAGES

This is the most accurate way of curing bacon and ensures that it's always consistently seasoned and cured. For this preparation, you will need a scale.

1 pork belly, *preferably skin-on*	Whole black peppercorns, *cracked beneath a saucepan*
Kosher salt	
Brown sugar	1 bunch thyme
Pink curing salt	
Garlic cloves, *smashed with the side of a chef's knife*	

Weigh the pork belly in grams and record its weight. Calculate 2 percent of that weight, and measure that weight in kosher salt. For example, if your belly weighs 2,000 grams (close to 4½ pounds), you'll weigh out 40 grams salt, which is about 2⅔ tablespoons. Weigh out half the weight of the kosher salt in brown sugar (20 grams, or about 4 teaspoons, in the example above). Weigh out 0.25 percent of pink salt (5 grams in our example, or about 1 teaspoon). Combine the kosher salt, brown sugar, and pink salt and stir till it's uniformly mixed.

Rub the mixture all over the pork belly. Put it in a 2-gallon/7.5-liter zip-top bag and add the remaining ingredients. Rub the ingredients around to distribute them. (If you don't have a large enough bag, wrap the belly well in plastic wrap and put it on a rimmed baking sheet that will fit in your refrigerator.) Refrigerate the belly for 7 days, redistributing the seasoning two or three times during the week.

Remove the belly from the bag or plastic wrap. Rinse it thoroughly and pat it dry. Put it on a rack set in a rimmed baking sheet. Place the sheet in your oven and turn the oven to 200°F/93°C. Remove the sheet when the meat reaches 150°F/65°C, 2 to 2½ hours.

Alternatively, you can hot-smoke the meat in a smoker. If you're using a grill, set it up to smoke using wood chips and smoke on indirect heat for 1 hour, then finish it in a 200°F/93°C oven to 150°F/65°C.

If you have used skin-on belly, cut off the skin while it's still warm and reserve it to use in soups, stews, and stocks. Allow the bacon to cool and then refrigerate, cutting slices or lardons as you need them. If you intend to freeze some or all of the bacon, slice or cut it into lardons before you do.

ON MAKING BREAD

Making bread is easy, especially if you have a scale. A basic bread dough breaks down to 5 parts flour to 3 parts water by weight, plus a little yeast and salt. That's it. What you do with that combination is what makes the bread good or not so good. This is the basic bread baker's percentage: 100 percent flour, 60 percent water, 3 percent yeast, and 2 percent salt, all by weight.

Weight is important primarily because flour measured by volume can differ by as much as 50 percent, depending on the type of flour you use, how you scoop it, and the humidity in your kitchen. So, if you have a recipe calling for 4 cups flour, you might end up using anywhere from 1 pound/450 grams flour to 1½ pounds/680 grams flour—a big enough difference to determine the success of your bread.

There are only a few steps to making bread once you've measured out the ingredients: First, mixing the dough till it's so elastic you can stretch a piece to translucency. Second, letting it rise, covered, until it has doubled in volume (this is called fermenting in baker's parlance because it's during this stage that it develops flavor). Third, punching down the dough to release gases and redistribute the yeast, so that it has fresh flour to feed on, and letting it relax so that it is amenable to shaping. Fourth, shaping the dough, whether into a baguette or boule, or in a loaf pan. Fifth, letting it rise again so that it has a nice airy crumb (known as proofing, an old bakers' term derived from the notion that the rising proved that the dough had active yeast). And sixth, baking it.

You might go so far as to say there is a seventh step: not eating it the minute it comes out of the oven, something very hard to do. But you must restrain yourself so that the bread's interior finishes baking as it cools.

If you're intent on making a BLT from scratch, I recommend harvesting your own yeast—the resulting bread is much more flavorful. This is easy, too, since wild yeast is already present in flour. Just combine 2 tablespoons all-purpose flour and 2 tablespoons water in a container and let it sit, uncovered, at room temperature. Add the same amount of flour and water each day. After about 3 days, you should see bubbles beginning to break through the surface—this means your starter is active. Now pour out half the starter, then add the same amount of flour and water that you poured off, twice a day, to feed the starter. When it is very bubbly (which could be a week or more, or less, depending on your environment), it's ready to use.

To make bread using a starter, simply combine 1 part starter, 1 part water, and 2 parts flour, then add up the weights and calculate 1 percent salt. So, if you wanted a 2-pound/900-gram loaf, you'd use 8 ounces/225 grams starter, 8 ounces/225 grams water, 1 pound/450 grams flour, and ⅓ ounce/9 grams salt (a couple teaspoons).

Even if you don't make a starter, you can mimic the effects of one by making what's called a preferment, a kind of sourdough hack. Bread gets much of its flavor from the activity of the yeast. The longer the yeast has to feed (and multiply) on the flour, the more carbon dioxide and alcohol it releases. This, among other things, adds flavor. If you know you'll be baking bread tomorrow, mix 5 ounces/140 grams flour and 5 ounces/140 grams water together and stir in ¼ teaspoon yeast. Cover it with plastic wrap and let it sit overnight until you're ready to bake. When you are, combine your ingredients, but remember to subtract 5 ounces/140 grams each water and flour that you will add in the form of your preferment, and you can reduce the amount of yeast by ½ teaspoon, since the yeast population in the preferment will have grown.

A note about no-knead breads and how they're cooked: The baker and cookbook author Jim Lahey came up with a bread recipe that requires no kneading. Rather, it lets yeast and time do the kneading. One of the things yeast does is basically knead the dough from the inside, micro-kneading. The very slack dough sits untouched for 12 to 18 hours, then is turned out onto a floured surface, folded to give it some structure, allowed to rise, and baked in a covered Dutch oven. I don't particularly love the no-knead bread (though many, many people do—it's published on the *New York Times* website if you're curious and want to try it), but what was a revelation to me was the Dutch oven.

When I took my intro to bread baking class at the Culinary Institute of America, we baked our breads in a big professional deck oven, and with a press of a button you could inject steam into it as soon as the loaves went in. This moist environment facilitated the initial oven spring, or quick initial rise, and helped create a very crisp, flavorful crust. This is difficult to do in a home oven—some people jerry-rig it with ropes or chains or stones and shoot water onto the loaves to create the steam—but when you pop your dough into a Dutch oven, the moisture the bread releases is trapped in this fairly small enclosure, matching the effect of the steam injection of a deck oven. It's a brilliant idea.

BASIC DUTCH OVEN BREAD
MAKES 1 (2-POUND/900-GRAM) LOAF

This is a perfect all-purpose dough and makes a great boule, especially if you cook it in a Dutch oven (a technique introduced by the baker Jim Lahey), which traps the moisture the bread gives off and helps create a delicious crust. But you can also stretch it thin and long, stipple it with your fingers, rub oil on it, and bake it for ciabatta. Or you can turn it into pretzels (page 290). It relies on the standard procedure: Mix the dough, let it rise to double its size (the fermenting stage, in bakers' parlance), punch it down, shape it, let it rise again, then bake. Once you feel comfortable with this dough, how it ferments and rises, feel free to try other proportions, using more water and different flours, such as spelt.

20 ounces/600 grams bread flour or all-purpose flour (*about 4 cups*), *plus more for dusting*

1 ½ cups/360 milliliters water

2 teaspoons active dry yeast

2 teaspoons kosher salt, *plus more for sprinkling* (*optional*)

Olive oil, *for brushing* (*optional*)

Combine the flour, water, and yeast in the bowl of a standing mixer (or a mixing bowl if kneading by hand) and mix with a dough hook (or sturdy spoon) till a dough forms. Add the salt and continue mixing (or kneading) until the dough is very smooth and elastic. Pull off a piece of dough; if you can stretch it so that it becomes translucent, the dough is properly mixed. This should take a few minutes in a mixer. Be careful, because it's possible to overmix the dough using the mixer, in which case it won't have quite the same rise. (It's difficult to overknead dough by hand.)

Cover the bowl and allow the bread to rise for 2 hours, or until it's doubled in volume (times can vary depending on how hot your kitchen is). If the dough begins to deflate, it has risen too long and may be compromised to some extent.

Preheat your oven to 450°F/230°C. Put preheat with the oven. (If you don't have a Dutch oven, put a baking sheet or baking stone in your oven to preheat.)

Transfer the dough to a floured board and punch it down to release the gas and redistribute the yeast. Cover it with a dish towel and let it rest for 10 minutes. Shape the dough into a boule by cupping the dough between both hands and moving the boule around in a circle until it forms a tight ball.

Put the boule in the hot Dutch oven (or on the baking sheet or stone). Slash a cross or a hashtag in the top of the bread. Brush with olive oil and sprinkle with coarse kosher salt if you wish, put the lid on the Dutch oven, and bake for 30 minutes. Remove the lid and continue to bake, uncovered, for another 15 to 30 minutes. When it's done, the bread will sound hollow when tapped. If you want to be sure it's done, use an instant-read thermometer: It should read at least 200°F/93°C.

Remove the pan from the oven and let the bread cool completely before slicing it.

SANDWICH BREAD
MAKES 1 (2-POUND/900-GRAM) LOAF

If you want to make a softer bread with a more delicate crumb, and one with a classic sandwich bread shape, here is a dough that uses buttermilk as both a gentle flavoring device and as a fat to soften the bread.

Both the Basic Dutch Oven Bread (opposite) and this sandwich bread work well for a hearty BLT. I would use this bread for a from-scratch Turkey Club (page 293).

18 ounces/480 grams bread flour or all-purpose flour (*about 3½ cups*)

1½ cups/360 milliliters buttermilk

1 large egg

1 tablespoon honey

3 ounces/90 grams room temperature butter, *cut in thirds*

1 teaspoon active dry yeast

1 tablespoon/15 grams kosher salt

Egg wash: 1 large egg mixed with 1 tablespoon milk (*optional*)

Combine the flour, buttermilk, egg, honey, butter, and yeast in the bowl of a standing mixer (or a mixing bowl if kneading by hand) and mix with a dough hook (or sturdy spoon) till a dough forms. Add the salt and continue mixing (or kneading) until the dough is very smooth and elastic. Pull off a piece of dough; if you can stretch it so that it becomes translucent, the dough is properly mixed. This should take a few minutes in a mixer. Be careful, because it's possible to overmix the dough using the mixer, in which case it won't have quite the same rise. (It's difficult to overknead dough by hand.)

Cover the bowl and allow the bread to rise for 2 hours, or until it's doubled in volume (times can vary depending on how hot your kitchen is). If the dough begins to deflate, it has risen too long and may be compromised to some extent.

Transfer the dough to a floured board and punch it down to release the gas and redistribute the yeast. Cover it with a dish towel and let it rest for 10 minutes. Shape the dough into a boule by cupping the dough between both hands and moving the boule around in a circle until it forms a tight ball. Then roll the boule back and forth into a cylinder the length of your loaf pan.

Coat the loaf pan with cooking spray. Place the dough in the pan, cover it with a towel, and let it rise for 1 hour.

Preheat your oven to 450°F/230°C.

When the dough has risen, remove the towel and make one slash lengthwise along the top of the dough. If you would like a beautiful browned crust on top, brush the egg wash over the top of the loaf. Put the pan in the oven. Bake for 30 minutes, then reduce the heat to 375°F/190°C and continue to bake for another 30 minutes, or until it's done. It should sound slightly hollow when tapped and an instant read thermometer should read at least 200°F/93°C or higher. Allow it to cool completely before slicing.

Note: Use this recipe to make individual rolls (see page 290).

MAYONNAISE
MAKES ABOUT 1 CUP/240 MILLILITERS

Mayonnaise made at home is one of the few preparations that is so different from its store-bought counterpart that there should be different names for them. I love to make mayonnaise. And if you use a whisk attachment with an immersion blender, it doesn't take any real effort. But whisking it by hand is also very satisfying, and a bit of a workout.

   Having enough water to maintain the emulsification is important. You don't need much (and the lemon juice serves this function as well). If you like a lemony mayonnaise, use a full tablespoon of lemon juice. If you want to hold back, begin with two teaspoons of lemon juice and one of water. Have a little of each on hand as well, to add as you wish. If the mayonnaise begins to look too thick, add a few drops of water. If you want more acidity, add more lemon. You can add more lemon than you think you need, as you won't be eating it straight, so don't be shy.

   Homemade mayonnaise has a texture like nothing else, far superior to the gelatinized stuff in a jar. Moreover, you can control the flavor, adding lemon and even aromatics. I'm partial to minced shallot macerated in lemon juice—so good with artichokes and asparagus. Adding freshly minced herbs, such as tarragon, transforms it into a magical sauce. Try it on potatoes or boiled cauliflower, or use it on a fried egg sandwich.

   Or just plain, on your BLT from scratch.

1 tablespoon minced shallot	½ teaspoon kosher salt
1 tablespoon lemon juice	1 large egg yolk
1 teaspoon water (*plus more as needed*)	¾ to 1 cup/180 to 240 milliliters vegetable oil

Combine the shallot, lemon juice, and salt in a large bowl. Allow it to sit for at least 10 minutes. Whisk in the egg yolk, then whisk in 1 or 2 drops of vegetable oil. Then slowly begin pouring in the remaining vegetable oil in a thin stream, whisking continuously until you have a thick, creamy sauce. Marvel at the taste and consistency.

1. This is mayonnaise: egg yolk, lemon juice and water, seasonings, and oil. (Note the dish towel curled beneath the bowl to stabilize it during whisking.)

4. Whisk constantly as you add the oil. Remember, you can also stop whisking if your arm is tired; the mayonnaise will only break if too much oil is added too quickly or there is not enough water to maintain the emulsion.

2. I begin by mixing the yolk into the lemon juice-water, then adding just a drop, maybe two, of the oil and whisking it thoroughly into the yolk to establish the emulsion. I can then pour the oil in a thin stream, whisking constantly.

3. Once the emulsion has clearly taken hold, you can add the oil in a thicker stream.

5. At this point you can add as much oil as you wish, provided you have enough water.

6. Mayonnaise should be so thick it won't fall from the whisk. If you have added all your oil and it is still soupy, you have a broken mayonnaise. Start it again whisking the broken mayonnaise into a teaspoon of water (and a second yolk if you wish) and it should all come back together.

ON ASSEMBLING THE BLT

First, bake your bread and let it cool.

Since you've gone to the trouble of curing your own bacon, make use of that slab and cut several ½-inch/1-centimeter-thick slices. You can cook these on the stovetop by starting them in plenty of water to tenderize them, then letting the bacon crisp up when the water cooks off. Alternatively, you can wrap the slices in aluminum foil and bake them in a 250°F/121°C oven for an hour, then finish by searing them on the stovetop. The important thing is that they are tender enough to bite through without being tough and making the sandwich hard to eat.

While the bacon is cooking, go out to your garden and pick some lettuce and tomato.

Whip up your mayonnaise.

If you started the bacon in the oven, sauté it in a hot pan to brown and crisp the exterior (of course, if you'd rather slice it, that's fine, too).

When you're ready to assemble, slice and salt your tomatoes. Slice as many pieces of bread as you need and toast them. Slather one side of each piece of toast with mayonnaise. Set the bacon slabs on half of the toast slices. Top the bacon with tomatoes. Top the tomatoes with lettuce. Close the sandwiches with the other mayo-slathered toast slices. Slice the sandwiches diagonally and serve.

HOMEMADE PRETZELS MAKES 16 (2-OUNCE) PRETZELS

Pretzels are simply bread dough that has been coated with a lye solution and baked. Lye is a base, and every bit as burning as a powerful acid when mixed with water, so do be careful, especially if baking with kids. Wear rubber gloves if you're concerned, but I find that working carefully with spatulas is fine. The general rule of thumb is 4 percent lye by weight—that is, 4 grams lye for every 100 milliliters water. Do use parchment paper as the lye may discolor your baking sheet. Order food-grade lye (which is powdered) and chunky pretzel salt or flaky Maldon salt for garnish. These will be traditional pretzels with a crisp crust and soft, chewy interior.

1 recipe dough for
Basic Dutch Oven
Bread (page 284)

4 teaspoons lye

1 quart/1 liter water

Salt, for garnish
(*see headnote*)

Punch down the risen bread dough, divide it into 16 balls, and let them rest, covered with a towel, for 10 minutes. Roll each ball into an 8-inch/20-centimeter rope, cross the two ends, and flip it over, attaching the ends to the inner rounded part of the pretzel and leaving the nubs extended for a traditional pretzel shape. You can also simply bake them as is for pretzel rods. Cover the pretzels with a towel and let rise for 30 minutes.

Preheat your oven to 425°F/220°C. Line a rimmed baking sheet with parchment paper. Mix the lye into the water in a sauté pan over medium heat until dissolved. Choose a pan that will allow you to submerge the pretzels completely in the water. Remove the pan from the heat.

Using one or two slotted spatulas or spiders, lower each pretzel into the lye mixture for 10 seconds or so, then put it on the lined baking sheet. Garnish the pretzels with salt. Bake for 10 to 12 minutes, until dark brown and cooked through.

POPPY ROLLS

Use the Sandwich Bread recipe on page 285 to make individual rolls: After the dough has gone through its first rise, punch it down and let it rest for 5 or 10 minutes covered with a dish towel. Divide the dough into eight equal pieces, shape them into tight balls, and put them in a skillet in a ring or however you wish to bake them. Brush them with egg wash and sprinkle them with poppy seeds. Bake for 45 minutes, until cooked in the middle (if you're unsure, a thermometer inserted into the middle of one should read *above* 200°F/94°C). Allow to cool for at least 30 minutes before using. These are best eaten the day they are baked but they can be wrapped in foil and frozen for up to a month.

Other Breads and Sandwiches

THE TURKEY CLUB SERVES 4

Other Breads and Sandwiches

The turkey club sandwich is simply a BLT on top of a turkey sandwich. This recipe might not have made it into this book had my wife and I not taken a trip to Minneapolis. Ann's favorite sandwich is the turkey club, and given the opportunity to order one, she usually does. She's especially fond of the turkey club at a restaurant called Gregg's in her hometown of Providence, Rhode Island. There they roast and slice their own turkey breast and serve it as a double-decker sandwich—toast, turkey, toast, bacon-lettuce-and tomato, mayo, toast—cut in triangular quarters and held together with toothpicks.

But in Minneapolis, no matter where we went, no one made it properly. The first one was a turkey, lettuce, and tomato sandwich, cut in half diagonally. The next was the same, only this one did have bacon. At the third place she ordered it, we made sure it would be a double-decker with tomato-bacon-lettuce. Yes, we were assured; it was a traditional turkey club. And it will be cut in quarters? Yes, said the waiter. "*Diagonally*?" I confirmed. "Of course," he said.

The very same waiter arrived with the sandwich, set it before my wife, and vanished. It was a BLT with turkey, cut in half. Lengthwise.

I think it's a matter of respect. When I was at the Culinary Institute, they had an actual diagram of a proper turkey sandwich in my lunch cookery booklet. But now, the turkey club has become the Rodney Dangerfield of the sandwich world.

Let's take it back. Make it for dinner one night, with a side of fries and a salad. Put toothpicks on your shopping list, preferably the kind with colorful frilly ends.

The turkey club is especially good if you use turkey breast you roast yourself. Given how easy it is to roast a breast on the bone (and that's key—on the bone keeps it moist), it's not bad simply to have around all week for sandwiches. (Save the bones to add to your next Easy Overnight Chicken—and Turkey—Stock, page 38.)

Be sure to put the mayonnaise on all three sides of the toast that will face the interior of the sandwich (make that four sides if you want to do both sides of the middle slice); this fat barrier will prevent tomato juices from soaking into the bread and making it soggy, and it ensures that all bites of the sandwich are nice and moist.

12 slices white or whole-wheat sandwich bread, *toasted*

Plenty of mayonnaise

1 pound/450 grams sliced turkey breast

12 to 16 slices bacon, *cooked*

4 to 8 slices tomato, *lightly salted*

4 bright green, crisp romaine lettuce leaves

16 fancy toothpicks

Spread each piece of toast with a goodly amount of mayonnaise—don't be stingy. Divide the turkey among half of the pieces of toast. Top with another piece of toast, mayonnaise side up. Rest 3 or 4 pieces of bacon on top of this, then the tomato, then the lettuce. Put the final piece of toast, mayonnaise side down, on the lettuce. Put a toothpick into each quadrant of each sandwich. Slice each sandwich diagonally into quarters and serve.

THE REUBEN SERVES 2

However this sandwich came into being (Wikipedia lists numerous possible origins), I'd go so far as to say that if you haven't made your own Reuben, you don't really understand what a truly remarkable sandwich it is. The combination of cured beef, tart sauerkraut, a rich Russian dressing, and melted Swiss cheese, piled on rye bread and fried like a grilled cheese sandwich, is outstanding. It has all the great components of any satisfying dish: crunch, juiciness, fattiness, and the tart taste of a pickled vegetable. I know that you can buy Russian dressing, but it's so easy to make (see opposite) that there's hardly a need to. As always, the better the bread, the better the sandwich. It's worth making your own rye if you like to bake bread (see opposite). Or buy a good loaf at a bakery you like and trust. This is a great from-scratch sandwich as well, especially since home corned beef (page 224) is superior to store-bought. For extra credit, grow your own cabbage and ferment it (see page 296).

Reubens are great to make in batches because you can start them in a hot skillet on the stovetop, flip them, and transfer them to the oven, where they finish cooking while you set the table or open the wine. These can be so thick that flipping them can be hard. If you have toothpicks on hand, secure each side of the sandwich with two toothpicks, breaking them off at bread level (the sandwich will collapse somewhat when it finishes, making the toothpicks easy to remove).

I use mayonnaise on the outside of the bread because it's easier to spread straight from the refrigerator than butter and has the same effect on the bread when fried, but feel free to use butter instead (I do the same for grilled cheese sandwiches, by the way). And note that the cheese goes on both pieces of bread for the sandwich. There is a lot of liquid and juiciness in this sandwich, and the cheese barrier prevents the bread from getting soggy.

Serve with an arugula or watercress salad, dressed with some lemon and a drizzle of olive oil.

½ cup/90 grams sauerkraut, homemade (page 296) *or store-bought*

12 ounces/340 grams sliced corned beef, homemade (page 224) *or store-bought*

4 slices good rye bread

Mayonnaise *as needed*

4 to 8 slices Swiss cheese (*enough to completely cover each slice of bread*)

½ cup/120 milliliters Russian Dressing (opposite)

Preheat your oven to 300°F/150°C.

Put the sauerkraut in a small saucepan and bring to a simmer on the stovetop. Put the corned beef in a bowl with a couple tablespoons of water, cover with plastic wrap, and microwave for 30 seconds to warm the meat. Leave covered until ready to use.

Coat one side of each slice of bread with mayonnaise. Put them, mayonnaise side down, on a cutting board. Cover each plain side of bread with a layer of cheese. Divide the corned beef between two of the bread slices. Top the corned beef with the warm sauerkraut, using tongs and letting any excess liquid drain off. Spoon the dressing over the sauerkraut and top each sandwich with the second piece of bread, cheese side down.

Heat an oven-safe skillet over medium-high heat. Add the sandwiches and cook until the bread is nicely browned, 2 to 3 minutes. Flip the sandwiches, cook for 30 seconds, then put the pan in the oven for 10 to 15 minutes, until the bottoms are browned and the sandwiches are heated through. Serve warm.

RUSSIAN DRESSING

MAKES ABOUT 1 ½ CUPS/360 MILLILITERS

Somehow, when I was in fourth grade, I was taught in a home ec class how to make Russian dressing in an old mayonnaise jar. I couldn't believe how delicious carrots and celery were when I dipped them in—beat the hell out of Pop-Tarts and pretzels as an after-school snack. When I went looking for contemporary versions on the internet, I was surprised to find that so many used ketchup. I used chili sauce back then, and so does my partner in Charcuterie, Brian Polcyn (we included his version in that book). Brian also uses diced white onion, but this version uses my standby, shallot in lemon. While working on this book, I texted him to ask if he made Russian dressing often. His response: "Only when I'm rushed." Pun noted, but it's true—that's how fast it comes together.

If you're making this just for a batch of Reubens (opposite), halve the recipe. But you might want to make the whole recipe—I think Russian dressing is due for a comeback. It makes a great accompaniment to a crudité platter. Make it with your own mayo (page 286), and it's out of this world.

½ shallot

Kosher salt *to taste*

1 tablespoon lemon juice

1 cup mayonnaise

¼ cup chili sauce

1 tablespoon prepared horseradish

1 ½ teaspoons Worcestershire sauce

Plenty of freshly ground black pepper

Other Breads and Sandwiches

Mince the shallot. Midway through mincing, give it a good pinch of salt. Finish mincing. Combine it with the lemon juice in a ramekin and let it sit for 10 minutes.

Combine the remaining ingredients in a bowl. Add the macerated shallot. Stir to thoroughly combine all the ingredients. Store in an airtight container in the refrigerator for up to 3 days.

HOW TO MAKE RYE BREAD

The Basic Dutch Oven Bread recipe (page 284) can be used to make an excellent rye simply by using rye flour in place of some of the white flour. The basic ratio here is 3 parts white flour to 2 parts rye flour. So, that would be 12 ounces/340 grams bread flour or all-purpose flour and 8 ounces/225 grams rye flour. The same mixing, fermenting, shaping, and rising techniques used for basic dough apply here. Add 1 to 2 tablespoons of caraway seeds to the dough as you're mixing.

HOW TO MAKE SAUERKRAUT
(OR NATURAL PICKLES FROM ANY VEGETABLE)

Other
Breads and
Sandwiches

Sauerkraut is another one of those preparations that you can buy anywhere, but it tastes so different from what you can make at home in a week that the store-bought stuff should be called something else.

Using the magical proportion of the 5 percent brine (which I learned from my first instructor, chef Michael Pardus), you can pickle a single jar of sauerkraut in 5 to 7 days. It will have that distinctive sauerkraut tang, the same pickled cabbage flavor, but it will also have a crunch, a brightness, and a freshness that you can't get any other way.

Indeed, any vegetable can be pickled this way with great results. Make your own carrot and daikon pickle for a homemade Bánh Mì (page 298). Or pickle your own Thai chiles, then seed and chop them to garnish anything from a sautéed steak to roast chicken to any of the curries in chapter 8. The flavor of the chile pickling liquid—salt water alone—creates its own delicious tart condiment to be sprinkled on anything that needs a little kick. Or make your own kimchi, with cabbage and daikon and Korean chili paste (the chef Judy Joo has a fantastic paste recipe online).

Of course, it's best to use a scale, but if you don't have one, you can still make a close-enough 5 percent brine using Morton's coarse kosher salt: 1 tablespoon weighs just about ½ ounce/14 grams.

2½ cups/500 grams water

1 ounce/28 grams kosher salt (*about 2 tablespoons Morton's kosher salt*)

Vegetables of choice, *sliced or chopped as desired*

Combine the water and salt in a saucepan and heat on the stove till the salt is dissolved (or use a bowl in the microwave). Let cool to room temperature.

Fill a 1-quart/1-liter canning jar with your vegetables, then pour in the brine almost to the top. Put plastic wrap over the mouth of the jar. Use a clean stone or other small weight (I use a shot glass) to push the vegetables and the plastic wrap down, then fill the rest of the jar (and the shot glass) with more brine. Fit the lid on loosely (the fermenting vegetables will release gas) and set the jar on a plate or tray (some of the brine will eventually spill over).

Fermenting is best done in normal to cool room temperatures. In the summer, if your kitchen is hot, spoilage bacteria can take over (it will look like foam and scum and mold), so find the coolest spot available.

The vegetables should be nicely pickled after 7 days (perhaps even 5) and ready to use. For long-term storage, make a 3 percent brine and cool to room temperature. Drain the pickled vegetables (taste the liquid; you may want to reserve some for use as a vinegar or seasoning alternative, especially when pickling chiles). Pour the 3 percent brine over them, cover, and refrigerate for 2 to 3 weeks.

TO PICKLE CABBAGE FOR SAUERKRAUT

Cabbage is one of the few vegetables I routinely add extra aromatics to when pickling.

Prepare the brine as above. Fill your jar with finely sliced cabbage. Push 2 or 3 peeled garlic cloves and 2 bay leaves into the center of the cabbage. Fill the jar with brine, cover it with plastic wrap, and press the cabbage down with an appropriate glass or other weight. Refill the remainder of the jar and cover loosely. (Alternatively, press the plastic wrap down well below the rim of the jar and, holding it down, fill the jar so that the weight of the brine and the plastic wrap barrier hold the cabbage down, then cover loosely.)

Brine at cool room temperature for 5 to 7 days. Serve hot or cold, or refrigerate in a 3 percent brine as noted above.

THE FRENCH DIP   SERVES 4

This is a great dish to serve a lot of people; simply slow-roast the beef ahead of time. There are any number of worthy add-ons—you might top with caramelized onions or cheese—but in the end, as my beloved says, "It's all about the juice."

Of course, you can use leftover prime rib or other beef, or even sliced roast beef from the deli. If you have enough stock on hand, reduce 3 cups/710 milliliters down to 2 cups/480 milliliters for an even heartier flavor. Serve with a Classic Caesar Salad (page 151) and you've got a perfect meal.

4 French rolls

1½ pounds/680 grams sliced roast beef

2 cups/480 milliliters One-Hour Beef Stock (page 142)

Preheat your oven to 400°F/205°C.

Warm the rolls in the oven for 10 minutes. Heat the beef, covered in a microwave or in the oven with the buns, till it's warm and the fat is succulent.

Heat the stock just to a simmer and divide among four ramekins for dipping.

Cut the French rolls open, stuff them with the beef, and serve with the dip.

THE BÁNH MÌ   SERVES 4

I include this recipe here because it makes use of three preparations in this book: slow-roasted pork, meat loaf (traditionally this would be a country pâté), and pickled vegetables. But this classic Vietnamese sandwich is first of all about the bread: a French roll with a thin but crunchy crust and a soft crumb. They're hard to find if you don't have a Vietnamese bakery near you, so feel free to use a well-made baguette. Or, by all means make your own rolls (see the Note below).

With all that bread and meat, you need to make sure you've got plenty of fat in the form

of mayonnaise to keep it succulent—mix some Sriracha with it to keep those flavors zinging.

¾ cup/180 milliliters mayonnaise

2 to 4 tablespoons Sriracha

Juice of ¼ lime, plus 4 lime wedges *for garnish*

4 French rolls, lightly *toasted and cut open*

12 ounces/340 grams (8 thinnish slices) Meat Loaf (page 85) or country pâté

12 ounces/340 grams Slow-Roasted Pork Shoulder (page 212), *sliced and reheated in a microwave or oven until warm*

20 or so cucumber slices

1 cup/100 grams pickled carrot and daikon (see page 296)

4 or 5 jalapeños, *seeded if desired and thinly sliced*

Leaves and thin stems from 1 bunch cilantro

Combine the mayonnaise, Sriracha, and lime juice and stir till combined. Slather both sides of the interior of the rolls with the mayonnaise.

Layer the sandwiches with the meat loaf slices, slow-roasted pork, cucumber, pickled carrot and daikon, jalapeño, and plenty of cilantro. Serve each with a wedge of lime.

Note: To make your own baguettes, make the dough for Basic Dutch Oven Bread (page 284), punch it down, and divide it into six pieces. Form each into a mini boule, cover with a dish towel, and let rest for 10 minutes. Roll each piece into a cylinder about 6 inches/15 centimeters long. Cover with the towel again and let rise for 50 minutes. Put your baking stone or rimmed baking sheet in the oven and preheat the oven to 425°F/218°C. When the dough is ready, place the boules on the hot stone or baking sheet and make two or three diagonal slashes across the top to score them. Bake for 25 to 35 minutes, until done.

THE EGG SALAD SANDWICH
SERVES 4

The egg salad sandwich was once ubiquitous, but it seems we stopped caring about it. When it's done well, it's almost indecent how good it is. But you have to pay attention. You need great seasoning, a delicious mayonnaise, a little crunch, a touch of acidity, and some spice. And this is the one sandwich that I actually prefer on store-bought white bread, lightly toasted. But since this sandwich is all about the egg, spring for organic, cage-free if you can.

There are many ways to hard-cook an egg. If you have a pressure cooker, use that—it makes a lot of eggs so much easier to peel. But if you don't, put them in a saucepan and cover them with 2 inches/ 5 centimeters water. Bring the water to a boil, then remove the pan from the heat and cover it. Let the eggs sit for 13 to 15 minutes, then transfer them to an ice bath till they're thoroughly chilled.

Oh, and if you want to add some crispy chopped bacon, I don't think anyone will hold it against you. Some roasted red pepper, diced, might add some nice color. Diced avocado—oh, man, that would be great (in which case, use lime on the red onion instead of lemon, but reduce it by a quarter— lime is a little stronger than lemon). There's so much you can do with a simple egg salad sandwich.

¼ red onion, *cut into small dice (about ¼ cup)*

Kosher salt and freshly ground black pepper *to taste*

2 tablespoons lemon juice, *or more to taste*

10 hard-cooked large eggs, *peeled and chopped*

2 celery ribs, *cut into small dice*

¼ teaspoon piment d'Espelette powder or cayenne, *or more to taste*

1 cup/240 milliliters mayonnaise

8 slices white bread, *lightly toasted*

4 to 8 cold lettuce leaves

Rinse the onion under hot tap water and put in a bowl lined with paper towel to drain. Season aggressively with a good four-finger pinch of salt. Let it sit a few minutes, then remove the paper towel and sprinkle the lemon juice over the onion. Let it sit for 10 more minutes while you prepare the rest of the sandwich (peeling and chopping the eggs, chopping the celery, toasting the bread).

Combine the eggs, celery, Espelette powder or cayenne, black pepper, and the lemony red onion. Stir gently to combine. Stir in half the mayonnaise. Taste and add more salt if it needs it. Continue adding mayonnaise till it looks creamy and moist. Taste and evaluate for seasoning: Does it need more salt, pepper, spice, or lemon? Adjust accordingly. Divide among four slices of toast, then top with lettuce and the remaining toast. Cut the sandwiches on the diagonal. Serve with champagne if you have it; they go so well together.

HOW TO MAKE PITA
MAKES 8 LARGE PITAS

Pita bread looks impressive but is remarkably simple to make. Simply follow the Basic Dutch Oven Bread (page 284) ratio of 5 parts flour to 3 parts water, but replace some of the white flour with wheat flour—the same proportions as for rye bread (page 295), in fact. So, you'll need 12 ounces/340 grams bread flour or all-purpose flour and 8 ounces/225 grams whole-wheat flour.

Mix and ferment (initial rise) as with the sandwich dough. Then, after you punch the dough down, portion the dough into 3-inch/8-centimeter balls and allow to rise again. Meanwhile, preheat your oven to 425°F/218°C, with a baking stone or a rimmed baking sheet in the oven. When the dough has risen, roll each ball out to about ⅓ inch/ 8 millimeters thick, then bake on the stone or baking sheet until they puff and turn golden brown, about 5 minutes. Use as desired. Wrap them in aluminum foil and freeze if not using that day.

Other Breads and Sandwiches

FALAFEL WITH TAHINI SERVES 4

The amazing chickpea becomes falafel with the help of herbs and seasonings, and then it becomes a sandwich, with the standard garnishes except for one important addition, thanks to Ann, who wouldn't stop talking about the roasted eggplant at L'As du Fallafel, a kosher sandwich shop in Paris that serves what some call the best falafel anywhere. It makes wonderful sense to add eggplant to this sandwich. It adds a depth of flavor that none of the other ingredients can provide, plus a welcome hit of moisture. The falafel almost becomes secondary to the warm, creamy eggplant—but not quite. With tahini and a little peanut butter for extra-nutty flavor, this is now one of my favorite sandwiches. Or you could skip the pita and turn this into a falafel and roasted eggplant salad—add more lemon to the tahini and thin it further to use as a dressing.

For the falafel:

1½ cups/300 grams dried chickpeas, *soaked overnight in water and drained*

1 cup fresh parsley leaves

¾ cup cilantro leaves

½ cup/60 grams diced onion, *diced*

2 cloves garlic, *smashed*

2 tablespoons lemon juice

2 teaspoons ground cumin

2 teaspoons ground coriander

1 teaspoon kosher salt

¼ teaspoon cayenne powder

Vegetable oil, *for pan-frying*

For the tahini sauce:

½ cup/120 milliliters tahini

1 tablespoon creamy peanut butter

1 garlic clove, *smashed and macerated in 3 tablespoons lemon juice*

1½ teaspoons cumin

½ teaspoon smoked paprika

¼ teaspoon cayenne pepper (*optional*)

For the sandwiches:

6 (½-inch/1-centimeter-thick) slices peeled eggplant

Kosher salt *to taste*

1 cup very thinly sliced red onion

6 tomato slices

Extra-virgin olive oil

2 pitas, store-bought or homemade (see page 299), *cut in half*

Hummus, store-bought or homemade (page 253; *optional*)

12 thin cucumber slices

4 leaves head lettuce or butter lettuce

Combine all the falafel ingredients except the oil in a food processor and pulse until everything is ground and mixed into a fine meal texture. Form into 20 or so balls the size of golf balls.

Pour enough oil into a deep skillet to come halfway up its sides. Heat the oil over high heat to 350°F/175°C. Working in batches, fry the falafel balls until deep golden-brown, 2 minutes or so. Turn the balls over and cook until they are uniformly browned and cooked through, 2 to 3 more minutes. Transfer to paper towels to drain.

Combine all the tahini ingredients in a food processor and process until smooth, scraping down the sides as necessary. With the blade running, add enough water to thin the sauce to the desired consistency, up to ½ cup/120 milliliters or as needed. Set aside.

Preheat the oven to 425°F/218°C.

Salt the eggplant slices liberally on both sides and let sit for 10 minutes. Liberally salt the red onion. Gently salt the tomato slices while you're at it.

Rinse the eggplant, pat dry, brush both sides with olive oil, and arrange in a single layer on parchment paper on a rimmed baking sheet. Roast for 20 to 25 minutes, until tender. You can also broil them to put some color on them.

Rinse the red onion under hot tap water, then pat dry.

Warm the pitas in the oven for 5 minutes or so. To make the sandwiches, first sauce the pitas with the tahini sauce and hummus (if using). Be generous, as you don't want your sandwich to be dry. Then distribute the falafel, eggplant, tomato, onion, cucumber, and lettuce evenly among the pitas.

Indian-Style Curries

CHAPTER 10

The Profiterole

In the world of the professional restaurant, there is a long-standing divide between the savory kitchen and the pastry kitchen. Often the savory cooks will denigrate the pastry cooks as being too froufrou, and pastry chefs will denigrate the cooks as imprecise cretins. It's always in good fun, especially as savory cooks tend to be imprecise cretins and it takes considerably more skill (and decorum) to be an excellent pastry chef than it does to be an excellent savory chef.

The fact is, very few savory chefs become famous pastry chefs (Stephen Durfee did it at the French Laundry, out of necessity, and he created some desserts that are still renowned). Michel Richard was one of the best pastry chefs in both his native country, France, and his adopted country, America, and he went on to be every bit as innovative in the savory world at his many restaurants. But it's hard to think of many others with that kind of ambidextrous virtuosity.

The pastry kitchen and the hot kitchen are different territories, with their own rules and weather.

In France, according to the New York chef Jean-Georges Vongerichten, born in Alsace, apprentices typically started their education in the pastry kitchen. At least that was his experience. And while he longed for the action of the savory kitchen, looking back, he says he was very lucky to begin in pastry because it taught him precision. In the pastry kitchen, he learned how to weigh and measure with exactitude, skills that would serve him well no matter where he went.

I am a savory cook—that's the world I know and feel comfortable in—but even cooks and cretins such as myself need to have a firm handle on desserts and confections. I don't know anyone who doesn't like something sweet at the end of a meal. (My favorite dessert concludes this chapter and is, I dare say, the easiest and fastest recipe in the book—and yes, it truly is my favorite way to conclude a meal.)

But in the spirit of cooking from scratch, I considered what dessert might represent desserts generally and also be a gateway to a variety of techniques and lessons that can be applied to all cooking. I am a Francophile and thus chose a classic French dessert: the profiterole. I adore its three main components both for their deliciousness and for the lessons contained in each. As with the savory preparations featured in this book, the profiterole gives me an opportunity to take one dish that employs multiple uses and show how versatile each is and where each might lead.

Profiteroles show us the remarkable pâte à choux, a kind of batter-dough hybrid made with eggs, butter, milk, and flour. This concoction features in several dessert preparations in addition to profiteroles, including cream puffs and éclairs, churros, and sugar-cinnamon doughnuts. The profiterole is a kind of ice cream sandwich, so it is also a lesson in ice cream and, therefore, custard, since ice cream is just a vanilla custard, frozen. Of course you can purchase really good vanilla ice cream, but you can make the best ice cream yourself, and once you do make your own, you can vary it in infinite ways—I especially love a spicy Mexican chocolate ice cream.

But when you know how to make a great ice cream, you also know how to make a great pastry cream, which is just that same vanilla custard thickened with starch (you could also thicken it by baking it in a water bath for crème brûlée). And that simple pastry cream, even on its own, is compulsively delicious. Pipe it into a profiterole shell for a cream puff. Elongate that cream puff, fill it, and glaze it with chocolate sauce for a chocolate éclair. Spread it on multiple layers of crêpes to make a crêpe cake. Or whip some butter into it for a delectable icing, sometimes referred to as French buttercream, for cupcakes.

Making custard leaves you with egg whites, which freeze remarkably well, so no need to throw them out. These can be turned into meringues, which beget their own category of desserts. Since I was a child, I've loved sweet meringues baked till they're crunchy—such a marvel they seemed to me. And these can in turn become the base or vessel for pastry cream and berries, a dessert called pavlova.

And this singular classic French dessert, the profiterole, finishes with the world's easiest sauce, chocolate sauce (ganache), which really is so easy it's a wonder that people buy it in jars. As with all these preparations, you can take them in various directions once you know how chocolate and cream coalesce, to make ice cream, a tart, chocolate truffles.

There are recipes and techniques earlier in this book that work as beautifully in the sweet kitchen as they do in the savory kitchen. The pie dough for the Chicken Pot Pie (page 54) will be used here for a berry pie with a lattice crust, because lattice crusts aren't just cool to create and regard, they function to top the pie with a flavorful crust while allowing the abundant moisture in the berry filling to cook off. And it also provides an opportunity to make the easiest kind of pie there is, the French upside-down pie known as tarte Tatin—apples cooked in sugar and simply topped with dough, baked, and turned out onto a plate.

All these desserts are relatively simple—the pie is perhaps the most labor intensive of the bunch—because I like to present something sweet and delicious at the end of a meal, but, frankly, as a savory chef, I want desserts with only a few simple steps. When you're running behind (as I so often find myself doing) but still want to serve a satisfying dessert, the crumble or streusel technique, topped with melting ice cream, never fails to please; it's the lazy cook's tarte Tatin and every bit as delicious.

In the end, all the basic preparations connect to one another. Cooking is not a collection of individual recipes but rather a gorgeous lattice of connected techniques and ingredients that can all be taken in varying directions. Knowing these interconnections liberates you in the kitchen.

The Profiterole (309), a classic restaurant dessert, offers a few valuable lessons. FIRST, you will learn the wonders of pâte à choux, a fancy French name for a boiled pastry dough that is not as intimidating as it sounds. Once you've mastered it, you can make PÂTE À CHOUX PUFFS (310), light, airy pastry rolls that will be filled with homemade VANILLA ICE CREAM (313) and topped with CHOCOLATE SAUCE (313) also known as Chocolate Ganache. For a unique twist, you could substitute CARAMEL SAUCE (313) which I will show you how to make. Those airy puffs can be filled with PASTRY CREAM (314) or CHOCOLATE PASTRY CREAM (315) to make CREAM PUFFS (314) and they can also take a walk on the savory side with the addition of cheese, in which case they're called GOUGÈRES (310).

Once you have pâte à choux in your arsenal, you will want to try your hand at deep frying it to make CHURROS (316). And that chocolate ganache we made for the profiteroles? Easy as pie, and also fills an incredibly tasty CHOCOLATE TART (318), which uses my 3-2-1 PIE DOUGH. (chapter 2, 81)

Another useful and simple technique in the pastry kitchen is meringue, the basis for a crispy, delicious PAVLOVA WITH WHIPPED Cream and BLACKBERRY BLUEBERRY COMPOTE (322) and the basis for meringue is egg whites, which you will have leftover if you've made vanilla ice cream or pastry cream, both of which require yolks only. AND once you're making the berry compote, an excellent way to use berries that are on the verge of turning over-ripe, you ought to prepare enough to fill a BLACKBERRY-BLUEBERRY PIE (324) The French turn pie on its head with the classic TARTE TATIN (329) assembled on upside down apple pie with no top (bottom) crust, thinly sliced apples hitting the hot pan and caramelizing delectably in the process NO time for such fussiness? An APPLE STREUSEL (330) is the way to go. As simple a dessert as there is, but sweet and crispy and a fabulous end to any meal. BUT you dont want it to end, right? THE LAST DESSERT: Chocolate and Whiskey (332) my favorite way to say fini!

THE PROFITEROLE
From Scratch

MAKES 16 TO 18

Cream puffs sandwiching ice cream, finished with chocolate sauce: This is simply one of the best desserts there is, and it's as easy to make as it is impressive. This is an especially easy from-scratch dish, especially given that two of the three components can be made days before serving and the other can be made hours ahead of time. I'll give all the recipes for a from-scratch version, but please, don't *not* make this because of the ice cream—a good store-bought vanilla works great. Or you can use a basic pastry cream to make Cream Puffs (page 314), or simply fill the puffs with flavored whipped cream.

While you could buy a jar of chocolate sauce—I'm sure there are terrific ones out there—it's so incredibly easy to make that it seems hard to justify spending money on a premade sauce. But again, everyone's circumstance is different.

The only thing you can't really buy are the cream puffs. Happily, the preparation takes only about 10 minutes, and the return on that investment is great.

I recommend serving either one profiterole per person for a light dessert or three for those who spend all dinner looking forward to dessert.

1 recipe Pâte à Choux Puffs (page 310), *preferably warm*

1 recipe Vanilla Ice Cream (page 313) *or store-bought ice cream*

1 recipe Chocolate Sauce (page 313), *warm*

Slice the pastry puffs and put them on plates. Scoop one ball of ice cream for each profiterole and make a sandwich of each. Drizzle the chocolate over and serve.

Pâte à choux from scratch begins with four ingredients.

PÂTE À CHOUX PUFFS
MAKES 16 TO 18 PUFFS

1 cup/240 milliliters whole milk	Scant 1 cup/ 120 grams flour
8 tablespoons/ 115 grams unsalted butter	4 large eggs

You don't even need a recipe for this preparation if you remember the basic ratio of the four ingredients: by weight, 2 parts each eggs and milk, 1 part each flour and butter. Or, if you prefer to measure by volume, it's 2 parts each eggs, flour, and milk and 1 part butter.

It's a fascinating dough because the flour is essentially boiled in the milk and butter until it gelatinizes and forms a paste, into which you stir the eggs. The eggs make it puff and give it flavor, the flour and liquid provide its bread-like structure, and the butter contributes tenderness and richness. The resulting dough can be fried, boiled, or baked, all with differing results. It's one of my favorite things to make.

These puffs are best served warm, but you can make them several hours ahead of time and let them sit, uncovered, at room temperature. You can also pipe them onto the parchment and put the baking sheet in the freezer, then bake from frozen at the last minute.

Preheat your oven to 425°F/218°C. Line a rimmed baking sheet with parchment paper.

Combine the milk and butter in a small saucepan and bring to a boil over high heat. When the butter has melted, reduce the heat to medium and add the flour. Stir the mixture vigorously with a wooden spoon or stiff spatula until it forms a paste and pulls away from the sides of the pan, a minute or so, then remove the pan from the heat. Allow it to sit for a few minutes.

Break 1 egg into the mixture and stir with a wooden spoon or stiff spatula until the choux paste absorbs the egg completely. The paste will look shiny and slick; when the egg is incorporated, the dough will be shaggier. Repeat with the remaining eggs, one at a time. (If you're making a bigger batch of choux pastry, you can use a stand mixer with the paddle to mix the eggs in.)

Transfer the choux paste to a piping bag with a straight ½-inch/1-centimeter tip. Pipe golf ball–size mounds onto the parchment. If they form tips when you pull the bag away, dip your finger in a bit of milk and tap them down. Bake for about 25 minutes, until they are golden brown and cooked within—taste one to make sure!

ON THE SAVORY SIDE: GOUGÈRES

The same choux pastry that makes cream puffs for profiteroles can be used to make gougères, or cheese puffs. They are a superb appetizer or passed hors d'oeuvres. Simply add ½ to ¾ cup/30 to 45 grams grated Parmigiano-Reggiano to the dough as you mix it. If you have a stand mixer, use it fitted with a paddle; this whips more air into the dough for greater lift. Then, after piping the puffs onto the parchment, top each with a sprinkle of more grated cheese. Bake and serve immediately. Or go all out and fill them with some form of whipped cheese—say, Boursin lightened with whipped cream. Simple and delicious.

1. Bring milk and butter to a simmer.

2. When the butter has melted, add the flour.

3. Stir vigorously with a stiff wood spoon or spatula.

4. The flour absorbs the water and gelatinizes to form a paste.

5. Remove the pot from the heat and crack an egg into the pot, stirring immediately, before the egg has time to cook.

6. Stir until each egg is fully incorporated (the paste will appear shiny and slick but then will lose its shine and become almost shaggy when the egg is in) before stirring in the next egg.

7. Pipe balls of choux paste onto parchment, tamping down the tips with a wet finger.

8. Bake until browned and cooked through. It should look like a little cabbage—"choux" is French for cabbage, thus "cabbage paste."

VANILLA ICE CREAM MAKES ABOUT 1 QUART/1 LITER

This is a straightforward vanilla ice cream and, to me, what ice cream is all about: a clean vanilla custard, frozen. Dairy is heated with the vanilla, whisked into the creamed yolk and sugar, strained, chilled, and spun in a machine. (The recipe calls for milk and cream, but feel free to use all half-and-half.) Save the egg whites! They keep for months in the freezer and can be used for Whiskey Sours (page 120), angel food cake, a royal icing, or a Pavlova (page 322); just slice off what you need as you need it.

2 cups/480 milliliters milk	1 to 2 teaspoons pure vanilla extract
2 cups/480 milliliters heavy cream	10 large egg yolks
1 vanilla bean	Scant 1 cup/ 180 grams sugar

Combine the milk and cream in a small saucepan. Slice the vanilla bean in half lengthwise and scrape the seeds into the pan; add the scraped pod. Bring the milk and cream to a simmer over high heat, then remove from the heat and allow the pod to steep for 20 to 30 minutes.

Combine the yolks and sugar in a bowl and whisk till they're uniformly combined.

Remove the pod halves from the milk and cream and bring back to a simmer. Pour about ¼ cup of the hot milk and cream into the egg-sugar mixture, whisking as you do. Pour in a little more and continue whisking, then add the remaining milk and cream.

Strain the mixture into a clean bowl and chill in the refrigerator. Freeze according to your machine's instructions.

CHOCOLATE SAUCE (CHOCOLATE GANACHE) MAKES ABOUT 1 CUP/ 240 MILLILITERS

This couldn't be simpler: Combine equal parts chocolate and hot cream in a bowl, wait a few minutes, then slowly whisk and watch the cream and chocolate coalesce as if by magic into a gorgeous silky chocolate sauce (feel free to call it by its fancy French name, ganache). Warm, it's pourable. Cold, it's stiff and can be shaped into truffles and rolled in cocoa powder (if you want the ganache to be firmer when cool, reduce the amount of cream by 25 percent). It's an incredibly versatile sauce. Pour it over berries, a tart, ice cream, or, of course, cream puffs filled with ice cream for profiteroles. Because there are only two ingredients, the quality of the chocolate is paramount.

½ cup/120 milliliters cream	4 ounces/ 110 grams high-quality bittersweet chocolate, *broken into large pieces*

In a small saucepan, bring the cream to a simmer over medium-high heat—keep an eye on it, as it will boil over the pan in seconds once it comes to a boil. Put the chocolate in a bowl and pour the hot cream over it. Wait for 2 or 3 minutes, then whisk till it's uniformly combined.

Store leftovers in an airtight container in the refrigerator for up to 1 week. Soften it carefully in the microwave, 20 seconds or so, until you have the consistency you like.

CARAMEL SAUCE

I included a recipe for Bourbon Caramel Sauce (page 79) in chapter 2 because it goes so nicely with the bread pudding there. But I might have included it here because of its similarity to chocolate sauce. Ganache is equal parts cream and chocolate; caramel sauce is equal parts cream and cooked sugar. It can be flavored (with whiskey, for instance), and it can be enriched (cook the sugar in butter and add a squeeze of lemon or apple cider vinegar for butterscotch sauce). You can make it thicker or thinner by increasing or decreasing the amount of liquid you use. The more liquid added, the looser it will be.

CREAM PUFFS
MAKES 16 TO 18

Other Pâte à Choux Pastries and Cream-Filled Treats

Cream puffs are simply the same puffs used for profiteroles but filled with pastry cream rather than ice cream. While a profiterole is a substantial dessert—puffs, ice cream, and chocolate sauce—cream puffs make for a simpler after-dinner sweet, if you want something that's not quite a full-on dessert. Or make a lot of them to create an elaborate croquembouche, a sculpture of puffs "glued" to one another with caramel—a conical shape or other structure can make a festive centerpiece for holiday buffet table. The choux puff is endlessly versatile.

1 recipe Pastry Cream (at right) or Chocolate Pastry Cream (opposite)

1 recipe Pâte à Choux Puffs (page 310)

Spoon the pastry cream into a piping bag fitted with a ¼-inch/6-millimeter tip. Poke the tip through the bottom of each choux puff and fill it. Hold at room temperature until ready to serve.

PASTRY CREAM
MAKES ABOUT 2 ¼ CUPS/530 MILLILITERS

Pastry cream is compulsively eatable as soon as you make it, like the best vanilla pudding you've ever had. Add cooked tapioca pearls for a perfect tapioca pudding; add kirsch or framboise for flavor. It can be used to fill Cream Puffs (at left), to take the place of the whipped cream in a Pavlova (page 322), or to layer with crêpes to make a Crêpe Cake (page 321). And here's a secret: It's the same recipe for Vanilla Ice Cream (page 313), halved (though I like the added richness of a few more yolks and butter, of course). It's simply thickened with cornstarch rather than by lowering its temperature. But even with the minor ingredient alterations, you could freeze this as you would ice cream.

You can make any amount you wish—just remember to use 2 tablespoons of cornstarch per 1 cup/240 milliliters half-and-half.

2 cups/480 milliliters half-and-half

1 vanilla bean

1 teaspoon pure vanilla extract

8 large egg yolks

½ cup/90 grams sugar

¼ cup cornstarch mixed with ¼ cup water or milk

4 tablespoons/60 grams unsalted butter, *cut into 4 pieces*

Pour the half-and-half into a small saucepan. Slice the vanilla bean in half lengthwise and scrape the seeds into the pan; add the scraped pod. Bring to a simmer over high heat, then remove from the heat and allow the pod to steep for 20 to 30 minutes. Remove the pod halves and discard them (or put them in your sugar bowl to perfume your sugar). Add the vanilla extract.

Combine the yolks and sugar in a bowl and whisk till they're uniformly combined. Prepare an ice bath large enough to put your pan in (you will need to cool the mixture quickly to complete it).

Return the cream just to a simmer over high heat, then reduce the heat to medium-low. Pour about ½ cup/120 milliliters of the hot half-and-half into the egg-sugar mixture, whisking as you do. Then pour that egg mixture into the remaining half-and-half in the saucepan, whisking to combine it all. Add the cornstarch slurry and turn the heat to medium, stirring continuously until the pastry cream has thickened to the consistency of pudding. Remove the pan from the heat and stir in the butter, stirring continuously until the butter has melted.

Plunge the pan into the ice bath, continuing to stir until the pastry cream has stopped cooking and is smooth and creamy. Store in an airtight container in the refrigerator for up to 3 days.

CHOCOLATE PASTRY CREAM

MAKES ABOUT 3 CUPS/710 MILLILITERS

The principle used to make a ganache, in which hot cream melts and then combines with chocolate, also works with a custard to make chocolate pastry cream.

Other Pâte à Choux Pastries and Cream-Filled Treats

2 cups/480 milliliters half-and-half

1 vanilla bean

1 teaspoon pure vanilla extract

8 large egg yolks

½ cup/90 grams sugar

8 ounces/225 grams bittersweet chocolate, *chopped*

¼ cup cornstarch mixed with ¼ cup water or milk

4 tablespoons/60 grams unsalted butter, *cut into 4 pieces*

Pour the half-and-half into a small saucepan. Slice the vanilla bean in half lengthwise and scrape the seeds into the pan; add the scraped pod. Bring to a simmer over high heat, then remove from the heat and allow the pod to steep for 20 to 30 minutes. Remove the pod halves and discard them (or put them in your sugar bowl to perfume your sugar). Add the vanilla extract.

Combine the yolks and sugar in a bowl and whisk till they're uniformly combined.

Put the chopped chocolate in another bowl. Return the cream just to a simmer over high heat, then reduce the heat to medium-low. Pour about ½ cup/120 milliliters of the hot half-and-half into the egg-sugar mixture, whisking as you do. Then pour that egg mixture into the remaining half-and-half in the saucepan, whisking to combine it all. Add the cornstarch slurry and turn the heat to medium, stirring continuously until the pastry cream has thickened to the consistency of pudding. Remove the pan from the heat and stir in the butter, stirring continuously until the butter has melted.

Pour the hot pastry cream mixture into the bowl of chocolate, stirring and folding the chocolate into the pastry cream as it melts. Store in an airtight container in the refrigerator for up to 5 days.

CHURROS MAKES ABOUT 8

Other Pâte
à Choux
Pastries
and
Cream-Filled
Treats

This classic treat is served all over Mexico, and it couldn't be easier: Pâte à choux dough is deep-fried, then rolled in cinnamon-sugar. To make churros properly, you will need a pastry bag and a star tip (which you can get at most kitchen supply stores or online). The star-tipped shape increases the surface area and helps give the churros better structure so that they can be made long. But if you don't want to bother, you can pipe the pâte à choux out of the corner of a plastic bag and cut them into 2-inch/5-centimeter lengths. These are best served warm—happily, this is easy to do as they cook in just a few minutes.

For the cinnamon-sugar:

½ cup sugar

2½ tablespoons cinnamon

For the churros:

1 recipe Pâte à Choux (page 310)

2 tablespoons sugar

2 teaspoon pure vanilla extract

½ teaspoon cinnamon

1 quart/1 liter vegetable oil *for frying*

Mix together the sugar and cinnamon and set aside.

Make the churros: Make the pâte à choux per the instructions, adding the sugar, vanilla, and cinnamon to the milk-butter mixture. Put your dough into a pastry bag fitted with a star tip.

Heat the oil in a large, heavy pot over high heat until it reaches 375°F/190°C. Working in batches if necessary, pipe the choux dough into the oil, using a knife to cut the dough as it comes out into 6-inch/15-centimeter pieces. Cook until the churros float and turn golden brown. Transfer them to a plate lined with paper towels. When they have drained, toss them in the cinnamon-sugar till they are well coated. Serve immediately.

CHOCOLATE TART SERVES 8 TO 10

This tart takes two common preparations—All-Purpose 3-2-1 Dough (page 81) and Chocolate Ganache (page 313)—to a wonderful and elegant conclusion. Here the ganache ratio is reduced somewhat because I'm adding a small amount of egg and flour. I like to flavor it with Grand Marnier and orange zest because I'm a sucker for the chocolate-orange flavor pairing; snooty pastry chefs may tell you this is a cliché, and you can certainly omit the orange or sub in something else if you like.

I finish it with more grated orange zest on top, but you could also garnish it with whipped cream or chopped cashews or—perhaps the finest garnish—drizzles of Caramel Sauce (page 313) and a light sprinkling of Maldon salt. Or, since chocolate and raspberry are also a great pair, make Blackberry-Blueberry Compote (page 323) with 2 cups/300 grams raspberries and spread it across the top of the tart in a thin layer.

This is but one strategy for making a chocolate tart. If you don't want to bake it, you can make Chocolate Pastry Cream (page 315) and pour it right into a baked pie or tart shell. The texture is not quite as fine, but it's still delicious. A standard pie plate or 10-inch/25-centimeter baking dish can take about 3 cups/710 milliliters filling.

For the crust:

1 ¼ cups/180 grams all-purpose flour

1 tablespoon sugar

Kosher salt

4 ounces/120 grams unsalted butter, *chilled and cut into large dice*

4 tablespoons ice water

For the filling:

1 ¼ cups/300 milliliters half-and-half

1 teaspoon pure vanilla extract

8 ounces/225 grams bittersweet chocolate, *coarsely chopped, or bittersweet chocolate chips*

2 large eggs

2 tablespoons sugar

¼ cup Grand Marnier *or other flavoring* (*optional*)

2 tablespoons/ 30 grams unsalted butter

Grated zest of 2 oranges

Maldon salt *to taste* (*optional*)

recipe continues

First, make the crust: In a mixing bowl, combine the flour, sugar, and a pinch of salt. Rub the flour mixture and butter with your fingers until you have small beads of butter and plenty of pea-size chunks. Add just enough ice water to bring the dough together. Shape it into a disk, wrap in plastic, and refrigerate for at least 15 minutes or up to 2 days.

Preheat your oven to 350°F/175°C.

Roll the dough into a circle large enough to fill a tart pan. Place the dough in the tart pan and trim to fit the pan. Put a sheet of parchment paper or aluminum foil in the pan and fill it with dried beans or pie weights.

Bake the tart shell for 20 minutes. Remove the parchment or foil and the beans, poke holes in the bottom of the crust with a fork, and continue baking until the shell is golden brown, 15 to 20 minutes longer. Leave the oven on.

Meanwhile, make the filling: Combine the half-and-half and vanilla in small saucepan and bring to a simmer over high heat.

Put the chopped chocolate in a bowl and, when the half-and-half is simmering, pour the cream over it. Allow it to sit for a couple minutes, then whisk it to blend the dairy and chocolate.

In another bowl, combine the eggs, sugar, and Grand Marnier (if using) and whisk to combine. Whisk this mixture into the chocolate. Then whisk in the butter. When the butter has melted, sprinkle in the flour, whisking until it's incorporated, then mix in the zest from one orange.

Pour the mixture into the baked pie shell and bake for 20 minutes. Allow the tart to cool to room temperature, then chill in the refrigerator until set. Serve cold or at room temperature, garnished with zest from the second orange and a gentle sprinkling of Maldon salt, if using.

CRÊPE CAKE SERVES 8

This is a very simple and satisfying dessert making use of two other preparations in this book: crêpes layered with pastry cream. You can make the crêpes as much as 4 hours ahead of time; feather them on a plate once they've cooled a little so that they don't stick to each other. Then cover and hold at room temperature until you're ready to assemble the cake.

You can finish the cake in several different ways, but it does need to be completed for an appealing presentation. A very simple finish is to cook the eighth crêpe till it's browned, then place it, browned side up, on top of the cake and simply dust with confectioners' sugar just before serving. Or, since it's a very soft dessert, you might want a crunchy element, so you could top it with chopped Heath bars. (My mom used to make a soft angel food cake for my birthday every year and top it with these chocolate caramel candies.) You might instead prefer to top the cake with Blackberry-Blueberry Compote (page 323) or Chocolate Sauce (page 313). With the berry or chocolate sauce, you might make this an elegant plated dessert, spooning a circle of sauce onto each plate and placing a slice of cake on it, or drizzling the sauce over each individual slice.

If you would like to serve more, prepare half again as much pastry cream and crêpes and make a twelve-layer cake.

Other Pâte à Choux Pastries and Cream-Filled Treats

1 recipe Pastry Cream (page 314)

8 Crêpes (page 87)

Optional toppings:

½ to ¾ cup/ 120 to 180 milliliters Blackberry-Blueberry Compote (page 323) or Chocolate Sauce (page 313), chopped Heath bars, and/ or confectioners' sugar

Make the pastry cream up to the point when you're cooling it in the ice bath. Let it cool only long enough to stop it from cooking, but don't let it become totally chilled or it won't be easy to spread. Place one crêpe on the serving dish you intend to use. Spread 3 or 4 tablespoons pastry cream over the top of it. Place the second crêpe on top of the first and spread pastry cream on top. Repeat with all the crêpes, leaving the eighth crêpe bare on top, ready for your toppings. Cover the cake with plastic wrap and refrigerate until it's thoroughly chilled, at least an hour depending on your refrigerator.

When ready to serve, finish the cake with a sauce or topping of your choosing.

PAVLOVA WITH WHIPPED CREAM AND BLACKBERRY-BLUEBERRY COMPOTE SERVES 6

Pavlova, sweet meringue cooked till crisp, is one of my favorite desserts. The pleasure is in its texture, delicately crispy on the outside and chewy on the inside. It's more than enough reason to save your egg whites when making ice cream, pastry cream, or any custard. Purportedly named after the Russian ballerina Anna Pavlova, it is most frequently served with berries and cream. In spring, simply use your choice of fresh berries and whipped cream. In winter, when good-quality South American berries are abundant in American grocery stores, I love to make a simple compote.

Egg whites can be fickle. A drop of yolk or any fat in your mixing bowl and they may fail to become meringue at all. Room-temperature egg whites work best, so try to separate the eggs 10 to 20 minutes before you begin whipping them. (Take a tip from my friend and ace pastry chef Shuna Fish Lydon and whip them on low for 4 or 5 minutes, just to coax them along before you whip air into them.) I add a little acid in the form of lemon juice to stabilize the egg white (others use a dried acid, cream of tartar). Flavor it with a little vanilla or Grand Marnier or brandy or eau de vie if you wish.

If you want to keep the meringues very white, bake them at or below 225°F/107°C. But if you need them done faster, bake at 250°F/121°C; just know that they will take on a little color, which may be what you like.

You can shape them any way you wish. Ina Garten, whose books I admire, likes to shape the meringue into one large form and serve it whole, like a tart with berries and whipped cream. This is a great way to serve pavlova. But you can also spoon it into single-serving portions or pipe it into precise shapes, such as the shape of a bowl to carry the berries and cream. Or spread them into cookie shapes and serve them as berry and cream sandwiches (French macarons are essentially egg white cookies, usually flavored with almond meal and brightly colored, with a creamy filling). There's no end to what the pavlova can do.

The ideal ratio is equal parts by weight of egg white and sugar, or roughly 2 tablespoons sugar for every egg white. To increase this recipe to serve more, add one egg white for every two extra servings you wish to make.

For the pavlova:

3 large egg whites

1 teaspoon lemon juice

1 teaspoon pure vanilla extract *or other flavor of your choice*

½ cup/90 grams sugar

For the whipped cream and berry compote:

½ cup/120 milliliters heavy cream

1 teaspoon pure vanilla extract

2 to 3 tablespoons sugar

1 recipe Blackberry-Blueberry Compote (page 323)

Make the pavlova: Preheat your oven to 250°F/121°C. Line a rimmed baking sheet with parchment paper.

In the bowl of a standing mixer or using an immersion blender, whip the egg whites gently for a few minutes to warm them up. Then whip on high. When the mixture becomes frothy, add the lemon juice and vanilla and continue to whip just until the whites come off the beater in a ribbon and barely hold a peak. Continue whipping on high as you gradually add the sugar. Stop mixing when the meringue is shiny and bright white and holds a stiff peak.

Spoon or pipe the meringue into whatever shapes you wish onto the prepared baking sheet. Bake for 1 hour, then turn off the heat and leave them in the oven until they're cool. Or, if you have time, after the 1 hour at 250°F/121°C, reduce the heat to 200°F/93°C, leave the oven door ajar, and bake for another 30 minutes, then turn off the oven, close the door, and let them cool in the oven (the idea is to dehydrate them rather than cook them).

To make the whipped cream, in the bowl of a standing mixer or using a hand mixer, whip the cream till it has thickened slightly, then add the vanilla and, while still whipping, the sugar. Continue to whip until the cream holds soft peaks.

To complete the pavlovas, dollop some cream on top of the meringue and spoon the compote over the cream.

BLACKBERRY-BLUEBERRY COMPOTE   MAKES 2 CUPS, ENOUGH FOR 8 TO 10 SERVINGS

Tarts, Pies, and Pavlova

I chanced upon the felicitous combination of blackberries and blueberries when I noticed that a container of each had been pushed to the back of the fridge and would go bad if I didn't use them that day. So, I put them in a pan and tossed them with sugar and water, brought it to a simmer, and cooked the berries down gently. For the next several weeks I had the compote to add to Greek yogurt or toast in the morning or with ice cream as a dessert. And when we had friends over for dinner, I used the compote for a Pavlova (page 322) with the help of inexpensive egg whites.

Because this is thickened with starch, it is as stiff as jam when chilled. If you'd rather serve it syrupy, simply omit the cornstarch.

1 cup/150 grams blueberries	¼ cup water
1 cup/150 grams blackberries	1½ tablespoons cornstarch mixed with 2 tablespoons water (*optional*)
¼ cup sugar	

Combine the berries, sugar, and water in a saucepan and bring to a simmer over high heat. Reduce the heat to low and cook, stirring occasionally, for 15 to 20 minutes, until the berries are falling apart and the liquid has become viscous.

If you would like a thicker consistency, stir in the slurry of cornstarch and water. When the berries return to a simmer, the cornstarch will have thickened them. Transfer to a bowl and serve hot or allow to chill in the fridge. Store leftovers in an airtight container in the refrigerator for up to 2 weeks.

BLACKBERRY-BLUEBERRY PIE SERVES 8

This is, essentially, Blackberry-Blueberry Compote (page 323) cooked in All-Purpose 3-2-1 Dough (page 81). But you can use any fruit with minor adjustments. Berries and peaches and other soft fruits tend to give off larger amounts of liquid, requiring more thickening (cornstarch). Other ingredients, such as rhubarb, are very tart and require more sugar. But it's all common sense, and if you pay attention to one or two pie preparations, you should be able to make a pie without a recipe. Just remember that a standard pie plate holds 5 to 6 cups/900 grams fruit.

One pie dough recipe makes enough for both a bottom and top crust, and part of the fun of making this pie is creating a beautiful interlocking lattice for the top crust. This is appealing to look at and also allows the water from the berry filling to cook off more efficiently. Don't mix the berries with the sugar until you have cut your lattice strips and you're ready to fill the pie shell because the berries quickly begin to release their juices once they're combined with sugar.

This is a straightforward berry pie with no seasoning, just pure berry flavor, which is all I think it really needs. But feel free to add a dose of grated lemon zest or a teaspoon of ground cinnamon if you wish. And since you're going to the trouble of making a pie with a gorgeous lattice crust, you might as well give that crust a gorgeous sheen by brushing it with egg wash.

---

1 recipe All-Purpose
3-2-1 Dough
(page 81)

¾ cup/135 grams
sugar

½ cup/240 grams
cornstarch

3 cups/450 grams
blackberries

3 cups/450 grams
blueberries

Egg wash: 1 large
egg mixed with
1 tablespoon milk
(*optional*)

Preheat your oven to 425°F/218°C.

Divide your dough in half. Roll out one half so that it's large enough to fill your pie plate with about 1 inch/2.5 centimeters overhang, and place it in the pie plate.

Roll out the second piece of dough into a 10-inch/25-centimeter square for the lattice crust.

When you're ready to fill the shell and make the lattice, combine the sugar and cornstarch in a large mixing bowl and mix them together well. Add the berries and toss well until they're evenly coated. Pour the contents of the bowl into the pie shell.

Make the lattice crust. Trim the strips to the edge of the pie plate and fold the bottom crust's overhang over the edges of the strips. Pinch and crimp the dough together. Brush the crust with the egg wash if you wish.

Put the pie on a rimmed baking sheet to catch any drips and bake for 1 to 1¼ hours, until the fruit is bubbly and thick and the crust is golden brown. Set the pie on a rack and let it cool completely before cutting into it.

1. Cut the second piece of dough into strips. Use a fluted pastry wheel if you have one. If you want to be very precise feel free to use a ruler. I like my strips to be about ¾ inch/2 centimeters wide. You'll need at least 9 strips and as many as 11, so choose the best ones. Make them thicker if you wish. They'll shrink slightly when baked.

2. When you've cut your strips and preheated your oven, mix the berries with the sugar, and pour them into the pie shell (don't mix the berries with sugar ahead of time or the sugar will begin to pull liquid from the berries).

5. Recover pie with the folded strips, then fold the other two strips back, then lay another strip vertically across the pie. Fold the horizontal strips back.

6. Continue this alternating process until you have completed the lattice.

3. Lay five strips (or more if you wish) horizontally across the pie so that they extend over the edges.

4. Fold every other strip back over itself all the way back and lay a strip vertically across the pie. Fold the horizontal steps back over the pie and the two unfolded strips.

7. Using scissors or a pairing knife, cut the lattice strips so they're not overhanging the edge but can become part of the crust. Crimp the edges of the dough to seal the lattice strips and make a good-looking rim.

8. Brush the crust with egg wash for a beautiful, browned finished pie.

Blackberry-Blueberry Pie. Pure berry flavor.

TARTE TATIN SERVES 8

This is little more than an upside-down pie. True to French country cuisine, it's utilitarian and uses only inexpensive ingredients. It's simple to make, but it does take some attention while the apples cook. You simply layer sliced apples on top of sugar and butter and cook on the stovetop until the apples and sugar begin to caramelize. When you see the juices and sugars beginning to brown, that's when it's time to cover it with All-Purpose 3-2-1 Dough (page 81) and get it in the oven. You can do this in a cast-iron or stainless steel skillet, but the apples can stick, so I prefer an oven-safe nonstick pan for this.

My favorite apple for baking is the Braeburn, but Granny Smiths or any other tart, crisp variety will work. For an appealing presentation, restaurant kitchens will carefully fan the bottom layer of apples (which will become the top when it's turned out) in a circular pattern, but it's fine to add your apples haphazardly if you wish. Serve it with ice cream or a dollop of crème fraîche.

*Tarts,
Pies, and
Pavlova*

For the apples:

½ cup/90 grams
sugar

4 tablespoons/
60 grams unsalted
butter, *cut into 5 or
6 pieces*

6 large apples
(*about 3 pounds/
1.5 kilograms*), *peeled,
cored, and cut into thick
slices*

½ teaspoon ground
cinnamon (*optional*)

For the crust:

1 cup/150 grams
all-purpose flour

Kosher salt

6 tablespoons/
90 grams unsalted
butter, *chilled and
cut into large dice*

3 to 4 tablespoons
ice water

Preheat your oven to 350°F/175°C.

Prepare the apples: Put the sugar in an 8- to 10-inch/20- to 25-centimeter oven-safe nonstick skillet and shake the sugar into an even layer. Scatter the butter pieces on top. Then layer your apples on the butter and sugar and put the pan over medium heat. Once the apples start dropping their juices and the sugar dissolves, lower the heat to medium-low and cook the apples, undisturbed, till they're very soft, about 20 minutes. Sprinkle the cinnamon on midway through cooking, if using. Press down on the apples occasionally and rotate the pan on the burner to make sure they're cooking evenly.

Meanwhile, make the crust: Combine the flour, a pinch of salt, and the butter for the crust. Pinch the butter until it's in little chunks and bits. Add just enough ice water to bring it all together. Shape it into a disk, wrap it in plastic, and refrigerate it till you're ready to roll it out.

When the juices have begun to brown and the apples are very soft, roll out the dough. Cut a circle about 10 inches/25 centimeters in diameter. Place it over the apples and tuck in the edges all around. Bake on the middle rack until the crust is golden brown, about 20 minutes.

Let the tart rest for 5 to 10 minutes, then put a plate over the pan and carefully invert the tart onto the plate. Remove the pan and serve.

APPLE STREUSEL SERVES 8

When time is very limited, making a Tarte Tatin (page 329) is out of the question. But you still need to have something to offer for dessert, so skip the slow caramelization of the apples. Don't even peel them. Just quarter them, remove the core, slice into thin wedges, and make a streusel topping. Pop it in the oven before you sit down to eat, then serve it hot with ice cream, whipped cream, crème fraîche, or good Greek yogurt.

I offer two topping options here: one very common recipe for the seriously last-minute dessert and a second recipe that easily elevates the dish if you have nuts and rolled oats on hand. The first topping recipe is so basic that my wife rarely bothers with a food processor when she makes it; she just coats the apples with the dry topping ingredients and drops chunks of butter on top. You could also just use room-temperature butter and mixing everything together with a fork.

While you can buy almond meal (ground almonds), since you're already using a food processor to make the second topping option, I prefer to use whole almonds. This allows you to give your almonds a chunkier texture, but if you have almond meal on hand, that's perfectly fine as well.

4 or 5 crisp, tart apples (*such as Braeburn or Granny Smith*), *cored and cut into thin wedges*

¼ lemon

Basic Streusel Topping (if using):

1 cup/150 grams all-purpose flour

1 cup/200 grams sugar

8 tablespoons/ 115 grams unsalted butter

1 teaspoon ground cinnamon

¼ teaspoon ground cloves (*optional*)

Almond Streusel Topping (if using):

¾ cup/100 grams raw, skin-on almonds, or ¾ cup/100 grams almond meal

½ cup/60 grams all-purpose flour

¾ cup/135 grams granulated sugar

¼ cup packed light or dark brown sugar

1 teaspoon ground cinnamon

¼ teaspoon ground cloves or allspice

8 to 12 tablespoons/ 115 to 175 grams unsalted butter, *cut into small pieces*

¾ cup/75 grams rolled oats

Preheat your oven to 350°F/175°C.

Butter an 8-inch/20-centimeter skillet or a 9-by-13-inch/22-by-33-centimeter baking dish or other appropriate vessel. Spread out the apple wedges and squeeze the lemon over them (catching any seeds), then toss the apples with the lemon. Press the apples so they are all at an even level.

If making the basic streusel topping: Combine all the ingredients in a food processor and pulse till well combined. Top the apples evenly with the streusel mix.

If making the almond streusel topping: Put the almonds in a food processor and pulse until the almonds have the consistency of meal. Add the flour, both sugars, the spices, and 8 tablespoon/115 grams butter and pulse till well combined and the streusel has a mealy texture. Remove the blade and stir in two-thirds of the oats. Top the apples evenly with the streusel mix. Sprinkle the remaining oats over the top. If desired, scatter another 4 tablespoons/ 60 grams butter evenly across the top.

Bake until the top is browned and crisp and the apples are bubbly, about 1 hour. Serve warm. (Have leftovers for breakfast.)

THE LAST DESSERT: CHOCOLATE AND WHISKEY SERVES 2

The Last Dessert

4 ounces/110 grams good chocolate

4 ounces/120 milliliters good whiskey

This is my idea of the perfect conclusion to a meal: It encourages you to stay at the table just a little bit longer, to enjoy your companions, to carry on the conversation.

You need to make sure you and your guests have similar tastes (some guests at a dinner party may be big on dessert, something to take into consideration). If you're offering a simple chocolate and whiskey conclusion to four or more people, it's fun to be able to offer a choice of whiskeys. My preference is a heavily peaty single-malt scotch, such as Lagavulin or Laphroaig. But chocolate goes particularly well with an excellent American bourbon—Michter's, Woodford Reserve, or

Blanton's, for instance. These caramelly, smoky flavors go especially well with chocolate, and the total effect is greater than the sum of the parts.

My appreciation for the pleasure of simplicity and richness began at a restaurant near our West Village apartment where my wife and I regularly eat. We grew accustomed to seeing two big chunks of excellent chocolate arrive with our bill. One time we decided to order a whiskey to enjoy with it; this was such a pleasure that it became customary. But I didn't realize how much I loved concluding a meal this way until the restaurant cut back and began serving foil-wrapped bites of mediocre chocolate. This was no good at all. The custom ended, thus reminding me that we often don't appreciate something until it's taken away.

And what better thought to end on: Imagine not being able to cook beautiful food. Imagine if there were no grocery stores, or butcher shops, or farmers' markets. That is, imagine if we didn't have an affordable and abundant supply of fresh food. Imagine if everything we ate came in cans and boxes, the same food available everywhere at convenient marts and department stores.

Of course, that won't happen. Indeed, our food only gets better and better, and the places to buy it increase yearly. I would argue that never in the history of humankind have we had a more bountiful, more nutritious, more delicious variety of foods to cook and share with our family and the people we love. And the more we take advantage of this bounty, the more we ensure its continuance. Rejoice.

Happy cooking and *bon appétit.*

Recipe Timetable

MAINS, SIDES, AND DESSERTS

A true timetable for these recipes is difficult to calculate, and here's why: a dinner of Lexington BBQ with rice and sautéed Brussels sprouts takes less than 30 minutes—but only if you put the pork shoulder in the oven hours earlier, if not the day before. So, all told, the meal takes 6 hours and 30 minutes, but only 30 minutes of active work.

If you go by total time and active work, as many recipes today do, steak au poivre is in the less-than-30-minutes category for active time. But I presume you'll want more for dinner than that—at least a salad, if not some fries or mashed potatoes as well. That's likely going to push your time past 30 minutes. Duck takes two to three days to confit properly, but once you have duck confit on hand, it's the definition of convenience food—heat and serve in under 30, with potatoes done in ten minutes if you dice them small enough.

With this in mind, only about five of these meals are in the 1½ to 2-hour range. (The "seriously from scratch" recipes, of course, can take a day, a weekend, or months—that's why they're actually timeless!) Just about every full meal here, with side dishes, can be made in an hour. I like to plan on spending an hour start to finish when I make a weeknight meal. If I need to get food on the table fast, that limits my choices—I'd go with pasta or a seared steak and a salad, an omelet and a salad—but it doesn't have to limit the quality of your meal. If you've thought ahead and have some duck confit from a couple of months ago, or you corned some beef, or slow roasted a pork shoulder, any number of meals are 30 minutes away. These under-30 meals, meals that take 30 minutes if you've cooked or preserved the meat ahead, are starred.

Again, choose meals for which you have a comfortable amount of time in which to prepare them.

LESS THAN 30 MINUTES

ABOUT AN HOUR

1½- TO 2-HOUR RANGE

PROJECTS

RECIPE COMPONENTS

These are sauces, stocks, spices, and components that
will elevate your cooking and make your meals complete.

SAUCES, SPICES, AND ACCOMPANIMENTS

STOCKS

BREADS AND DOUGHS

PRESERVING FOOD

COCKTAILS

ACKNOWLEDGMENTS

First thanks go to my editor, Michael Sand, for sticking with me during this whole mysterious process of creating a well-crafted book out of a lifetime of seemingly disconnected cooking experiences. Thank you, Michael, for your intelligence, precision, elegance, and friendship.

Deb Wood is an uncommon art director who, sitting with her laptop in a rocker in my loft in Providence, Rhode Island, surprised me with the cover of this book, then followed through by creating the entire design of *From Scratch*. Deb's work was made possible by the magic that photographer Quentin Bacon (and his ace digital technician, Kristen Walther) worked on the food coming out of a home kitchen. Managing editor Lisa Silverman and associate production director Denise LaCongo held all the parts of the production of this book together. And I continue to be grateful for Gabby Fisher, one of the best publicists I've been able to work with. Books are a team effort, and all these people made this book happen.

Oh, and one small addition to that list. From her private outpost in suburban Boston, Karen Wise copyedited the manuscript. Our relationship goes back and goes on, and it's difficult to describe the mind capable of such technical grammatical precision while also refining the narrative arc of a cookbook.

Special mention must be made of two young cooks and culinarians: Mariamelia Valdez Heredia and Owen Macca. They were students at Johnson & Wales University when they came to assist in preparing the food for the photo shoots. Their reliability, precision, working-clean-ness, and professionalism were fundamental to the images in this book. They have a standing recommendation from me to any chef who wants an asset in their kitchen. And Bruce Tillinghast, former chef-owner of New Rivers in Providence—thanks for your work and generosity and intelligence during those shoots. And for your friendship always.

More thanks. My wife, Ann Hood, an elegant writer and perhaps the most generous soul I know, read every version of this and kept me moving forward. And eating my food! And also cooking for me throughout—how lucky am I to be married to a such fabulous cook and writer and reader? I'd like to thank her kids, Sam, an eager cook and eater, and daughter Annabelle, who may never eat another lasagna again.

And I would like to thank my kids, James and Addison, who grew up eating my food, experiments and all (and never hesitated to offer critical feedback). Keep on cooking, James! And, Addison, thank you for introducing me to Jean-Georges's pea pancakes.

I've worked with many chefs, such as Jean-Georges and others mentioned explicitly in this book, chefs whose talents go far beyond the food they make—teachers, all of them. My first mentor and teacher, Michael Pardus—I would not be here had it not been for him. I continue to work and write books with Brian Polcyn—my dear friend and teacher. And Thomas Keller—above all, he led me toward the greatest skill in the kitchen: the ability to *see*, to be observant, to know how to think while cooking.

Index

Editor: Michael Sand
Designer: Deb Wood
Production Manager: Kathleen Gaffney

Library of Congress Control Number: 2018958265

ISBN: 978-1-4197-3277-5
eISBN: 978-1-68335-653-0

Text copyright © 2019 Michael Ruhlman

Photographs by Quentin Bacon, copyright © 2019 Abrams
Photograph on page 340 by Ann Hood
Illustrations on pages 4, 14–23, and 352 by Dave Konopka
Hand lettering on pages 29, 59, 93, 126–27, 157, 189,
210–11, 238–39, 274–75, and 306–307 by Deb Wood

Jacket © 2019 Abrams

Printed and bound in the United States

10 9 8 7 6 5 4 3 2 1

Abrams books are available at special discounts when
purchased in quantity for premiums and promotions as
well as fundraising or educational use. Special editions
can also be created to specification. For details, contact
specialsales@abramsbooks.com or the address below.

Abrams® is a registered trademark of
Harry N. Abrams, Inc.

ABRAMS The Art of Books
195 Broadway, New York, NY 10007
abramsbooks.com